"Can regular companies become innovation powerhouses? *Eat, Sleep, Innovate* answers with a resounding 'Yes!' and then shows you exactly how to do it. Written by experienced practitioners, filled with fresh thinking, and infused with both humor and hands-on advice, this is an invaluable guide for making creativity a daily habit within your team or organization."

— **THOMAS WEDELL-WEDELLSBORG,** author, *What's Your Problem?*; coauthor, *Innovation as Usual*

"So you've done the 'innovation theater' thing and have the dead Post-It notes to prove it. Still frustrated that your great innovative ideas never see the light of day? This wonderful new book by Scott Anthony and his colleagues may be just what you need to clear out the day-to-day behaviors that are often the most significant hidden barriers to innovation. It's practical and full of interesting examples from both the corporate world and the not-for-profit world. On top of all that, it's a lot of fun to read! It deserves a space on that crowded library shelf."

— **RITA GUNTHER McGRATH,** professor, Columbia Business School; author, *Seeing Around Corners*

"Now more than ever, the world needs innovation. A potent mix of behavioral science, innovation practice, and vivid case studies, this book is a wonderfully insightful and practical guide to breaking down the common barriers to innovation and building the rituals, habits, and culture that allows it to flourish every single day."

— **VIJAY GOVINDARAJAN,** Coxe Distinguished Professor, Tuck School of Business at Dartmouth College; *New York Times* and *Wall Street Journal* bestselling author

"This book represents an important integration of theory and practice on driving change. The beauty is in the detailed guidance on how to unleash your organization's innovation potential."

— **LINDA HILL,** Wallace Brett Donham Professor of Business Administration, Harvard Business School; coauthor, *Collective Genius*

"As an incumbent enterprise challenged by rapidly shifting customer behaviors and markets, we were looking to transform into a more customer-centric organization. The approach described in *Eat, Sleep, Innovate* gave us the insights, focus, and inspiration to create and hard-wire a culture of innovation. A bold and encouraging read."

—**THOMAS FISCHER,** Chairman, MANN+HUMMEL

"*Eat, Sleep, Innovate* offers astute advice for every company leader looking to thrive in the digital era. This engaging book, written in a very accessible style, tackles head-on the hard issues of creating an innovative 'culture by design' with lots of practical techniques and motivating case studies—including my favorite, DBS Bank."

—**PETER WEILL,** Chairman, Center for Information Systems Research (CISR), MIT; coauthor, *What's Your Digital Business Model?* and *IT Savvy*

"Many organizations pay lip service to the idea of having a culture of innovation. Yet, too often, the results are as impactful as the sticky notes from last month's brainstorming session. The practical tools in this in-the-trenches handbook will help you and your organization rethink how you can enable innovation on a day-to-day basis and drive lasting culture change."

—**TOM FISHBURNE,** founder and CEO, Marketoonist; author, *Your Ad Ignored Here*

"A joy to read, this book is brimming with useful ideas about how all of us can be nudged, reminded, and cajoled to be brilliantly innovative. The BEANs concept is so addictive, you'll be inspired to create your own."

—**ZIA ZAMAN,** founder and Managing Partner, Beaver Lake Capital; Chief Innovation Officer, MetLife Asia

"Many companies want to know how they can best emulate iconic companies like Amazon, Alibaba, and Alphabet. But the real opportunity for organizations is to build on their own strengths to create a thriving culture of innovation. *Eat, Sleep, Innovate* provides concrete, practical advice for individuals and companies that aspire to accomplish extraordinary things."

—**CHRIS YEH,** coauthor, *Blitzscaling* and *The Alliance*

"Today's uncertainty demands innovation at an unprecedented pace and scale, combined with the ability to align different mindsets from different stakeholders. *Eat, Sleep, Innovate* is an inspiring and practical guide to help organizations—from family-owned businesses to government authorities—innovate with true impact."

—**CHRISTOPH BRAND,** International Advisor, Goldman Sachs

"This book is a unique and powerful contribution to improving how we think about and practice innovation. Because it's grounded in reality, it will allow your innovation efforts to take off."

—**STUART CRAINER** and **DES DEARLOVE,** founders, Thinkers50

# EAT
# SLEEP
## *Innovate*

# EAT

# SLEEP

# *Innovate*

## How to
## Make Creativity
## an Everyday Habit
## Inside Your Organization

*Scott D. Anthony*

*Paul Cobban / Natalie Painchaud / Andy Parker*

HARVARD BUSINESS REVIEW PRESS
BOSTON, MASSACHUSETTS

The web addresses referenced in this book were live and correct at the time of the book's publication but may be subject to change.

Library of Congress Cataloging-in-Publication Data.

Names: Anthony, Scott D., author. | Cobban, Paul, author. | Painchaud,
    Natalie, author. | Parker, Andy (Business consultant), author.
Title: Eat, sleep, innovate : how to make creativity an everyday habit
    inside your organization / Scott D. Anthony, Paul Cobban, Natalie
    Painchaud, Andy Parker.
Description: Boston, Massachusetts : Harvard Business Review Press, [2020] |
    Includes index.
Identifiers: LCCN 2020026429 (print) | LCCN 2020026430 (ebook) |
    ISBN 9781633698376 (hardcover) | ISBN 9781633698383 (ebook)
Subjects: LCSH: Creative ability in business. | Corporate culture. |
    Technological innovations. | Success in business.
Classification: LCC HD53 .A56 2020  (print) | LCC HD53  (ebook) |
    DDC 658.3/14—dc23
LC record available at https://lccn.loc.gov/2020026429
LC ebook record available at https://lccn.loc.gov/2020026430

The paper used in this publication meets the requirements of the American National Standard for Permanence of Paper for Publications and Documents in Libraries and Archives Z39.48-1992.

# Contents

**Introduction**                                                                    1

The World's Greatest Untapped Source of Energy

*Part One*

## LAYING THE FOUNDATION

1   **The Responsibility of the Many**                                        15

COMPANION CASE STUDY . . . 33
Creating "Innovation Chefs" at The Salvation Army

2   **The Shadow Strategy**                                                    41

COMPANION CASE STUDY . . . 51
From Damn Bloody Slow to Best Bank in the World

3   **Hacking Habits**                                                          63

COMPANION CASE STUDY . . . 82
BEANs in Hyderabad

4   **Conducting a Culture Sprint**                                            87

*Part Two*

## TIPS, TRICKS, AND TOOLS

**5   Phase 1**                                    119
Discover Opportunities

**6   Phase 2**                                    137
Blueprint Compelling Ideas

**7   Phase 3**                                    153
Assess and Test Ideas

**8   Phase 4**                                    173
Move Ideas Forward


**Conclusion**                                     193
Starting a Movement


Appendix                                           205
Notes                                              227
Index                                              235
Acknowledgments                                    243
About the Authors                                  249

# EAT

# SLEEP

# *Innovate*

*Introduction*

# The World's Greatest Untapped Source of Energy

Hello, reader. We are going to have fun and meet some interesting characters, we promise. First, however, let's detail the essence of this book in plain, simple language.

This is a book about innovation. More specifically, it is about how to make innovation a day-to-day habit in your organization. You eat every day, you sleep every day, and today's quickly changing world means you should innovate every day. Hence the title *Eat, Sleep, Innovate.*[1] This book is a practical guide for building a culture of innovation where the behaviors that drive innovation success come naturally.

If you work in a large organization and consume articles and books about innovation, you may be thinking, *Hmmm, culture of innovation? I've heard this before. What's next? Another story about the wonders of some*

---

1. The authors proposed *Unleashing Innovation* or *Hacking Innovation* as a title. Our publisher thankfully had a much better idea (although it did take some getting used to on our part)! And hello, footnote reader. We are glad to have you with us. The notes section at the end of the book has sources and references. The footnotes are here to expand on the text and to have a bit of fun (see, it isn't a boring book). You don't really need to read them. But you should.

*hypergrowth company that spends luxuriously on the food in its cafeteria and the trimmings in its game room?*

If you're skeptical, we understand. We've been on the frontlines of innovation efforts and have seen the good, the bad, and the ugly. In our experience, companies are well-intentioned—they want to innovate and they want to build a stable of creative employees—but their attempts usually fail, or, in some cases, completely backfire. Hence the skepticism.

In our quest to unpack and help leaders create cultures of innovation, we have formed an obsession—not with BATs and FAANGs[2] but, rather, with NO-DETs: normal organizations doing extraordinary things.

Here is a brief story about one such NO-DET: DBS, one of Southeast Asia's largest banks. Its history is intertwined with its home country, Singapore, which broke off from Malaysia to become an independent country in 1965. Three years later, Singapore's government founded the Development Bank of Singapore to take over financing activities from the Economic Development Board. That bank grew to become Singapore's largest bank and was renamed DBS in 2003.

Asian banks are generally conservative, highly regulated organizations. Singapore has a well-earned reputation as an orderly, rule-abiding country. A new CEO, Piyush Gupta, joined DBS in 2009, the same year that Paul joined.[3] Over the last decade, DBS has become recognized as a global leader in innovation, winning numerous accolades and becoming the most valuable publicly traded company on Singapore exchanges. Did it buy a high-growth startup and outsource innovation to it? No. Did it dramatically turn over its workforce, replacing boring bankers with mischievous millennials? No. Did it order people to innovate? No.

2. BAT is the acronym for Chinese internet giants Baidu, Alibaba, and Tencent (with market capitalization of $1.1 trillion); FAANG is for Facebook, Apple, Amazon, Netflix, and Google (with market capitalization, including Google's parent Alphabet, of $4.1 trillion). While these companies are all interesting, their cultures are too intertwined with their origin stories and charismatic founders (like Jack Ma, Jeff Bezos, Sergey Brin, and Larry Page) to be easily replicable.

3. That's coauthor and faithful Norwich City Football Club supporter Paul Cobban. You'll see Paul, along with Andy, Natalie, and Scott, throughout the manuscript. We debated whether to call each of these people "coauthor" upon first reference in every chapter, but we figure you, dear reader, are smart enough to follow along without such a reference.

It's easy to assume that people can't change. That lifetime workers have well-worn habits and lack the requisite knowledge to adopt cutting-edge technologies. Many DBS leaders assumed just that. But a few years ago, Adrian Cockcroft, then a development leader from Netflix, came to visit DBS.[4] Cockcroft described how another bank had visited Netflix and had bemoaned the fact that Netflix clearly had an advantage in attracting young, talented engineers. Cockcroft made two observations. First, he told the bank that the average Netflix engineer was forty years old. Second, he noted that he had hired a good proportion of his engineers from banks and had simply "gotten out of their way."

The innovators had always been there. It just took something to bring them out.

In *Eat, Sleep, Innovate,* you'll learn more about how DBS went from lagging in its local market to being globally recognized as an innovation powerhouse. You will see how the HR department of a leading telecommunications company started an innovation movement and how UNICEF uses its broad reach to find innovative ways to help children around the world. These and other organizations featured in this book are normal. They look like where most people in the world work. But *Eat, Sleep, Innovate* will show how they are, like all organizations, capable of doing extraordinary things.

\* \* \*

Close your eyes and imagine a sunset on a beach, with lapping waves and a gentle breeze. You probably pictured an idyllic landscape and are starting to think about a future vacation (see the sidebar "COVID-19 and Innovation"). Beyond beauty, what else is in this picture? Untapped energy. Wind, water, and light all carry tremendous energy as they move through the world, their intermingling cycles infinitely renewable. You can see and feel their energy directly. But for it to be useful, you must capture, store, and channel it to a useful end versus letting it naturally diffuse and spend itself.

4. As of the writing of this book, Cockcroft was at Amazon Web Services.

# COVID-19 and Innovation

Let's address the elephant in the room.[a] We think the odds are high that the "vacation" reference triggered thoughts about the bright red line separating 2019 and 2020. Indeed, the writing and editing process of *Eat, Sleep, Innovate* coincided with the COVID-19 pandemic. When we submitted the final draft manuscript to our publisher in early February, concern about the virus was largely contained to China. By the time we got the edited manuscript back in mid-April, most of the world was under lockdown.[b] By the time the book comes out in October, circumstances will be different in ways that no one can be quite sure of, and readers in 2021 and beyond will be in yet different circumstances.

Uncertainty increases the need for innovation. In the second quarter of 2020, the world had to confront a range of unanticipated issues, ranging from ensuring the sanctity of global supply chains to figuring out how to virtualize work and school to confronting various socioeconomic issues. Additionally, places where remote work perpetuates will have to deal with new challenges such as fostering a common culture without reinforcing physical rituals.

This book is not a specific a guide to "flatten the curve" of COVID-19 or navigate a "new normal" post-COVID-19. Rather, it is a guide to make creativity a habit inside your organization. The pages that follow include a few direct references to COVID-19, including detailing how DBS used its innovation capabilities to help it respond quickly and thoughtfully to the new reality of remote operations. We will put specific thoughts related to COVID-19—and any subsequent big event—on the book's companion website, www.eatsleepinnovate.com.

a. Or, if you'd prefer, the elephant on the Zoom.

b. After returning to Singapore from a trip to the United States in mid-March, Scott spent fourteen days isolated in a corporate apartment. He got out and enjoyed six days of glorious freedom before Singapore announced a "circuit breaker" that closed schools, restaurants, and most businesses for the next two months.

Now close your eyes again and picture the sort of never-ending cubicle farm you would see in movies like *Office Space* or in cartoons like Dilbert. Your mental image is probably a lot less idyllic. You might be thinking again about your next vacation. Beyond gray walls and a desk, what else is in this picture?

*Organizations have untapped innovation energy.*

Untapped energy, in the form of the organization's innovation capacity. Every organization houses deep veins of raw human ingenuity or partially formed ideas that could be transformed into massive value if they could only be liberated from their burial spots within the unyielding rock walls of the organization. Even when innovation energy is expended, it is often spent inefficiently or chaotically, yielding at best only a fraction of its potential utility.[5]

The central argument in *Eat, Sleep, Innovate* is that the world's biggest untapped source of energy isn't the wind, water, or sun. It is inside existing organizations, which are brimming with innovation energy. Today that energy is largely constrained and contained. You need to release, harness, and amplify it. This book will show you how.

* * *

A few years ago, Scott was in Cambodia with his family.[6] He was visiting an inspirational organization, a socially oriented venture that provided employment for thousands of desperately poor Cambodian artisans who hand-created garments, carvings, statues, and more. While visiting a silkworm farm connected to the venture, the Anthony family saw a bright blue box. It was called the Ideas Box, and the text on the front said it was "for you, for your colleagues, for your well-being." Sounds

---

5. The doodle that goes with this paragraph is from Paul, who contributed more than fifty distinct doodles for this book. If you are looking for a different memento from your wedding, give him a buzz!

6. Scott Anthony, one of the book's coauthors. (We're going to stop doing this soon.)

inspirational, right? Look closer. The box had a lock on it. And the lock was so rusted, it was clear that it not been opened recently—or, perhaps, *ever.*[7]

Companies seeking to spark innovation often instinctively copy artifacts they see in other innovative companies. Maybe they install a well-stocked cafeteria with bright colors or provide scooters. But quick-and-easy artifacts that are simply bolted on and don't represent and reinforce leadership's real vision lack soul. And soulless artifacts simply function as "innoganda," or innovation propaganda.[8] While

**A locked ideas box**

innoganda can generate a burst of energy at first, it typically leads to cynicism over the long term.

Culture is a complex, interdependent system. It's easy to do something different in a single meeting. But having something that changes the day-to-day actions of hundreds, if not thousands, of people is hard. You simply can't change a system by doing a thing.

*Innoganda leads to cynicism, not impact.*

\* \* \*

This book lays out a system-level way to encourage and enable people to think and act beyond the status quo. Our approach sits at the inter-

---

7. One of our favorite reviewers (Karl Ronn) said, "This should be an Internet meme." Scott's fourteen-year-old son would consider it life-changing if his dad were connected to a meme. Maybe not in a good way, though. He is fourteen, after all.

8. Some call this "innovation theater." Innoganda is shorter. Take that, Steve Blank and Eric Ries (but read their stuff; it is great).

section of four streams of research: organizational culture, habit change, innovation-enabling behaviors, and innovation-enhancing structures and systems.[9] The four of us—Scott, Andy, and Natalie, as advisers at Innosight, and Paul, as a practitioner at DBS—are connected to and passionate about this literature. Over the last few years, we have sought to augment the literature with additional primary research and field experience (including a 2017–2018 project between Innosight and DBS) to create a practical toolkit that brings clarity to the often-fuzzy topic of culture change. Our perspective is that success requires focusing on changing people's daily habits through a series of interventions, and then ensuring that the new habits stick and scale. We'll have plenty of time to go into specifics, but here's the "Cliffs-Notes" version:[10]

1. Culture change starts by getting granular and defining the specific behaviors that enable innovation success. We like to say that innovators are curious, customer-obsessed, collaborative, adept in ambiguity, and empowered. But the desired behaviors may vary from company to company.

2. You have to acknowledge and defeat a tough enemy called the shadow strategy—the hidden but powerful forces that prioritize today over tomorrow. Doing this requires moving beyond innoganda campaigns to concerted efforts to shape day-to-day habits.

3. To succeed in these efforts, borrow from the habit-change literature to encourage desired be-

*Don't just bring in bean bags. Create behavior enablers, artifacts, and nudges (BEANs).*

---

9. You can see the books we found most influential in each stream in the "Culture of Innovation Bookshelf" in the book's appendix.

10. Natalie and Scott remember, um, augmenting their detailed reading of assigned books in high school with these short synthesis guides known for their signature yellow and black covers. They definitely never replaced reading the book. For sure.

haviors and overcome identified blockers by hacking people's habits with BEANs: behavior enablers, artifacts, and nudges.

4. You can create an alpha version of a culture of innovation for your team, group, or department via a six-week sprint that includes a focused BEANstorming session.

5. Ensuring that change sticks and scales requires integrating day-to-day habits into supporting systems and structures, most notably those that determine how your company allocates resources.

Here is a more detailed roadmap for readers who like to know what they are getting into. We have broken the book into two parts. Part I lays the book's foundation with four long-form chapters and three companion case studies.[11] Chapter 1 starts with definitions. The phrase "culture of innovation" itself is a barrier, as it is typically used in such a vague and ambiguous way and is ascribed to so many wildly different situations that it has become almost meaningless. We define a culture of innovation as *one in which the behaviors that drive innovation success come naturally.* Chapter 1 parses this definition, describes the behaviors that drive innovation success in plain language, and shows those behaviors in action at UNICEF. Following this chapter is a detailed case study describing how The Salvation Army's Eastern Territory is seeking to create more "innovation chefs." Chapter 2 starts with a puzzle. Why is it that humans are born innovators, but organizations struggle with it? A story about Scott's son "Happy Harry" and Microsoft missing the search-advertising market highlights the problem (the shadow strategy that institutionalizes inertia), and the ensuring case study about DBS's journey shows it is solvable.

How do you create a culture of innovation? Don't bring in foosball tables. Don't run useless campaigns exhorting people to give it their all on Wacky Idea Wednesday, Free-Thinking Friday, or, heaven for-

---

11. A typical business-book chapter is roughly six thousand words, or about twenty pages in print. The chapters and case studies in part I of this book range in length from about one thousand to eight thousand words, and the DBS case study is actually longer than the chapter that precedes it. For those looking for monotonic consistency, we apologize, but this is, after all, a book about creativity and innovation. Go with it!

bid, Special-Purpose Sunday. Instead, follow the guidance of chapter 3 and hack habits with BEANs. Inspired by the habit-change literature, a BEAN is a behavior enabler, artifact, and nudge. We'll describe what a successful BEAN looks like, and share stories of BEANs that work, such as DBS's Gandalf Scholarship, Tata's Dare to Try award, and Adobe's Kickbox program. The case study after this chapter details an intervention at a DBS tech center in Hyderabad and describes keys to successfully creating a BEAN.

Chapter 4 will draw on a case example from the HR department at a large Asian telecommunications company to provide step-by-step guidance on how to conduct a six-week sprint capped by a BEANstorming session to develop practical interventions and catalyze a group of change agents.

Part II of *Eat, Sleep, Innovate* contains practical tips and tools and inspiring stories to help you drive culture change that sticks and scales. Short sections are organized into chapters tied to the phases a would-be innovator must follow: discovery (chapter 5), blueprinting (chapter 6), assessing and testing (chapter 7), and moving forward (chapter 8). Each phase contains example BEANs, "BEAN boosters" (that help amplify the impact of selected BEANs), case studies, and practical tools.

*Eat, Sleep, Innovate* concludes with reflections, a process for culture change, and our call to action. The book's appendix contains reference material: our culture of innovation bookshelf, a culture-change literature review, and our "bag of BEANs," with brief summaries of 101 BEANs. The book's companion website has a range of additional tools and templates to help you put the ideas of *Eat, Sleep, Innovate* immediately into action.

* * *

While the four of us come at the problem from different perspectives, we are united in our goal to address the challenge of constrained, contained innovation potential. We are convinced that organizations are capable of so much more than they realize. We've seen firsthand the awesome power of established organizations combining the unique assets that they've built over the years with behaviors that are consistent with successful innovation. The book draws on our collective seventy-plus years of field experience working with organizations all around the globe on these challenges and decades of accumulated research from some of the world's leading academics—but that doesn't mean it is easy.

Culture change is not a paint-by-number exercise. The solution for your organization needs to be tailored to your unique goals, current context, and history. This should be good news for leaders who might look admiringly at innovation icons like Apple, Disney Pixar, Google, or 3M while simultaneously sensing that these models are not replicable within their own walls. What we will share are battle-tested ideas that work, providing you with the language, the tools, and—perhaps most critically—the confidence to create your own culture of innovation.

Part One

# LAYING THE FOUNDATION

**PART I OF *EAT, SLEEP, INNOVATE* LAYS THE FOUNDATION FOR** the argument of the book.

- Chapter 1 and its companion case study details the book's core terms of reference, most notably the idea that a culture of innovation is one in which the behaviors that drive innovation success come naturally.

- Chapter 2 describes the core challenge facing organizations seeking to create such a culture: institutionalized inertia powered by the shadow strategy. Its companion case study shows how DBS overcame this challenge.

- Chapter 3 and its companion case study develop the idea of behavior enablers, artifacts, and nudges (BEANs) to encourage desired behaviors and overcome identified blockers.

- Finally, Chapter 4 provides a detailed view of how to run a six-week culture sprint capped by a two-day activation session that includes structured "BEANstorming."[1]

---

1. For those stressed out, wondering why there is no companion case study for Chapter 4, it is pretty simple: the case study is intertwined with the chapter. Relax. As Ralph Waldo Emerson said, "A foolish consistency is the hobgoblin of little minds."

1

# The Responsibility
# of the Many

It was early September 2017. Victoria Maskell, based in UNICEF's Panama office, was sitting in an emergency meeting about Hurricane Irma, "looking at the terrifying swirl of red with yellow, green and then blue edges moving towards the Caribbean." The hurricane, which had strengthened into a Category 5 storm, would do considerable damage once it hit landfall, and Maskell was looking for ways to support emergency preparedness for local populations that might be otherwise unreachable.

Her thoughts turned to U-Report, a mobile empowerment platform created by UNICEF, an international United Nations agency that provides children with access to health and education. UNICEF had created the platform to take advantage of its reach in close to two hundred countries, using social messaging and SMS channels on mobile phones to gather dipstick opinions on topics of interest to UNICEF's partners and stakeholders. Maskell recalled how UNICEF had used U-Report to answer questions and provide information about the Zika virus and a recent deployment to Peru after severe flooding. In both instances, UNICEF "used U-Report on a very, very small scale to understand the situation of young people and to send some 'stay safe' messages."

Maskell thought U-Report could be a great way to spread information about a predictable disaster like a hurricane. So she worked with representatives from seven other UNICEF offices, including Christopher Brooks, senior digital and data specialist at UNICEF who was working in New York, and James Powell, global U-report coordinator based in Bangkok, Thailand, and seven UN online volunteers. The team provided around-the-clock coverage, providing information and receiving and processing questions from around the globe. UNICEF sent information to more than 25,000 U-Report members and answered 8,000 individual questions on the platform. For 80 percent of the youth reached, U-Report was their only source of information regarding how to prepare for the hurricane, and 80 percent of users said they had shared information with more than one person.

UNICEF received hundreds of messages of thanks. A fifteen-year-old in the East Caribbean wrote, "I don't know how to explain myself, but in my fifteen years this is the first hurricane I've ever been through, and it really scared me. But I don't know how to tell you that the information you sent me was some of the best information I got, and I shared it with my whole family by telephone. Thank you."

After the storms passed, U-Report allowed UNICEF to get a better grasp of where help was most necessary and to mobilize an appropriate response.

"We sometimes forget the power of the global community, but a global team allows us to respond quickly. U-Report aims to bring about social change and champions the very idea of a global community," Maskell said. "One of the brilliant things about the U-Report community is that we share best practices and we grow as a global set of colleagues with one clear aim in protecting children and young people when they need it most."

Nobody had mandated Maskell to act. There was no senior leader painting a bold strategic vision. No one needed to invent a technological breakthrough. The effort came from normal people acting in a way that allowed them to come up with a creative solution to a difficult problem. That's innovation in action.[1]

---

1. As a postscript to the U-Report story, in the COVID-19 crisis, UNICEF used a chatbot feature it built on the platform to get information out to five million people and released a white-label version of U-Report so it could be used more broadly.

In this chapter, we're going to dive deep into the actions that make Maskell and others like her innovative—because there are Victoria Maskells in every organization. They're creative, curious, and inventive, and they thrive if their habits, instincts, and behaviors are allowed to flow naturally. That, in essence, is what a culture of innovation is all about. Let's now unpack what innovation truly means and explore the benefits of a culture of innovation.[2]

## What We Talk about When We Talk about Innovation

Our formal definition of innovation has five simple words: "Something different that creates value."[3] *Something* is intentionally vague. People often think innovation is about creating new technologies. But that would mean only a narrow group of people are involved—engineers or white-lab-coat-wearing scientists—and that's not the case. Take Scott's grandfather. Robert N. Anthony Sr. was a renowned professor who earned a place in the Accounting Hall of Fame for writing dense, dry academic textbooks with scintillating titles like *Management Control in Nonprofit Organizations*  but he was an innovator as well.

In the early 1960s, Anthony Sr. introduced the first version of a very different type of book, called *Essentials of Accounting*. It was *not* a dense, dry academic textbook that required an expert instructor to understand. It was a do-it-yourself workbook for nonexperts, filled with self-directed exercises that, in essence, would allow readers to teach themselves the

---

2. There was some debate among the writing team about the examples in this chapter and the case study that follows being exclusively from not-for-profit organizations. The argument was that the examples are rich and different than what appears in most innovation books and certainly fit the principle described in the introduction of focusing on NO-DETs: normal organizations doing extraordinary things. For those in commercially oriented organizations, don't worry. Your time will come.

3. Andy, Natalie, and Scott have been in a long-running (albeit friendly) dispute with Innosight colleague Dave Duncan about this definition. He prefers "Something new that creates value," because *new* reflects the Latin roots of the word *innovation* and requires people to stretch thinking to push the novelty of their idea. We prefer *different* because it makes clear that smart adaptation of an existing idea also counts as innovation.

basics of accounting. At the end, you couldn't run the control function for a nonprofit organization, but you could grasp the difference between a debit and a credit, calculate days receivable, make greater sense of the financial press, and have more informed conversations with people in your finance department. The book, which reached its eleventh edition before Anthony Sr. passed away in 2007 (with a twelfth edition published posthumously), sold more copies than all of Anthony Sr.'s other books combined.[4] The innovation here wasn't a whiz-bang technology; it was a different way to teach accounting.

We use the word *different* in our definition over more dramatic words, like *breakthrough*, because it reminds us that one of the highest-impact paths to innovation is paved by making the complicated simple and the expensive affordable. Reading *Essentials of Accounting* is arguably *worse* than receiving face-to-face instruction from a skilled academic who can explain concepts and provide real-time feedback, but its success shows this doesn't matter. Its simplicity and affordability opened up a much broader market, following the path of what Innosight cofounder and Harvard Professor Clayton Christensen famously dubbed *disruptive* innovation.

Finally, the definition's most critical words: *creates value*. These words separate innovation from precursory activities like invention and creativity. Those activities are no doubt important, but until you have turned a spark of creativity into revenues, profits, or improved process performance, in our eyes, you have not innovated. The focus on creating value reminds us that innovation isn't an academic activity; it is an active one.

Let's say you are creating a presentation about innovation. What icon would you put on the title slide? The answer for most people is instantaneous: the light bulb. Who invented the light bulb? It's a trick question. Most people will say Thomas Edison, but if you study the historical record, a number of people could claim credit for inventing the underlying technology. The reason we remember Edison is not because he was a

---

4. Scott was given three copies of *Essentials of Accounting*. The first was a birthday present from his grandfather when he turned . . . eight. (Thanks, Grandpa!) The second was right before he started his first job at a consulting firm. The third was right before he entered business school. That was the itch Scott's grandfather scratched: an easily accessible book that could be widely distributed by organizations wanting to increase their team's financial fluency.

great *inventor*—although, with more than 1,000 patents to his name, he was—but because he was an even better *innovator*. He was obsessed with the creation of value. Edison didn't work on just the technology; he pushed to develop an end-to-end system that would allow an end consumer to enjoy light. The world's first electricity-generating facility was owned by the Edison Electric Light Company, which operated in lower Manhattan. In 1889, that company merged with several other Edison-owned entities to create General Electric. Never forget Edison's most famous quote on this topic: "Genius," he noted, "is 1 percent inspiration and 99 percent perspiration." Unless you are sweating and driving the creation of value, in our eyes you have not innovated.

When we ask people to describe innovation in action, they often default to world-changing technologies like the light bulb, big-bang products like the iPhone, or game-changing services like Airbnb. All are excellent examples, but innovation comes in many different forms and flavors. For example, participants from various companies who have attended Scott's Harvard Business Publishing corporate learning webinars have suggested the following as innovation in action: developing a visual scorecard to track KPIs, using standing meetings to increase efficiency, performing remote-site monitoring, and even fostering the "organic development of stuff sharing areas for employees, including a jewelry swap table on one floor." These are all reasonable examples of something different that creates value.

You can find innovation everywhere if you have the right language to describe it. Innovation isn't the job of the few; it is the responsibility of the many. Accountants can do it. Not-for-profits can do it. Kids can do it (more on that soon). You can too. And today's quickly changing world demands that *all* of us improve our ability to do it—and that all of our organizations create cultures that support it.

## What Culture Actually Means

A culture of innovation sounds appealing, doesn't it? The phrase conjures up images of places that turn seemingly wild dreams into reality as a matter of course—places where new ideas flourish and where employees feel their voices are heard, their impact is felt, and their mark is left; and institutions that can nimbly adapt to and thrive within a world that is constantly zigzagging and increasingly slippery and unpredictable.

It isn't hard to name iconic companies that seem to have cultures of innovation—places like Google, Amazon, Disney Pixar, and Virgin. But what exactly constitutes these cultures? People often answer that question by talking about what they see. Perhaps the cafeteria features a former Michelin star chef whipping up vegan protein balls that taste sublime.[5] Or young employees might be zooming around on hoverboards. Maybe there's even a slide—of the playground and not the PowerPoint variety—in the middle of the office. It looks and feels fun, free-spirited, and open.

These visual indicators are what longtime MIT professor Edgar Schein described as "artifacts"—essentially, what you see when you look around an organization. While these might be *manifestations* of culture, artifacts are the tip of the proverbial iceberg—and not the defining attributes of a culture. For instance, in some contexts companies may ship in the foosball tables but see them gather dust, or they might hear snickers as senior leaders dutifully and awkwardly go down the slides; in other contexts the foosball tables and slides might become popular hotspots. There is more to the story than visible artifacts.

The word *culture* appears in popular aphorisms such as "culture eats strategy for breakfast" (attributed to Peter Drucker) and "culture is what you do when the managers leave the room," among others. But what exactly is an organization's culture? Schein's work looks beyond *what you see* in an organization to *what people actually do* on a day-to-day basis and, most critically, *what they think and believe.* As such, Schein defines company culture as "A pattern of shared basic assumptions that

---

5. Nothing at all against vegan protein balls. A Google search for "delicious vegan protein balls" returned 24,900,000 results. What a world!

the group learned as it solved its problems . . . [which have] worked well enough to be considered valid and, therefore, to be taught to new members as the correct way to perceive, think and feel in relation to those problems."

What exactly does that mean? Whenever an organization is still nascent or encounters a new problem, it has to figure out a way to solve it—perhaps people draw on their collective history, or perhaps they just try things until something works. And over time, an organization repeatedly encounters particular types of challenges—in creating new products and services, for example, or in selling, producing, or managing employee development. As the group finds a groove in addressing these challenges, their trial-and-error experimentation gives ways to standard processes, which eventually transform into routines or habits. Powering those habits are the assumptions that once were explicit but disappear into the fabric of the organization.

Here's an example. Imagine you go to a meeting where senior leaders are debating whether to fund a project. You might see that the discussion focuses primarily on the financial forecasts presented by a team. What led to that moment? Likely it was a series of organizational routines in which small teams gathered data, created spreadsheets estimating a project's financial impact, and shared those spreadsheets with leaders to garner feedback. But why? Why was there this routine of developing spreadsheets? And why did this work take place in small teams? If you asked those involved, they would probably say, "That's just what we do around here." The real answer, however, is that at some point in the organization's history, someone had learned that disciplined analysis was valuable; perhaps they had launched a project without it, and it ended up being catastrophic. At some point, they had also learned that teams outproduced work by individuals. Maybe they had a side-by-side comparison that justified that decision, or maybe it was a default setting that stuck. Whatever their path, over time, two assumptions coalesced: "The best results come from incorporating diverse perspectives," and "rigorous planning helps to avoid investment mistakes."

This is what makes culture so challenging. We see visible artifacts—like who says what at a meeting, what materials people bring, how an office is laid out, and so on—but below the surface of those artifacts are the ways people work, which are grounded in the assumptions, beliefs, and values the group holds. Culture isn't just what you see; it is what a group does and believes.

Schein's definition makes clear one of the biggest fallacies organizations fall prey to when seeking to boost their ability to innovate: they look at the hot innovative company of the day and seek to replicate the key practices of that company.

*Culture isn't what you see or say but what you do.*

"Oh, 3M has a '15 percent rule' to allow engineers to explore side projects? Let's copy that." Or, "Google has a 'moonshots' group that has the freedom to explore emerging technologies? Let's set one of those up!" Or "P&G has an 'open innovation' program designed to connect with individual scientists? Sure, sounds good." Each of those companies, however, have very distinct cultures that maximize the impact of those programs. What you see may be what you get, but if what you see doesn't *result* from what you've done or *reinforce* what you believe, then what you see is nothing more than a "soulless artifact" or innoganda.[6] Imagine, by analogy, that you see a beautiful orchid while on vacation in Singapore at the botanic gardens. You say, "I'd like to have one of those in my backyard in Minneapolis." It's obvious that the plant's environment here is different than the one in your backyard, but so are all the other things around the plant—the caretakers, the routines they follow, and so on.

In summary, a culture of *anything* (call it "X") is one in which people perceive X to be valuable; follow behaviors that enable them to achieve X on a routine, repeatable basis; and then reinforce those behaviors

---

6. That's innovation propaganda. We defined it all back in the introduction. This footnote is primarily for anyone who skipped the introduction. If you did, go back and read it. It's good!

with visual cues and other enablers. Hence, our definition of a culture of innovation is *one in which the behaviors that drive innovation success come naturally.*

## How Innovators Behave—and How Organizations Should Support Them

While many people still believe that innovation is a mystical activity that requires God-given skill, it is in fact a discipline. And like all disciplines, it can be managed, measured, mastered, and improved with careful practice. There is ample literature around the behaviors that drive successful innovation, such as *The Innovator's DNA*, by Clayton Christensen, Jeff Dyer, and Hal Gregersen, and publications by the Innosight team (most notably *The Innovator's Guide to Growth*, *Competing Against Luck*, and *Reinvent Your Business Model*). Our synthesis of this body of work highlights that innovation success traces back to five behaviors: great innovators are curious, customer-obsessed, collaborative, adept in ambiguity, and empowered; and great cultures encourage and reinforce these behaviors. Table 1-1 summarizes these behaviors, and the text below brings them to life by showing how each behavior contributed to another successful innovation at UNICEF.

### Behavior 1: Curiosity

Innovators are consistently searching for different and better ways to do things. They are explorers who are not content with resting on past success but believe they can always find a better way. That means they do the following:

- Keep an open mind, constantly asking, "What if . . . ?" and "How might we . . . ?"

- Avoid shutting down ideas by saying, "This is how we do things here"

- Adopt a problem-solver, versus a fault-finder, mindset

- Are perpetually paranoid about the future

TABLE 1-1

## Five behaviors that drive innovation success

| Broad behavior | Description | Specific behaviors |
|---|---|---|
| Curiosity | Question the status quo and consistently search for different and better ways to do things. | • Keep an open mind, constantly asking "What if . . . ?" and "How might we . . . ?"<br><br>• Avoid shutting down ideas by saying, "This is how we do things here."<br><br>• Adopt a problem-solver, versus a fault-finder, mindset.<br><br>• Be perpetually paranoid about the future. |
| Customer obsession | Relentlessly seek to develop an ever-deeper understanding of the jobs to be done of customers, employees, and stakeholders. | • Spend significant time with customers to understand their jobs to be done.<br><br>• Regularly create customer profiles and customer journey maps.<br><br>• Ensure all solutions are rooted in real needs and problems.<br><br>• Gain deep insight into how customers choose between solutions. |
| Collaboration | Incorporate cross-functional expertise resourcefully, recognizing that the smartest person in the room is often the room itself. | • Build cross-functional teams with diverse expertise and viewpoints.<br><br>• Actively seek external stimuli to borrow and adapt.<br><br>• Emphasize collective, versus individual, goals.<br><br>• Be transparent and frank while remaining respectful. |
| Adeptness in ambiguity | Act confidently, despite incomplete information; expect iteration and change; excel at experimentation; and celebrate judicious risk-taking. | • Focus on assumptions over answers.<br><br>• Constantly ask, "How can we learn more?"<br><br>• Design experiments to learn more about key assumptions.<br><br>• Embrace intelligent failure. |

| Empowerment | Exercise initiative, seek out and leverage resources, and make confident decisions. | • Show a bias toward action (ask for forgiveness, not permission). |
| --- | --- | --- |
| | | • Craft a clear and compelling story about the value of innovation efforts. |
| | | • Speak up when something isn't working. |
| | | • Embrace a growth mindset that sees possibilities, not a fixed mindset that sees constraints. |

Many of the countries UNICEF operates in face a problem, which is at the same time an opportunity. There are 1.8 billion people between the ages of 10 and 24 in the world today, nearly 90 percent of whom are in low- and middle-income countries. This is the largest cohort of young people in human history. Yet, many lack opportunities. Only 30 percent of the world's poorest children attend secondary school, and more than 50 million young people are on the move, running from conflict, poverty, and extreme weather. There is a vital window of opportunity to empower these youth by building skills and nurturing creativity, but such opportunity is at risk of being missed.

A proven way to empower youth and help them build skills is to have people from different backgrounds work together to solve problems. So a few years ago, a UNICEF leader in Kosovo wondered whether there was a way to bring youth communities together to solve social problems using human-centered design approaches. After all, young people have an intimate knowledge of local problems, and, armed with the right tools, are well positioned to design and implement solutions. That leader's fundamental curiosity, along with the desire to flip a problem into an opportunity, started the journey that resulted in a high-impact program called UPSHIFT, through which UNICEF convenes and supports local youth to become innovators.

## Behavior 2: Customer Obsession

Great innovators relentlessly seek to develop an ever-deeper understanding of the jobs to be done by customers, employees, and stakeholders.[7] That means they do the following:

- Spend significant time with customers (or for whomever you are trying to innovate) to understand their jobs to be done

- Regularly create customer profiles and customer-journey maps

- Ensure all solutions are rooted in real needs and problems

- Gain deep insight into how customers choose between solutions

The genius of UPSHIFT is that it involves the "customer" (local youth) directly in the creation of potential solutions. Consider the example of Sejnur Veshall, a young member of the Roma community of Prizren, a Kosovan municipality of about 100,000 people. "The Roma community in Kosovo definitely faces a lot of discrimination," Veshall said, "and even though I learned to be very vocal when this happened and always raised my voice against it, many others don't. It is Roma girls and women in particular who are most marginalized, oftentimes uneducated and trapped into housekeeping." The close connection to—indeed, the involvement of—the community creates instant empathy for areas that matter to would-be customers.

## Behavior 3: Collaboration

One of the most persistent findings in the innovation literature is that truly distinct ideas come at intersections, where different mindsets and skills collide. Great innovators incorporate cross-functional

---

7. A "job to be done" is a core Innosight concept popularized by our cofounder Clayton Christensen. As described in the book *Competing Against Luck*, a job to be done is the problem a particular customer seeks to solve in a particular circumstance. The idea is that innovations that make it simpler and easier for people to make progress against important problems readily gain traction, while those that either make life more difficult or target jobs that aren't relevant struggle.

expertise resourcefully, recognizing that the smartest person in the room is often the room itself. To be collaborative, innovators should do the following:

- Build cross-functional teams with diverse expertise and viewpoints

- Actively seek external stimuli to borrow and adapt

- Emphasize collective, versus individual, goals

- Be transparent and frank while remaining respectful

UPSHIFT shows collaboration at two levels. First, the team-based nature of the program encourages collaboration at a local-community level. Veshall led a team called Golden Hands, designed to teach Roma women to create and sell traditional decorative plates. "We wanted to teach Roma women an artisanal craft, build their professional skills, and help them turn this into a business," he said. "What Golden Hands is trying to achieve is to make Roma women active in their community and change attitudes towards the Roma people through providing spaces for socialization between people of different backgrounds

**Sejnur Veshall (second from right) and the Golden Hands team.**
*Source:* ©UNICEF/Marina.

and communities." Veshall's team organized workshops that included members of Roma and majority communities. "The involvement and integration of the Roma women in society through creating a decorative plates business is an important aspect of Golden Hands," Veshall said.

Second, collaboration within UNICEF has amplified UPSHIFT's impact by bringing it from one small country to many countries around the world, while continually improving it. A small, central innovation team has helped disseminate knowledge across the UNICEF network by convening in gatherings such as the UPSHIFT 2.0 conference. With forty people working on youth innovation around the globe, this conference created modular content and user guides that allowed local officers to adopt and adapt UPSHIFT. It created best-practice implementation guides to help form partnerships, develop workshops, drive engagement, and raise money. As of the writing of this book, UPSHIFT is in twenty-three countries, with plans to bring it to another fifteen. The program in Jordan targets the large youth population in refugee camps. In Vietnam, UNICEF has partnered with local schools to develop social innovation clubs, drive social inclusion, and develop solutions that address climate issues. In North Macedonia, a local team won $20,000 to support its idea of a mobile app called "Speak Out" to build a community of support for victims of bullying.

## Behavior 4: Adeptness in Ambiguity

Each early-stage innovative idea is the same: it is partially right and partially wrong. The trick is to know which part is which. Great innovators act confidently despite incomplete information, expect iteration and change, excel at experimentation, and celebrate judicious risk-taking. They know that the path to creating value will have twists and turns, fumbles and false steps, and setbacks and moments that feel like failure. Specifically, they do the following:

- Focus on assumptions over answers

- Constantly ask, "How can we learn more?"

- Design experiments to learn more about key assumptions

- Embrace intelligent failure

UPSHIFT's design directly encourages these behaviors. The program is based around the concept of a human-centered design bootcamp or "hackathon," where teams work to rapidly advance ideas. The content and guides created by a central UNICEF team (described above) help local UNICEF officers to work with partners to design and execute workshops in which teams can develop and experiment with ideas. The goal is to make things as tangible as possible, as quickly as possible. Involving the local community in the design of the solution makes it easy to get feedback on early-stage ideas, which helps with the iteration that is always part of the innovation journey. Typically, the most promising ideas receive further support and potentially seed funding, but every participant learns important new skills.

## Behavior 5: Empowerment

You can't do something that creates value unless you *do* something. That means exercising initiative, seeking out and leveraging resources, and making confident decisions. Innovators that are empowered do the following:

- Show a bias toward action (ask for forgiveness, not permission)

- Craft a clear and compelling story about the value of innovation efforts

- Speak up when something isn't working

- Embrace a growth mindset that sees possibilities, not a fixed mindset that sees constraints

Veshall's final reflection offers a powerful testimonial of how UPSHIFT enables empowerment:

> With remarkable mentorship and collaboration with the
> UPSHIFT team, Golden Hands was successful and everyone in

my community was surprised. This initiative gave me an epithet of a leader, which frightened me so much at first—suddenly I was not just Sejnur, a random young person, but a leader of a young team who organized events for the community and worked for the betterment of our situation. With the mentorship that the UPSHIFT team gave me, I came to embrace the self-confidence that came with the leadership role. After UPSHIFT, I returned to my community where I was raised, but now with much more confidence, greater access to networks and a professional experience of running a project, with greater desire to work more.

## The Benefits of Creating a Culture of Innovation

Creating and maintaining a culture of innovation isn't easy, but it's worth the effort. Since you are reading this book, you likely don't need to be convinced of that fact. But what if a skeptical colleague asks, "With all of the things we have going on, why pursue this?" One answer comes by way of a simple thought experiment. What would it look like, say, if your organization got better at solving problems and finding smart solutions like the ones we shared in this chapter?

But what if your colleague is more data-oriented? The big double-blind randomized study of innovative cultures hasn't been done yet—in part because, historically, it has been hard to even agree on what a culture of innovation means—but a significant body of evidence suggests its power. For example, in its 2006 "Most Innovative Companies" issue, *Bloomberg Businessweek* cited a Boston Consulting Group study that showed that innovative firms had a 4 percent total shareholder return premium over less innovative peers. That premium holds up in other studies. For example, in 2019, a team of Innosight consultants compared the total shareholder returns of the one hundred most innovative companies in a study by MIT, Glassdoor, and the S&P 500. The innovative firms enjoyed a 3.3 percent premium over a comparable set of companies over a ten-year period. Of course, we can't prove that causation doesn't work in reverse (improved returns create a perception that the company is innovative), but the consistency between the data is compelling.

You could also point out the data backing the benefit of each innovative way of working detailed in this chapter. Research by Adobe shows that fostering *curiosity* and creativity and questioning the status quo makes a company 3.5 times more likely to outperform peers in terms of revenue growth.

Further, in 2018, Forrester released two research reports on *customer obsession*. The first found that companies that show their customer obsession by providing great customer experiences see high stock-price growth. The second report (commissioned by Adobe) demonstrated that experience-driven businesses have happier employees and grow revenue more than 35 percent faster than non-experience-driven businesses.

The boost from *collaboration* appears even greater. A 2017 *Forbes* article reported that a joint study between the Institute for Corporate Productivity and a Babson College professor found that companies that promote collaborative work are five times more likely to be high-performing than those that don't.

Using agile methods to be *adept in ambiguity* is very much in vogue these days, and for good reason: Bain & Co. found that agile methods reduce project risk by 76 percent and increase team productivity by 84 percent. Harvard Business School professor Amy Edmondson has long touted the benefits of "psychological safety" and fail-safe environments, and Google's own research shows that psychologically safe teams exceed their revenue targets by almost 20 percent.

Finally, several studies show the value of *empowerment*. A multiyear academic study analyzing data from the Federal Human Capital Survey/Federal Employee Viewpoint Survey validated the widely held belief that empowering employees boosts their performance. Gallup's research on engagement shows that empowerment drives engagement, and engaged workforces outperform disengaged workforces by 21 percent in profitability and 20 percent in productivity.

Our hope is that the improved ability to define, measure, and purposefully shape a culture of innovation will, over time, lead to even stronger evidence that supports our conviction that it is a battle worth fighting.

# Chapter Summary

- ✓ Innovation is "something different that creates value." The vague-ness of the word *something* is a reminder that innovation is not the job of the few but the responsibility of the many. The phrase *creates value* distinguishes innovation from its precursors, such as creativity and invention.

- ✓ Culture is not just what you see; it is what you do, how you do it, and why you do it. That means that a culture of *X* is one in which people perceive *X* to be valuable, and they follow behaviors that enable them to achieve *X* on a routine, repeatable basis. A culture of innovation, then, is one in which the behaviors that drive inno-vation success come naturally.

- ✓ To maximize their chances of success, great innovators are curi-ous, customer-obsessed, collaborative, adept in ambiguity, and empowered.

- ✓ There is significant evidence for the benefits of creating a culture of innovation—most notably, persistent boosts to shareholder re-turns and improved team performance.

# Creating "Innovation Chefs" at The Salvation Army

Peter Drucker once called The Salvation Army "by far the most effective organization in the U.S." It is a charitable, faith-based organization that aids close to 23 million people a year. It is the second biggest recipient of donations in the United States, and eighty-two cents of every dollar donated to it goes toward programs for the needy.[1] Its mission is "to meet human needs in His name without discrimination." For example, after the terrorist attacks in the United States on September 11, 2001, thirty-eight planes and seven thousand passengers found themselves stranded in Gander, a small village in Newfoundland. The Salvation Army quickly mobilized with the Red Cross and the citizens of Gander to provide food, clothing, shelter, and comfort to the stranded passengers. "For a solid week, we did nothing but look after people. . . . We had no elaborate plan in place on what to do—we ran with common sense," one of its leaders said. "We did what needed to be done." The Salvation Army shows that a culture of innovation can exist at a large, established organization; it is what the introduction called a NO-DET (a normal organization doing extraordinary things).

In 1865, Methodist Reform Church minister William Booth and his wife Catherine founded The Salvation Army in London during a time of great societal divide. The Industrial Revolution had created tremendous wealth but had also subjected the impoverished people of East London to harsh conditions. The Booths felt traditional churches had failed people in need, so they took to the streets of London to serve

---

1. Generally, an efficiency ratio of over seventy-five cents is considered very high.

those who were poor, homeless, hungry, and destitute and wouldn't otherwise attend or be welcomed into church. The Booths committed to helping people at their point of need rather than from a central location. They designed The Salvation Army to serve two groups: the needy, who are the targets of their services, and the volunteers and supporters who provide the organization's labor and resources. They designed a flexible, lean, and "user-friendly" organizational model that keeps these two groups in close contact and adapts nimbly to their shifting needs.

The Salvation Army gives its ordained clergy, which it calls "officers," military titles, and it models its positions and titles on military structures. Thus, the international leader of The Salvation Army carries the title "General," and the country leader in the United States (based in Alexandria, Virginia) carries the title "National Commander." The Salvation Army divides the United States into four territories, with a territorial commander leading each territory. The four US territories are broken into thirty-nine divisions, each led by a divisional commander. Divisions consist of local centers for worship and service as well as various specialized centers. The focus of this story is The Salvation Army's Eastern US territory, which covers twelve states and includes Puerto Rico and the US Virgin Islands. For simplicity, we will refer to The Salvation Army when speaking about the entire organization and refer to the Eastern Territory when speaking about that region's specific localized efforts.

## Three Stories of Innovation in Action in the Eastern Territory

One of The Salvation Army's greatest strengths is its decentralized organization. Its international and national headquarters in London, England, and Alexandria, Virginia, are small, lean operations that primarily manage connections between chapters around the world. Decision-making power generally resides at the local level, with each chapter empowered to make decisions relevant to its community's unique needs and circumstances but also able to access territorial leadership and approval when appropriate. That structure feeds curiosity, customer-centricity, and empowerment, three key innovation behaviors. The three stories below follow the theme in chapter 1, showing how innovation, something different that creates value, comes in many different forms and flavors.

The first story begins with a visit to a local center by Eastern Territory IT Director Rich Gulley, Division IT Director Dave Dlugose, and Eastern Territory Innovation Department & Heritage Museum co-director Steve Bussey. It was clear the center was struggling and frustrated. Gulley and Bussey probed for the source of the frustration, conducting empathic research about frontline technological needs. They learned that, even though there was a national telephone number to call to donate items, people were overwhelming some local offices with up to sixty calls per day. Dlugose identified a simple phone-based solution: "Press two to connect to donations." This quick fix solved the problem. Local donation call volume dropped to zero and the national center efficiently ensured donations found their way to people in need. The solution was prototyped throughout New Jersey and scaled through the rest of the Eastern Territory. A simple idea, connected to a real problem and executed well, created real value.

* * *

The second story starts in Manchester, New Hampshire. In 2017, Captain Mike Harper and his Corps assistant Dan LaBossiere were looking for

**Mobile Joes, then and now.**
*Source: Left:* The Salvation Army USA Eastern Territorial Heritage Museum; *Right:* Captain Michael Harper, The Salvation Army.

a way to connect with the homeless in the community. They discovered a photo from a 1967 report of a young officer using a mobile beverage dispenser in emergencies and special events. Drawing inspiration from the photo, they purchased modern beverage-dispensing backpacks, which they wore while walking the streets to offer coffee and connect with homeless people. They called themselves "Mobile Joes," because they primarily used the backpacks for coffee.[2] Soon after the two young officers deployed Mobile Joes in Manchester, they found themselves on stage sharing the story with about a thousand colleagues at an Eastern Territory event in Maine. The officers shared the technical and practical aspects of the program and spoke about the personal impact they had been able to make. Audience members walked away from the event saying, "Hey, we can do that too." Conferences are a powerful way for ideas to spread throughout The Salvation Army, providing moments of serendipity and opportunities for collaboration. At these conferences, Bussey noted that it is common to hear people say, "Well, if they're able to do this, then I can try to do that as well." Often people have had an initiative fail in the past, but then, at a conference, they see elements of it working somewhere else. The goal is to help them learn to say, "Hey, maybe I can revisit this idea. Maybe it can work if I learn from their practices."

* * *

When people think of The Salvation Army, the first thing that often comes to mind are the bell ringers at Christmastime—those people who stand outside stores next to red kettles, collecting money for the needy. Today's decrease in the use of cash and coins and the parallel rise in digital payments clearly challenges this model. So during a Salvation Army national board meeting in Cleveland, one board member initi-

---

2. Paul and Andy found this example curious, which led us to realize that "joe," as slang for coffee, is unique to North America! One of our favorite reviewers, Thomas (we'll keep his last name in reserve until a future footnote!), responded to this moniker with "That's funny. In Denmark, we say, 'I could really use a hot cup of Paul right now. (No, not really.)'"

ated a dialogue between Apple and The Salvation Army to run an experiment with Apple Pay. The board member asked who might be interested in running the experiment, and Eastern Territory Director of Advancement Chaz Watson raised his hand. Thereafter, a 2018 experiment to allow donations via Apple and Google Pay in a few cities per-

**Mobile phone–based donations.**
*Source:* The Salvation Army National Archives.

formed well, setting the stage to expand the capability to more locations.

## How the Eastern Territory Is Strengthening Its Organic Culture of Innovation

The three innovation stories show the five innovative behaviors in action. In other words, the Eastern Territory shows strong signs of having a culture of innovation—a culture in which the behaviors that drive innovation success come naturally. No one at the organization (to the best of our knowledge) woke up and said, "Let's create a culture of innovation." Rather, the culture emerged from its unique mission and structure.

But there's risk in such a culture. An organization that doesn't know why it is succeeding with innovation might unintentionally change something that is working or miss opportunities to scale what's working and improve. Bussey uses a cooking analogy to illustrate the difference between an organization that deliberately sets out to cultivate a culture of innovation and an organization that just happens upon such a culture and lacks a strong grasp on what exactly makes it innovative. Consider, Bussey said, the difference between a French chef, who has been meticulously trained in precise culinary techniques, and an Italian grandmother, who follows her instincts and does what she learned from her parents and grandparents. Both chefs prepare delicious meals. The classically trained French chef is conscious of the precise ingredients and steps that make his meal great, and he can document and share these techniques. The Italian grandmother, on the other hand, trusts ingrained instincts based on history, practice, and genetics, making these practices more challenging to document, share, and teach to others.

An organization's strengths often defines its weaknesses. In the case of the Eastern Territory, the decentralization that fuels customer obsession and empowerment can make it difficult to scale successes. So, over the past few years, the territory has done several things to help strengthen its innovation culture. In 2012, the Eastern Territory created a group called the Salvation Factory, codirected by Steve and Sharon Bussey, to create more "innovation chefs." The Salvation Factory's purpose is consistent with William Booth's aspiration that "we must have new inventions of every kind." The Salvation Factory's website describes its Innovation Department as an "imaginarium, a space devoted to stimulating and cultivating innovative inventions. In this space, creative ideas are taken from inception and forged into reality; then distributed for use in The Salvation Army." The Salvation Factory specifically focuses on new initiatives that still contain a lot of ambiguity and aren't creating clear value for the organization. These are the initiatives on the periphery that aren't yet seen as a priority, and the Salvation Factory brings the structure, strategy, and resources necessary to move these transformational ideas forward. The Busseys and their team help make abstract ideas concrete through visual storytelling and prototypes and then support the integration of those ideas back into the broader Salvation Army system.

The Strikepoint grant program, created in 2015, is another structure that was initiated to strengthen the Eastern Territory's ability to innovate with impact. The intent of the program, according to Lt. Col. Jim LaBossiere, then division commander of the Salvation Army's North New England division, was to "encourage small bets."[3] An officer seeking funding for new ideas develops a narrative describing the statement of need, the target population, the desired outcomes, the staffing re-

---

3. LaBossiere now serves as program secretary, where he leads and supports program initiatives throughout the Eastern Territory.

quirements, the schedule, and the budget. A mission alignment council, comprised of departments such as legal, commercial, finance, property, and innovation, at both division and territorial levels, considers the requests. LaBossiere, who oversees the council, said, "If it is attractive, feasible, and aligns with our mission, then we say go for it. Our goal is to not stop new initiatives; it's to encourage them, and ensure proper steps are being followed and that we're not going to launch into something that we can't maintain or where we'll sacrifice some other part of the mission."

For example, Jamie Manirakiz, the Eastern Territory's anti-human-trafficking program coordinator, proposed an initiative for a focused effort to address issues related to human trafficking. The program grew from humble beginnings, serving one or two women a night, to a full-time drop-in center, seeing more than a hundred women a day, collaborating with law enforcement citywide, and offering a therapeutic residential program. Transparently tracking new mission initiatives helps transfer knowledge—for example, about what has received funding, how the program receives funding, and what has and has not worked—throughout the Eastern Territory. At the national level, leaders receive everyone's core mission profile electronically. They can see common denominators, challenges, gaps in funding, unmet needs, and big ideas. Leaders then take steps to empower more big ideas and subsequently guide their people through the creative process to identify and secure resources and ultimately make an impact. "Small victories lead to confidence and perhaps a deeper step of faith and a growing number of people involved in these types of projects," LaBossiere said. "It allows us to get past those, 'Oh, we don't have the money for it,' or, 'We don't have the space or the time.' Forget all that. Let's think of something amazing and see where we can go with it."

Finally, in August 2019 the Salvation Factory took over responsibility of the Eastern Territory's museum at its New York headquarters. "This fuses organizational memory, culture-building, and storytelling with the world of innovation," Steve Bussey said. "This gives us an opportunity to make these connections even more explicit and influence The Salvation Army worldwide." A great example of how the Salvation Factory integrates history to encourage collaboration and stimulate ideas is the design of exhibit in the museum called "InnoVision." Attendees are guided through a "hero's journey" with storytelling, visuals, and interactive displays to learn about, discover, and be inspired by innovations throughout The Salvation Army's history. The goal is to inspire participants to reach for similar goals, both for today and tomorrow. These types of museums, stories, and experiences can be a powerful way to celebrate an organization's past while also inspiring creativity.

# 2

# The Shadow Strategy

Why is innovation such an unnatural act inside most organizations? It isn't that the perceived importance of innovation is lacking. Survey after survey shows that executives believe innovation is a key to future success. It isn't a lack of investment either. Organizations spend huge amounts of money on innovation initiatives that range from making executive visits to Silicon Valley to creating special-purpose incubators.[1] And it isn't a lack of effort. Over the past two decades, many large organizations have tried it all: implementing open innovation programs, holding

**Word cloud showing perceived innovation blockers.**

1. We mentioned one of our favorite reviewers, Karl Ronn, in the introduction. Karl is a former Procter & Gamble executive who is now involved in the startup ecosystem in San Francisco. After reading this sentence, he wrote: "I tell people San Francisco has three industries. Tourism, innovation, and, the largest of all, innovation tourism. See our cathedrals. Go home inspired. And do nothing different." Innoganda!

innovation contests, giving people time and space to innovate, setting up corporate venture capital funds, and more.

In June 2017, Scott asked a group of one thousand top executives in the consumer and retail industries to use their mobile phones to answer a simple question: What single word describes what makes innovation a challenge for your organization? The word "fear" was inescapable, and "inertia" jumped out at him as well.[2] Scott connected the first word to an incident involving his son Harry and the second to innovation struggles at McDonald's and Microsoft. The insights from these stories explain how a critical challenge called the *shadow strategy* institutionalizes inertia and strangles innovation. This chapter details this core problem, and the companion case that follows shows the great strides DBS has made in overcoming it over the past decade.

## Happy Harry and Individual Constraints

Most of the time, Scott's eight-year-old son Harry is the kind of kid any parent would love to have.[3] He is quick to smile and laugh, has shockingly spiky hair, and can be reliably counted on to say something vaguely off the wall. His father is from the United States. His mother (Scott's wife, Joanne) is from England. Harry was fully manufactured in Singapore, born there in August 2011. But if you ask him where he is from, he is likely to say either "Mars" or "Harrylandia"—a mythical land where, depending on Harry's mood, he is a king, a god, or both.[4] Harry's nickname at school is "Happy Harry." Once, when asked to draw himself as a superhero, he didn't doodle Iron Man or Spiderman, he drew himself as "Captain Creative."

2. The word cloud also showed how hard the word *bureaucracy* is to spell in real time, as participants also submitted the words "beauracrwcy," "burocracy," and "beauracracy" (so close!).

3. Harry's mother, Joanne, insisted that Scott noted that Harry does, like any kid, have his whiny moments!

4. Harrylandia, you'll be happy to know, is replete with pigs, watermelon, and volcanoes. Who knew!

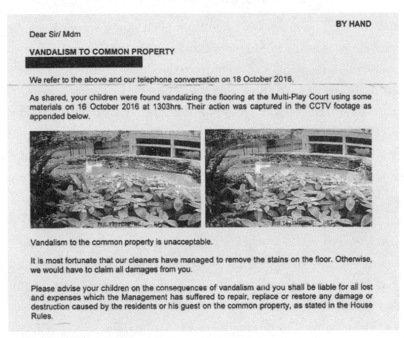

Dear Sir/ Mdm

**VANDALISM TO COMMON PROPERTY**

BY HAND

We refer to the above and our telephone conversation on 18 October 2016.

As shared, your children were found vandalizing the flooring at the Multi-Play Court using some materials on 16 October 2016 at 1303hrs. Their action was captured in the CCTV footage as appended below.

Vandalism to the common property is unacceptable.

It is most fortunate that our cleaners have managed to remove the stains on the floor. Otherwise, we would have to claim all damages from you.

Please advise your children on the consequences of vandalism and you shall be liable for all lost and expenses which the Management has suffered to repair, replace or restore any damage or destruction caused by the residents or his guest on the common property, as stated in the House Rules.

**Letter describing Happy Harry's chalk "incident."**

Imagine Scott's surprise, then, when he and his wife got a letter from their condominium association in Singapore in 2016, reporting an "incident" involving Happy Harry.[5] "Your children were found vandalizing the flooring at the Multi-Play Court using some materials," it read. "Their action was captured in the CCTV footage as appended below. Vandalism to the common property is unacceptable."

What had Harry had the audacity to do? It was a Sunday afternoon. The kids were bored. They asked Scott if they could go outside and use the chalk that Harry got for his birthday to create a baseball diamond on the basketball court. Not only did Scott sanction the behavior but, if the CCTV footage had been in high definition, you would have seen him on the court as well. The letter went on to say, "It is most fortunate that our cleaners have managed to remove the stain." Partially true and

5. Happy Harry was not yet five when the incident in question occurred. You can argue he was even happier then!

partially false. The stain was indeed removed. But it wasn't from cleaners. It was from a typical Singaporean Sunday-afternoon rainstorm.

Condo management was doing exactly what it thought it was supposed to do. In writing the letter, it was demonstrating something like the zero-tolerance "broken windows" theory that former New York City Police Commissioner William Bratton made famous when he cleaned up the city in the 1990s.[6] However, while such a stern warning would have been well warranted if Harry had used spray paint or written something religiously offensive, using chalk to express himself creatively is an entirely different thing.

Children enter the world as naturally creative, curious creatures. That's why recent kindergarten graduates generally outperform newly minted MBAs in the "marshmallow challenge," a timed competition to use spaghetti, tape, and string to build the tallest structure that will support a marshmallow on top. But what lesson does Happy Harry take from the letter? That creative expression, even benign creative expression, carries risks. The lesson gets reinforced as Harry grows up. School teaches him that there is a right answer and a wrong answer. Eventually, when he joins an organization, he will learn that there is a right way to do things and a wrong way to do things, and that the answer matters more than the question. That delivering against expectations is rewarded while trying something that doesn't work is punished. Left unchecked, all of this would lock down his natural curiosity. The resulting fear, or what the psychology literature calls "learned helplessness," inhibits innovation by individuals.

## Danger in the Dark

Imagine Harry all grown up. He now works in a large, established organization. He looks in the mirror and says, "You know what. I don't need my dad to tell me that innovation is good. The evidence is overwhelming.

---

6. The basic idea is that if you fix the small stuff, like broken windows and subway fare evasion, you change norms and expectations, and stop the big stuff from ever happening.

I can do this." He commits to overcome his individual fear and rerelease Happy Harry. Of course, he would have to deal with a basic challenge: he would have to strengthen his now atrophied innovation muscles. That's easy enough to address through conscious practice. But it is insufficient. Because the grownup Happy Harry faces a different and more devilish enemy: the shadow strategy that drives institutionalized inertia. Let's move from Harrylandia to the Golden Arches to learn more.

## Why Couldn't Dave Hoffmann Get His Bananas?

In 2014, Scott and Andy spoke to Dave Hoffmann about innovation at McDonald's.[7] At the time, Hoffmann led the fast food giant's operations in Asia-Pacific, the Middle East, and Africa.[8] That footprint covered close to 10,000 stores that produced $20 billion in annual revenues. Like many of the company's top leaders, Hoffmann had been with McDonald's for decades.

In 1993, a local franchise owner in Melbourne developed a concept called McCafé, which offered high-quality espresso-based beverages, fruit shakes, and bakery items at prices sharply lower than coffee chains like Starbucks or Costa Coffee (which was acquired by The Coca-Cola Company in 2018). The concept spread throughout Australia and now is embedded within McDonald's stores globally. By all accounts, the concept has been an amazing success. Yet something bothered Hoffman. "I keep saying I want bananas in the stores," he said. "And they never show up."

You may think, "Bananas? Who cares about bananas?" But all of us, at some point, push for our own versions of bananas, and get stifled— and understanding why we can't get sell-in is important.

Imagine the following scenario. Hoffmann makes his request at a meeting of top leaders. The meeting notes dutifully summarize his proposal. The proclamation winds its way through the organization to land

---

7. Andy is coauthor Andy Parker. We said we wouldn't remind you of this shocking first-name use in text again. But there you go—we did.

8. Hoffmann joined Dunkin' Brands in 2016 and became its CEO in 2018.

on the desk of a midlevel manager responsible for menu and operations at McCafé. Imagine this manager has already gone through the annual budgeting process, at which time new drink flavors and cakes looked more attractive than bananas. He now considers squeezing bananas in, but then he revisits the goals he agreed to at the beginning of the year. A key one was to reduce food wastage by 6 percent. Bananas are famously perishable, so adding them to the menu would threaten his ability to hit that metric. And after eighteen months on the job, he's *this* close to getting a coveted promotion. He also knows from experience that any off-budget request has to go through a review committee of midlevel managers who have a similar set of incentives. And as for Hoffmann, by now he has already gone back (appropriately!) to focusing on how to deal with the latest supply-chain or public-relations issue that has cropped up. Time gets away until, a few months later, he asks, "Hey, whatever happened to those bananas?"

In this story (and this is an imagined story, we have no idea if any of the specific discussions detailed above actually took place), it isn't bureaucracy or excessive risk aversion that squashes Hoffmann's bananas; it is simply the underlying systems that determine how resources get allocated. The core corporate machinery does the intended job of optimizing the current business model, and bananas and similar ideas end up a necessary casualty.

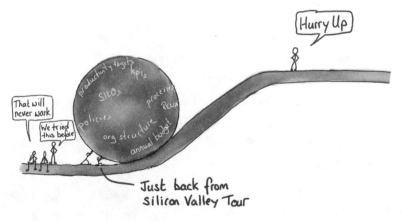

*Organizations do what they are designed to do.*

## Why Does Culture Eat Strategy for Breakfast?

Let's raise the stakes.

Imagine a deep-pocketed company that spots an opportunity to create a powerful growth business. A powerful chief executive officer, fully backed by the board of directors, declares the opportunity to be strategic. Resources are allocated aggressively to pursue the opportunity. But despite the stated strategic focus and resource allocation, the company ultimately loses the opportunity to an upstart that seems to lack all of the natural advantages enjoyed by the incumbent.

That's essentially what happened in the early 2000s when Microsoft was working on a solution that was eerily similar to a powerful business model at Google called AdWords. AdWords, the secret to Google's success over the past two decades, allows companies to "buy" keywords that tie advertisements to specific search terms. Companies pay only if someone actually clicks on an advertisement. As described in a brilliant 2009 *Wall Street Journal* article by Robert A. Guth, "Microsoft Bid to Beat Google Builds on a History of Misses," no individual decision doomed Microsoft's efforts. Instead, a series of subtle decisions led to Microsoft's miss. For example, Microsoft wanted to test search-based advertising on its MSN portal. But the portal's business leaders worried that the advertisements would draw users away from the banner advertisements that served as a lucrative source of revenue, so they made the search results hard for users to find. Disappointing test results were at least one factor that led Microsoft to deprioritize the opportunity.

Whether the innovation is big or small, the internal enemy is the same and results not from malice but, ironically, from success. Successful organizations become successful by repeatedly solving a problem. They grow by solving that problem more effectively and efficiently. They then develop habits related to how they solve that problem, and the rationale for the habits disappears into unstated assumptions ("That's just the way we do things around here.") Habits are reinforced by standard operating procedures, performance management systems, and operating metrics. In a stable world, engrained habits reinforced by systems and structures serve as a source of strength.

But in a *changing* world, with advancing technologies and lines between industries blurred, a blind adherence to these habits can be harmful, as institutionalized inertia inhibits necessary change. This is the fundamental paradox and the fundamental challenge facing leaders looking to create a culture of innovation: the systems that enable success in today's model reinforce behaviors inconsistent with discovering tomorrow's model. As one executive quipped, "We are organized to deliver predictable, reliable results. And that's exactly the problem."

The *shadow strategy* is the reason culture eats strategy for breakfast. After all, as noted by scholars from a field known as the "resource-based view," strategy isn't what you *say* you do—it is what you *actually* do. In the 2005 book *From Resource Allocation to Strategy*, Harvard Business School professor Joseph Bower and longtime Innosight adviser Clark Gilbert noted, "The strategy of a company is more than the statement of strategy as presented in company documents or written plans. It is the actual aggregation of commitments and their relationship to the realized strategy of the firm."

In simple terms, your strategy is:

- What marketing markets

- What engineering engineers

- What the sales team sells

- What production produces

- What finance funds

- How HR measures performance

All of these things are optimized to make today better and to improve or guarantee the bottom line. And all of them stand in the way of making tomorrow different.

A few years ago, Innosight surveyed close to one thousand executives. Only 12 percent of respondents said they had a growth strategy with at least a five-year-plus time horizon. More often, executives reported that "we are too busy executing" (36 percent) or "we have no process for creating one" (25 percent). *These companies absolutely have a long-term strategy: to keep doing exactly what they are currently doing.* The shadow strategy quietly tugs and nudges a company down a path of perpetuation, even if circumstances demand something drastically different.

In summary, organizations do exactly what they are designed to do—they execute a known and proven model. Imagine a leader breaks through the *individual* shackles described in Happy Harry's story. She dreams of becoming an innovation superhero who delivers all of the benefits of innovation to her organization. She has to come to grips with the reality that her biggest enemy is her own organization. The leader has to fight against *institutional* shackles—an intertwined strategy, operating metrics, processes, performance incentives, and decision criteria, all optimized to help the organization do what it is currently doing, only better, faster, or cheaper—not to help it do something materially different.

In *Seeing Around Corners*, Columbia University professor Rita McGrath shows that we have no one to blame for this problem but ourselves. McGrath describes a memorable experience running a workshop for a large multinational. She asks the group to list innovation blockers in their organizations. They provide the usual litany of responses, such as "Management wants near-term success," "Lack of customer focus," "Fear of failure," "Fear of cannibalizing our successful business," and "No career incentive to work on innovation/growth projects."

Here's what McGrath has to say about their responses:

> "What," I asked them, "does every single one of these barriers to innovation have in common?" After a few halting remarks, the penny dropped. Everyone is an internally imposed constraint. They are all there to protect and defend the orderly operation of the existing business and to keep it from being disrupted. More precisely, they are there to stop the kind of disruption that innovations can represent. And yet, if we collectively and consciously decide that these constraints can be addressed, we can move them out of the way. After all, God did not come down from heaven and declare, "There shalt be silos!"

As acolytes of process improvement guru W. Edwards Deming have noted, every system is perfectly designed to get the results it gets. Breaking this institutionalized inertia requires fighting against the shadow strategy.

The shadow strategy can be defeated, however; seemingly immovable organizations can become agile and innovative.[9] The case study that follows returns to Harry's home in Singapore to see one organization that did just that.

## Chapter Summary

- ✓ Human beings enter the world naturally curious and creative. All of us once were "Happy Harry."

- ✓ However, school and work constrain those natural tendencies, leading innovation muscles to wither.

- ✓ Organizations are designed to do what they are currently doing better, faster, or cheaper. Individuals who break free of self-imposed constraints must therefore wrestle against the shadow strategy, which institutionalizes inertia through reinforcing systems, structures, strategy, norms, and more.

---

9. The "immovable organization" is a Paul phrase. Run a thought experiment in which you consider how you would consciously create an organization that would never change. How much does it overlap with your organization?

# From Damn Bloody Slow to Best Bank in the World

Paul remembers vividly his first day at DBS in 2009: when he asked his taxi driver to take him to DBS, the driver said, "Ah, DBS—Damn Bloody Slow," referring to the notorious long queues that plagued its ATMs. That same year, when preparing to move to Singapore, Scott asked around for advice about which bank he should use there. No one said DBS. In fact, customer satisfaction scores ranked DBS fifth in Singapore, trailing locally based companies UOB and OCBC and global giants HSBC and Citi.

Now fast-forward a few years to 2016, when DBS was named the world's best digital bank by *Euromoney*, who noted, "It is demonstrably the case that digital innovation pervades every part of DBS." And by 2019, DBS became the first bank to simultaneously hold the titles Bank of the Year (*The Banker*), Best Bank in the World (*Global Finance*), and World's Best Bank (*Euromoney*).

How did that happen? A large portion of the answer is a concerted, cohesive effort to create a culture of innovation. These efforts have now paid dividends in many ways. Among them, customer satisfaction scores have gone from being industry-lagging to industry-leading, innovative efforts to redesign services have saved 250 million customer hours, and a digital-only offering in India and Indonesia has enabled new bank accounts to be created in minutes without a visit to a branch.

DBS's success story began in 2009, when Piyush Gupta took over as CEO. Gupta coupled substantial industry experience, gained from his long history at Citibank, with a dose of entrepreneurialism, learned from his helming of a (failed) startup called Go4i.com in the early

2000s. He became CEO at an interesting moment in the financial services industry—a time when many global banks were dealing with the aftereffects of the 2007–2008 global financial crisis. While many Asian banks emerged relatively unscathed, it was clear that more change was coming soon driven by the rapid emergence of nontraditional competitors such as Alibaba, Tencent, and Amazon.com and technologies such as digitization, cryptocurrency, roboadvisers, and peer-to-peer finance platforms. Gupta and his team concluded that DBS had to transform.

## Acting Like a 28,000-Person Startup

A key change for DBS was reframing its competition. No longer could it compare itself to other banks based in Singapore, like OCBC or UOB, or to big regional banks like ANZ. It also couldn't compare itself to global behemoths like JP Morgan Chase or HSBC—or even to small but nimble global banks like BBVA and ING. Rather, the pace of technological change meant it had to look less like a bank that biased toward regulatory compliance and more like a technology company that biased toward entrepreneurialism and innovation. As such, it decided to begin comparing itself to Google, Amazon, Netflix, Apple, LinkedIn (subsequently acquired by Microsoft), and Facebook. It didn't pick those companies haphazardly. If you put DBS between Netflix and Apple, it forms the acronym GANDALF, the long-bearded wizard from J. R. R. Tolkien's *Lord of the Rings* series. That, along with functioning like a "28,000-person startup," became evocative metaphors for DBS's future destination and presented clear contrasts from its state at the beginning of its transformation.

This change in orientation drove two fundamental shifts within DBS. The first shift related to technology. DBS made the strategic decision to insource technology operations to give it more control over its digital transformation. In 2009, almost all of its IT operations were outsourced. But by the end of 2017, DBS controlled 85 percent of its own IT operations. It had also moved two-thirds of its applications to the cloud to provide greater flexibility.

The second shift, which relates to the main focus of this book, was to encourage specific behaviors. This was the truly critical shift, because technology can't change itself; transformation happens only if technologists and businesspeople change what they do. So after some trial-and-error experimentation, DBS defined five desired behaviors of a 28,000-person startup (which, incidentally, overlap the five behaviors defined in chapter 1):

*Agile.* In order to adapt and move faster, DBS needed to go full-bore to embed agile principles so it could get fast feedback on ideas.

*Be a learning organization.* As a legacy company aspiring to be a digital company, DBS had a learning mountain to climb. Its technology people needed to learn fundamentally different paradigms around the cloud and automation, its businesspeople needed to become tech savvy, and its leadership needed to learn new decision-making approaches and how to unlock the company's curiosity.

*Customer-obsessed.* No one wakes up in the morning and says, "Hey, today's a great day to do some banking—let's all go to the bank." Banking tasks are typically part of a broader customer need or "job to be done." So DBS had to learn to go deep in understanding its customers' lives.

*Data-driven.* DBS had to accelerate its use of data analytics and embrace artificial intelligence. That fed into a desired shift from making decisions "by HIPPO" (the highest paid person's opinion) to making decisions with data.

*Experiment and take risks.* Conducting experiments is the best way to quickly get data to determine whether new ideas will address customer needs. Otherwise, it is too easy to fall back on the past practice of asking managers to put their reputations on the line by developing hefty business cases to make them successful.

The following stories describe these behaviors in action, showing how DBS innovated to enter new markets, save customers' time, and make families safer.

## Breaking into New Markets

Historically, DBS's stronghold has, naturally, been Singapore, where it is the clear market leader. During the 1980s and 1990s it became a regional bank by expanding into other regional markets such as Indonesia. In 2013 it began setting its sights on what historically seemed an aspirational market: India. DBS already had a small presence in the market, with fewer than 20,000 customers. How could it dramatically scale that number? The market's vast size and complexity meant DBS had to approach it in a fundamentally different way. Rather than a vast infrastructure of physical locations, it considered a digital-first offering that could allow it to scale up reasonably quickly without a big investment. It created a special-purpose team to design the offering. The team set a goal to create a mobile-only offering that would allow a customer to open an account, without going to a branch, in ninety seconds. That required thinking creatively about how to partner with local organizations like Café Coffee Day, a leading local coffee shop chain. It piloted the idea in 2015 and formally launched in 2017. Within two years it had attracted 2 million customers. Of course, that is still a relatively small number in a country with more than a billion people, but the innovative offering built a strong foothold in India and became the base of DBS's expansion into other markets. It also helped build DBS's digital fluencies. In 2017 it launched the world's largest banking application protocol interface (API), through which partners can invisibly integrate DBS's capabilities into their systems. By late 2018 it had demonstrated that digital customers are at least twice as profitable as traditional customers, setting the stage for further growth and expansion.

## Shortening Queues, Saving Millions of Hours

During its transformation journey, DBS constantly raised its ambitions. Before setting the bar at "best bank it the world," it aspired to become a leading Asian bank. How could it do that? Make banking joyful. How can banking be joyful? By disappearing from people's lives. That meant making DBS the world's first invisible bank while still providing high-quality service. So it set a new metric, called the customer hour, which measured the aggregate time customers spent waiting for the bank to complete tasks. It designed and executed 250 process-improvement events to remove operational waste from the system. Those events ended up saving more than 250 *million* customer hours, rocketing DBS from the bottom to the top of the customer satisfaction scores.

Today, DBS has the busiest ATM network in the world. How did it shorten its legendary ATM queues?[1] It combined careful customer observation with advanced analytics to identify opportunities for improvement. Some of those changes were invisible to consumers. For example, predictive analytics helped anticipate when machines would run out of cash and thereby optimize replenishment routes. Predictive analytics also helped anticipate mechanical failure. One surprising factor behind failure? Proximity to "wet markets" that sell fresh meat and fish. It turns out that ATMs and fish scales don't go well together. Other changes focused on the customer experience. For example, many customers would wait for their receipt to print, but it turned out they didn't actually want a receipt—they simply wanted to know their balance. So DBS added a feature that allowed customers to see their balance on the screen. It also had to think about when and how to show that balance. As it turned out, a significant number of customers, primarily males, were forgetting their cards in the machines. Close observation suggested that displaying the balance and the "Please take your card" message overwhelmed some customers. So, DBS separated the balance message from the "take your card" message, experimented with different time intervals between the message and the card's release, and added an audible alarm indicating that the consumer should take their card. DBS also made it easy for mobile users to quickly see their balances so that they wouldn't need to stand in line to use an ATM.

---

1. The long queues weren't entirely DBS's fault. Singaporeans like cash. A typical ATM has about 5,000 transactions a month. In Singapore, the average is ten thousand a month. The ATM with the highest frequency in the world resides in Singapore (Paul knows the location but is sworn to secrecy).

Another process improvement related to how DBS handled lost credit cards. Historically, when a customer reported a lost credit card, it would take DBS five days to return it. It set a goal of decreasing that time to a single day. Not only would the quicker turnaround time increase customer satisfaction, DBS reasoned, but a customer who doesn't have a credit card isn't using it. After delivering against its one-day goal, DBS phoned a customer and said, "Madam, how did you like getting your credit card back in a day?" The response, Paul believes, changed history. "It was great, thank you very much," she said. "But where is my debit card? I didn't just lose my credit card. I lost my handbag and all my cards in the shopping mall." This highlighted that, while innovating processes with an internal view has its benefit, an outside-in view often highlights broader opportunities to innovate. Focused research helped change the script used by call center representatives when customers reported lost cards. Rather than ask authentication questions with the implication that the customer was a criminal, representatives would express empathy and provide other useful information. Customer satisfaction scores went through the roof.

## Developing SmartBuddy

As DBS progressed with its transformation, it experimented with different tools, methods, and vocabulary to drive process improvement, customer experience, and innovation. For example, in response to an explosion of incoherent vernacular that confused its employees, DBS borrowed a model from the UK Design Council called double diamond, or 4D. The 4D model refers to four phases: Discover (identify a problem to solve), Define (detail the specifics of the problem), Develop (prototype and iterate solutions), and Deliver (finalize and launch the idea).[2] At a 2016 leadership offsite, DBS spent a full day training leaders on the concept. While historically, leaders had crafted solutions based on experi-

---

2. To plant a small seed, this model nicely maps the four phases of the innovation journey described in part II of the book.

ence or gut feel, this training taught them to "wallow in the problem," in order to uncover emotional, social, and functional jobs to be done, and then to experiment with different solutions.

A collaboration with Singapore's Ministry of Education to eliminate the need for cash transactions in public schools demonstrates this "wallow in the problem" methodology in action. DBS developed a prototype of a wristband that would allow cashless transactions and tied it to an app that allowed parents to provide allowances and set savings goals for their children. The solution, called SmartBuddy, also allowed children to transfer money into their own savings accounts. As DBS wallowed in the problem further, it discovered a related problem: parents were reporting concern about the safety of their children traveling to and from school. Based on this insight, DBS added a functionality to the app that would allow children to tap their wristbands on a reader in the school bus, which would then notify parents. SmartBuddy was subsequently launched across more than thirty schools in Singapore.

## Enabling Innovation

An innovative digital-only banking offering, shorter ATM lines, and a cashless solution that also helped parents feel safe show innovation in action at DBS. Or, in simple terms, they show "the what." The next two examples return to the beginning of the story to address "the how."

### BRINGING MOJO TO MEETINGS[3]

In 2016, DBS's top leaders gathered in Singapore to talk about how the bank was progressing. All agreed that though it had made headway, much work remained. A major blocker they identified was dysfunctional meetings that entrenched organizational inertia and hindered

---

3. You can't footnote a picture, but you'll notice a small illustration tied to this section. Every time a BEAN (behavior enabler, artifact, and nudge) is described in depth, Paul has doodled an image connected to it. You'll see forty-one more of these in the pages ahead (without captions, as that seems to defeat the point), and can find all of the details for the BEANs at www.eatsleepinnovate.com.

innovation. Most meetings at
DBS could be charitably described as inefficient. They
would often start and run late,
eating up time that leadership
could otherwise have spent on
innovation. Sometimes decisions were made, and some-

times they were not. People would dutifully arrive without a clear sense
of why they were there. Some participants were active, but many sat in
defensive silence. And it is this last point that was most salient. Meetings, DBS's top leaders concluded, were suppressing diverse voices and
reinforcing the status quo.

To fix those bad habits, DBS introduced a program called MOJO. It
was informed by research at Google that showed that having an equal
share of voice and psychological safety was critical to high-performing,
highly innovative project teams. MOJO promotes efficient, effective,
open, and collaborative meetings. MO refers to the meeting owner who
is responsible for ensuring that the meeting has a clear agenda, that
it starts and ends on time, and that all attendees are given an equal
say. The JO—or joyful observer—is assigned to help the meeting run
crisply and to encourage broad participation. The JO, for example, has
the authority to call a "phone Jenga," which requires all attendees to put
their phones in pile on the table. Perhaps most important, at the meeting's end, the JO holds the MO accountable, providing frank feedback
about how things went and how the MO can improve. Even when the JO
is a junior employee, he or she is explicitly authorized to be direct with
the MO. The presence of an observer and the knowledge that feedback
is coming at the end of the meeting nudges the MO to be mindful of
meeting behavior.

This approach, supported by physical reminders in meeting rooms
(small cards, wall art, and fun paper cubes that can be tossed in the
room) and a range of measurement and tracking tools, has had a powerful impact. Meetings at DBS no longer run late, which has saved an
estimated 500,000 employee hours as of 2019. Meeting effectiveness, as

gauged by ongoing employee surveys, has doubled, and the percentage of employees who feel they have an equal share of the voice in meetings has jumped from 40 percent to 90 percent. Improved efficiency and effectiveness doesn't mean meetings have become dull, however. Living up to their moniker, the JOs have even been known to give their feedback in verse. And legends have spread: at one meeting, the observer bravely told a senior executive who had lost his cool that the blowup had shut down all discussion. The executive welcomed the feedback, promising to do better next time. It's a story that still circulates, reinforcing the behavioral change DBS had hoped to drive with MOJO.

## THE INNOVATION TEAM THAT DOESN'T INNOVATE

It would be natural to assume that a centralized innovation team has driven the range of innovation stories at DBS. And it has, but perhaps in an unexpected way. In CEO Gupta's early days, he put in place a strategy to differentiate DBS based on its position in, and knowledge of, Asia. Underpinning the strategy were five pillars: Asian service, Asian connectivity, Asian relationships, Asian insights, and Asian innovation. Of the five, innovation proved the most challenging to get moving. There were a couple of false starts. The first iteration was to assemble some senior internal talent and ask them to develop ideas in a workshop. In parallel, DBS formed an advisory board of innovation experts to oversee the efforts. However, the workshop approach yielded unsatisfactory outcomes, and the innovation board members' expertise was too narrow and deep to help shape the innovation strategy effectively.

So DBS tested another approach. A new innovation head was hired to set up a small team that worked on potentially groundbreaking projects. However, the new team had difficulty selling its ideas to the rest of the company. This is a common challenge: organizations bring in people with innovation experience at other companies, isolate them, and expect them to work magic. But the magic often doesn't materialize. In DBS's case, the would-be magicians struggled to navigate through DBS's core organization, so they couldn't integrate DBS's core assets and capabilities into their ideas. Smart integration is critically important in a regulated industry like banking, where offerings need to comply with appropriate regulations and be slotted into complex systems.

By this time, the Asian service pillar was enjoying success by adopting a very inclusive approach. Everyone in the company was encouraged to participate, and, as a result, enthusiasm for improvement was spreading across the company. So DBS decided that the innovation portfolio should align with the customer experience program—which was led by Paul.

Paul gave the innovation team one rule: under no circumstance should it innovate. Why? Because the innovation team should be made up of evangelists, agitators, coaches, and guides that teach the *whole company* to innovate.

Many DBS employees, and especially leaders, believed that innovation was the special reserve of creative types—that average bankers could not be expected to innovate. To counter that perspective, the DBS team held programs to teach employees the processes involved in innovation. The first focus of these programs was to help leaders understand what it felt like to work at startup speed. The innovation team partnered with the HR learning team to create a series of weeklong events, which included three days of training on digital concepts. This week of events was then followed by a forty-eight-hour "hackathon," where executives were teamed with real startups to work on real business problems. The executives created working prototypes that they pitched to the CEO on the final afternoon.

The innovation team that doesn't innovate has made significant strides in its mission of raising the organization's overall innovation fluency and capabilities, helping DBS achieve its strategic objective of becoming a 28,000-person startup that is legitimately positioned to put the *D* in GANDALF.

## Coping with a Crisis

Finally, DBS's innovation capability helped its response to COVID-19, and COVID-19, perhaps a bit surprisingly, helped to strengthen DBS's innovation capability.

Following the 2003–2004 SARS epidemic, Singapore required that all of its companies develop business continuity plans. In early February 2020, the government moved its internal monitoring system to "orange," which required companies to limit the number of employees in offices at any given time; in April it executed a "circuit breaker" that mandated all but essential employees to work from home. DBS quickly moved to execute a bankwide effort to make the process as smooth and painless as possible.

Good innovators seek to empathetically understand their customers. In this case, the operations team quickly observed new challenges, such as the lack of "sense-based memory" that tied particular meeting rooms to particular meetings and the need to replace water cooler chat as an informal source of information. The team also noticed surprising concerns from employees, such as people being reluctant to turn on their cameras because they were embarrassed about their homes or feeling like managers asking them to turn on their cameras signaled mistrust versus a desire to make a more human connection.

A specific effort called "Project Lemonade" sought to rapidly develop tools and approaches to help combat these problems and enable virtual connection and collaboration. The project covered both "hard" issues, such as testing various technological platforms, and soft issues, such as defining simple rules for videoconference etiquette and determining how to use the chat function to augment key points and answer simple questions that could otherwise derail a discussion.

All of this helped to accelerate key ongoing behavior shifts. Agile practices such as daily team huddles became standard practices quickly. Senior leaders personally experiencing the pain of inadequate digital technologies helped to accelerate investments in critical upgrades. More widespread use of feedback tools helped DBS to be even more data driven in its decision making. Interestingly, early data showed improvement in meeting behavior, with higher degrees of collaboration and fewer emotional outbursts.

While at the time of the writing of this book significant uncertainty remains about the lasting impact of COVID-19, DBS's strengthening innovation capabilities position it well to be able to continue to rapidly adapt to, and indeed get in front of, key shifts.

* * *

Did MOJO catch your attention? It certainly caught ours.[4] It serves as a powerful, practical example of how to break the shadow strategy and encourage collaboration, a key ingredient to successful innovation. The next chapter provides the science behind MOJO's success and details a new tool for the would-be culture-changer: a behavior enabler, artifact, and nudge. Yes, it's finally time to dive deep into BEANs.

---

4. Well, it caught the attention of Andy, Scott, and Natalie. Paul, of course, helped to create MOJO. And has lots of mojo.

# Hacking Habits

Destin Sandlin had a simple question: How hard would it be to *unlearn* to ride a bike? So, the host of Smarter Every Day, a popular educational series on YouTube, asked a welder he knew to do something kind of strange: to change Sandlin's bike so that when he turned his handlebars *right*, the bike would go to the *left*, and vice versa. Sandlin was an engineer who understood the mechanics of bike riding and an avid rider who was well trained to handle a bike. How hard could it be?

Very hard, it turns out. "The challenge is much more complex than it might seem," a summary by the Arbinger Institute noted. "Several intricate processes—balance, coordination, steering, pedaling, and more—come together in the action of riding a bicycle. Our brains must precisely direct and coordinate each of these complex processes, meaning that learning how to ride a backwards bicycle requires a complete re-wiring of the neural pathways associated with bike riding."

Use BEANs to bust the status quo.

Sandlin's first ride went nowhere. It took him *eight months* of practicing five minutes a day before he could successfully ride the backwards bike. Then, of course, when he got back on a *normal* bike, he again went nowhere. Fortunately, it took only about twenty minutes for Sandlin to re-remember how to ride the normal bike.[1]

Now changing habits in an organizational context is quite different than in Sandlin's experiment. Riding a bike is deeply imprinted in muscle memory, requiring hard conscious work to unpack and unlearn. Few, if any, people spent their childhood running spreadsheet analyses, trusting market research over firsthand customer experience, or demanding answers when they should be asking questions. Still, the point remains: changing habits is hard. The shadow strategy descends and makes a well-intentioned organization functionally immovable. To learn how to encourage innovation behaviors, you have to hack habits with BEANs (behavior enablers, artifacts, and nudges). This chapter will detail key lessons from habit-change literature and share examples of some of our favorite BEANs. The companion case study that follows will then show the effectiveness of the conscious creation of BEANs at a DBS development center in Hyderabad.

## Lessons from Habit-Change Literature

The previous DBS case study detailed a program called MOJO, created to improve meetings and encourage collaboration.[2] Why does MOJO work? It rips a page out of the habit-change literature. Over the past few decades, psychologists have pinpointed why it is so hard to change habits and have provided a range of practical tools to facilitate habit change. Their way of thinking about change has now crossed over into mainstream culture via influential books such as *Switch* by Chip and Dan Health, *Nudge* by Richard H. Thaler and Cass R. Sunstein, *The*

---

1. Interestingly, it took his six-year-old son, who had less to unlearn and the higher neuroplasticity that comes with youth, only two weeks to learn how to ride a backwards bike.

2. It was only a couple pages ago, but if you are a nonlinear reader, here is the synopsis: The "MO" in MOJO is the meeting owner who sets the agenda and ensures wide participation. The "JO" is the joyful observer who intervenes if people are distracted and who provides public feedback to the MO. The program has saved hundreds of thousands of labor hours and helped dramatically improve the degree to which DBS employees feel their voices are heard in meetings.

*Power of Habit* by Charles Duhigg, and *Thinking, Fast and Slow* by Daniel Kahneman.

Similarly, our journey to the BEAN concept started by devouring the literature and studying historical habit-change programs. For example, one of the world's most successful habit-change programs, Alcoholics Anonymous, highlights themes that appear in the literature. Founded in 1935 by Bill Wilson and Dr. Robert Smith, over the past eighty-five years, the program has helped millions of people battle addictions to alcohol. The core of the program is simple, supported by mantras such as "one day at a time." The AA program recognizes how hard habit change is, so it attacks the problem on multiple fronts. Every member has a sponsor with whom they interact regularly, and members are encouraged to shape their living contexts to remove temptation: avoid meeting friends at bars, remove the booze from your house, and so on. The heart of the AA program is communal—at meetings, members work together to help each other—and is supported by physical artifacts such as tokens, which they earn when they achieve certain milestones.

Another successful program that follows a similar pattern is Weight Watchers, which in 2018 rebranded itself WW as part of a move from weight management to wellness management. Founded in 1963 in Queens, New York, by Jean Nidetch, WW is the most widely used weight management program in the world today, with more than 4 million active members. The points system at the core of the program simplifies the sometimes-complicated challenge of calorie counting and portion control. But more critical is the powerful social shaping that occurs during its meetings. Points and specific menu items help, but the meetings serve as the social glue that holds the program together.

These two programs—AA and WW—provide solid examples of how to modify an existing habit, while gaming companies show how to create new ones. It starts by following Atari founder Nolan Bushnell's maxim that games should be "easy to learn and difficult to master." That makes it easy for people to start and hard for them to stop playing a game, turning it into a habit. Games also typically have communal elements, where you can compete head-to-head or compare your score and progress to others. A variety of rewards motivate you to keep progressing. And, of course, there are sights and sounds that engage you with the game. When these factors come together, they result in amazingly addictive (and profitable) games such as *Super Mario, Candy Crush, Pokémon Go, Angry Birds,* and *Fortnite.* If it sometimes seems like the world is turning into a huge video game, it is because research shows that badges, rewards, and charts showing progress actually work.

Three themes connect these examples. First, habit change requires engaging both people's rational, logical side and their emotional, intuitive side. Second, habit change requires a multifront battle. Consider how AA and WW use a combination of mantras, nudges, and social interactions to change people's patterns. Third, the science of motivation shows how goal-setting, achievement, and social comparison and encouragement reinforce desired behaviors.

The enemy of innovation inside most organizations is institutionalized inertia that is reinforced in systems and norms. The antidote to inertia is to break old habits and form new ones. While most habit-change literature has focused on *individual* behaviors, such as stopping smoking, eating better, getting more regular exercise, and learning new skills, we posited that the principles of successful habit formation and change would be just as applicable to organizations.

As such, a few years ago a team at Innosight started to collect examples of interventions that promoted better innovation habits inside organizations. In the end, we collected more than one hundred examples, which we found in client organizations, in case studies from the Innovation Leader information service, and in corporate cultural documents compiled by Tettra, a Boston-area startup.

We picked the acronym BEAN because, like MOJO, the most successful programs combine the following:

- *Behavior enablers: Direct* ways to encourage and enable behavior change

- *Artifacts:* Physical or digital objects to *reinforce* behavior change

- *Nudges: Indirect* ways to encourage and enable behavior change

In the book *Switch*, Chip and Dan Heath borrow a Buddhist metaphor to describe the process of behavior change. They talk about a rider on an elephant going down a path. While the rider, representing the rational mind, might want to move in a new direction, the elephant, representing the emotional mind, continues to thoughtlessly trundle down the existing path. How, then, do you drive change?

Behavior enablers are direct ways to help the rider learn how to influence the elephant. A behavior enabler details the new script you want to follow and provides tangible, direct support to follow that script. To borrow language from Kahneman's *Thinking, Fast and Slow*, a behavior enabler engages "System 2," the slow, deliberate part of decision-making, which constitutes about 2 percent of our thinking. More specifically, behavior enablers might involve the following:

- Developing a routine or ritual, such as the "check in" that the MO follows in each meeting

- Having access to a coach or counselor, like AA's sponsor

- Building a wider community, such as those in the AA and WW meetings, to help directly reinforce the new behavior

- Creating simple checklists or user guides, like AA's twelve-step program or WW's points system

Nudges are indirect ways to support behavior change. In the elephant metaphor, a nudge changes the path itself, so the elephant moves in a new direction without consciously thinking about it. In Kahneman's language, nudges engage "System 1"—our fast, unconscious, automatic thinking system. In an organizational context, that might involve things like:

- Using what is known as "choice architecture" by making the desired behavior the "default choice" (such as in the famous example where the percentage of people who choose to be organ donors is almost completely explained by whether it is the default choice when applying for a driver's license)

- Having reminders (such as the notifications that wearable gadgets provide when you sit for too long)

- Creating and sharing stories (like the ones told at AA meetings)

- Using physical office design to facilitate specific behavior (similar to how AA suggests removing temptations from the house)

- Publishing "leaderboards" or providing other forms of comparison (a staple of any catchy game)

Finally, artifacts are the physical and digital reinforcers that connect the first two ideas. They are the signposts that help the rider remember what he or she needs to do. Example artifacts include:

- Prizes and trophies that recognize the new behavior (like the coins AA members earn to recognize a certain number of days of sobriety)

- Physical avatars that reinforce desired changes (such as the wizard Gandalf at DBS, which connects to DBS's aspiration to positively compare itself to Google, Amazon.com, Netflix, Apple, LinkedIn, and Facebook)

- Tokens (like the wizard hat and staff that DBS sometimes has at meetings to reinforce the Gandalf metaphor)

- Pictures and visuals that serve as background reminders

- Physical objects that sit on desks or in conference rooms

## BEANs at Innosight

As the language and the toolkit around BEANs began to emerge, Natalie, Scott, and Andy realized that Innosight had built two BEANs to support important change efforts.[3]

---

3. One thing we consistently see is that groups will tell us they don't innovate. We then give our definition of innovation (something different that creates value), and they realize they absolutely *do* innovate. They just didn't have the language for it. Similarly, we bet your organization has a BEAN or two that has helped to change or reinforce culture. Let us know if we are right, as we'd love to add more ideas into the bag of BEANs.

At the end of each year, Innosight has one-on-one discussions to get feedback from clients. A few years ago, as the leadership team reviewed the verbatims from client interviews, a surprising insight emerged. Innosight leaders had always assumed that the reason they won head-to-head battles against bigger consulting companies rested in its unique intellectual property or thought leadership. Yes, clients said, that wasn't unimportant, but everyone had some kind of intellectual property. What made Innosight different, clients said, was Innosight itself. There was just something different in how Innosight teams showed up and worked with clients. "They are a thought partner, invested in our success, fun to work with and humble but confident. Innosight genuinely wants to be driving impact," one client said. "They are a delightful group to work with. They have a great culture," another noted. This led to the leadership team's dusting off and refining a set of underlying values that had been formed early in Innosight's history but largely forgotten.

How does an organization encourage people to recurrently live the behaviors behind values like humility, transparency, collaboration, and inclusivity? The Innosight Different BEAN attacked this problem on multiple fronts. An anchor of the BEAN is an award given out by Innosight's managing partner every December. Behavior enablers include sharing detailed  descriptions of the values and desired behaviors and the annual routine of seeking award nominations via a simple SurveyMonkey survey. Select stories are shared at Innosight's year-end gathering, posted on Innosight's internal website, and fed to year-end reviewers to be captured and memorialized during the annual review process. There are many artifacts, including most notably:

- A physical award (which Andy won in 2014 and Natalie won in 2015!)

- A set of custom-created cartoons that now hang in Innosight's headquarters in Lexington, Massachusetts, and are included in pitch documents

- A video on Innosight's intranet that shows the values in action

- Rotating digital screens in the Innosight headquarters lobby, which greet visitors with values cartoons and Innosight impact stories

- Small desktop flip-books with additional cartoons that illustrate what it looks like when Innosight doesn't live up to its values[4]

Innosight provides further nudges for leaders to live up to Innosight Different by regularly running employee surveys that include questions about the degree to which leaders model the values.

The First Friday BEAN re-inforces a conscious effort to improve connectivity and col-laboration across Innosight. In normal times, Innosight's consultants spend a significant amount of time on the road, working side by side with its clients.[5] While this helps In-nosight deliver against a core value of impact, it can inhibit  community connectivity. First Friday is a ritual in which a significant portion of Innosight's North American and European employees gather in sessions nine times per year, with each session recorded and posted

4. Scott's favorite cartoon is of a client buried under PowerPoint slides that have been dumped from a truck. The tagline reads, "Now that's impact!"

5. And, of course, while this book is being written, Innosight consultants are spending all of their time at home interacting with colleagues and clients through videoconferences.

to the intranet for time-zone-challenged colleagues in Asia. One key nudge to encourage collaboration at these sessions is to have assigned seating to support the formation of new relationships. Interestingly, one of the surprising benefits Natalie and Scott noticed about the virtualization of life in the first half of 2020 is attendance to First Friday went up; there was no longer a divide between people in the room and people out of the room, and virtual breakout rooms made it easy to spur discussion.

Innosight has experimented with other ways to encourage collaboration, as well, which could someday turn into more fully formulated BEANs. For example, to create more connections, Innosight invites people participating in a training event or workshop to share their favorite song and artist before the session. Then a snippet of each person's song is played before and after breaks, with the group guessing whose song it is. Once the person is revealed, he or she shares what it is that makes the song special to him or her. It is a fun to way to accelerate the process of people getting to know each other, and at the end of the program you have a playlist.[6]

## What Makes a Successful BEAN

What makes a BEAN work? Studying the literature and looking at BEANs that work suggest six key ingredients.[7]

SIMPLICITY: Make it easy to adopt and remember.

Want to exercise more? Leave your running shoes by your bed before you go to sleep. Want a patient to remember to take medication? Ensure

---

6. Natalie stole this idea from a healthcare client. She recalls that one client picked a Metallica song that helped her through the last mile of a marathon, another loved Broadway musicals, and yet another loved country music because it reminded her of her family's ranch in Wyoming. At an offsite in October 2019, Scott picked Pearl Jam's "Betterman" (specifically the live version played in the August 7, 2016, concert in Fenway Park), and Andy picked "Agadoo" by Black Lace. Okay, he actually didn't, but this is a test from Scott to see if Andy would read the footnotes during the review process. He did. The song he actually selected was "Whole of the Moon" by The Waterboys.

7. Yes, the text that follows forms the acronym SPROUT. One reviewer felt that they had reached acronym overload at this stage in the manuscript, so we chose to have it as a gift to our dear footnote readers.

it is in a blister pack with the days of week on it. We're willing to bet you'll remember MOJO months after reading this book! Habit change is hard, so make it as simple as possible to start, which does mean spending time thinking of a memorable name for your BEAN.

PRACTICALITY: Connect it to existing routines.

The fewer things you have to change, the better. One of the biggest benefits of electric toothbrushes, for example, is a timer that turns the toothbrush off after the two minutes that dentists recommend. Behavior change with no thinking required! In the case of DBS, MOJO didn't require a completely new routine; it docked into an existing one—meetings already exist. They start and they (sometimes after what seems like forever) end.

REINFORCEMENT: Create physical and digital reminders.

As memorable as the name MOJO is, in the early days of any program, it is easy for people to revert to old habits and simply not take the time to appoint a MO, name the JO, check in, and check out. So when you walk into a conference room at DBS, you see visual cues—fun cubes that people can play with on tables and checklists on the wall—that serve as reminders of the MOJO program. These kinds of physical reminders help to nudge people to participate in the program.

ORGANIZATIONAL CONSISTENCY: Ensure it links to objectives, processes, systems, and values.

One of the most cited papers in the change literature is Steven Kerr's 1975 classic, "On the Folly of Rewarding A, While Hoping for B."[8] Effective BEANs don't encourage people to do one thing if the

---

8. The notes section in the back of this book has the formal reference for Kerr's work. The footnote is to acknowledge one of our favorite reviewers, who caught that there was a typo here reporting the paper was published in 1995. "I can report with complete objectivity that 1975 is in fact the very best year to be born in," the reviewer noted. A previous version of the manuscript described how Scott was born in that year, and that might have accelerated our efforts to figure out who this anonymous reviewer was, except he directly

company rewards them for something else or punishes them for that behavior.

UNIQUENESS: Create something fun and social and support it with stories and legends.

The name MOJO causes you to pause and say, "Tell me more." The name is easy to remember. Tying it to meetings ensures it is done in communal settings. Sharing stories (like the JO who provides feedback in verse or the brave JO who provided feedback to the senior leader) helps spread the idea.

TRACKABILITY: Build it in a way that it can be adjusted, measured, and scaled.

While there is a spirit of fun and creativity in MOJO, it is serious business: DBS tracks the effectiveness of meetings and knows that meetings with MOJO have double the effectiveness of those that don't. These measures allow DBS to track and improve MOJO. In 2018 DBS introduced a smartphone app (an early iteration of which is available in the public app store), both to aid in MOJO's application and to capture data that allows DBS to further improve the program.

## A Few of Our Favorite BEANs

Hacking day-to-day habits with BEANs is a key way to drive a culture of innovation. The text below discusses some of our favorite BEANs, grouped by the five behaviors described in chapter 1 (these BEANs are summarized in table 3-1), and includes prompting questions to help you create your own BEANs to encourage each behavior. Part II of the book details more than 20 additional BEANs, and the appendix has a list of

---

emailed us the thirteen pages of (hugely useful) comments he had on this book. Thanks, Thomas Wedell-Wedellsborg!

**TABLE 3-1**

## Our favorite BEANs

| Behavior | BEAN | Description | Behavior enabler | Artifact | Nudge |
|---|---|---|---|---|---|
| Curiosity | DBS's Gandalf Scholarship | Employees can receive S$1,000 (US$740) to study any topic of interest, as long as they teach it back to the organization | A step-by-step application guide | A companion website with videos of "teach-backs" | The name itself, which is a nudge toward DBS's culture-change "avatar" |
| Customer obsession | Amazon.com's Future Press Release | The practice of describing ideas via "future press releases" from a customer perspective | An in-meeting ritual of reviewing press releases versus PowerPoint decks | Physical memos | The meeting design |
| Collaboration | Boehringer Ingelheim's Lunch Roulette | An easy-to-use website to set up "lunch dates" with new people | Step-by-step instructions on the website | Collateral describing the program | Gamification via the roulette analogy, which encourages participation |
| Adeptness in ambiguity | Tata's Dare to Try | An annual prize and public recognition for teams that failed but learned something valuable | Prize guidelines that provide detailed descriptions of desired behaviors | A physical trophy | Supporting materials that spread stories about past winners |
| Empowerment | Adobe's Kickbox | A physical box with step-by-step experiment guides and a prepaid $1,000 debit card | Checklists, tools, and the debit card | A physical "box" given to participants | A kit that contains "levels," to nudge continued participation |

101 interventions in our "bag of BEANs." Further information about BEANs is available at www.eatsleepinnovate.com.

CURIOSITY. Another example of a well-crafted BEAN from DBS is the Gandalf Scholarship. As part of its aspiration to favorably compare with companies like Google and Apple, DBS set a goal of becoming a learning organization that constantly ques-  tioned the status quo. Historically, it ran leadership development in a traditional way, pushing in-class learning to identified employees, who were then encouraged to learn things that directly helped them improve their day-to-day work. The Gandalf Scholarship flipped the model on its head. Now, any employee can apply to receive S$1,000 (about US$740) to spend on a project of his or her choice—a course, books, a conference—that supports DBS's goal of becoming a learning organization. The only condition is that scholarship winners must teach what they've discovered to their colleagues. As of fall 2019, the bank granted more than 100 scholarships in areas from artificial intelligence to storytelling for managers, with the average recipient teaching close to an additional 300 people. DBS has recorded many of these "teach-backs" and posted them on an online channel with related articles and other information, creating virtual artifacts that have been viewed more than ten thousand times. The bank estimates that each dollar it spends on the scholarship has a positive impact on thirty times as many employees as a dollar spent on traditional training.

*Questions to consider: How can you help make sure your team doesn't get stuck in a rut? How can you encourage people to discover new things, even those that seem to be disconnected to their day jobs?*

CUSTOMER OBSESSION. One of Amazon.com's stated missions is to be the world's most customer-centric company. A ritual to reinforce this mission relates to how Amazon managers propose new ideas. At most

companies, ideas are detailed in PowerPoint documents replete with facts and figures. The thicker the
deck, the better the idea. At Amazon.com, instead
of a PowerPoint deck, managers create a Future
Press Release that they imagine will accompany the
launch of the finished product. The press release
doesn't start with the idea; it works backwards from

the customer job to be done. And it must contain frequently asked questions, which again encourages the idea submitter to look at the world
through the customer's eyes. When it comes time to discuss the idea,
rather than have the idea presented, meeting attendees silently read
the press release before engaging in discussion.

*Questions to consider: How can you make sure your team takes a
customer-first perspective? What visual cues can you create? Are there
regular questions or idea description mechanisms like Amazon.com's
future release that can help?*

COLLABORATION. When David Thompson worked in the US arm of phar-
maceutical manufacturer Boehringer
Ingelheim (BI), he created an innovative
way to inspire internal collisions that foster
collaboration. Thompson's idea came from
a problem all of us have encountered. He
entered the corporate cafeteria one day and

noticed his usual lunch companions weren't there—and he didn't recognize any of the other faces in the room. He envisioned—and then in two
days, with help from a friend, prototyped—a simple website where people
could find random lunchmates. They called the idea Lunch Roulette. Participants who sign up indicate the dates they are interested in participating and the locations they are willing to travel to. The click of a button
then creates a match and an automatic calendar invite. Upon its rollout,
hundreds of people immediately signed up, including the CEO. "A lot of

times, a CEO only talks with someone who has been prescribed for them. With Lunch Roulette, he doesn't know who he'll be paired with and neither does the other person," Thompson said. "Both can learn something from the other. After all, if we don't have people who can learn both up and down, then we have the wrong people in both levels."

*Questions to consider: How can you encourage physical or virtual collaboration? Are there ways to make it easier for people to meet and work together?*

ADEPTNESS IN AMBIGUITY. Being adept in ambiguity requires being able to handle the inevitable false steps, fumbles, and, yes, failures that come along with innovation. A power-

ful BEAN that helps to reinforce this tolerance comes from the Tata Group, India's largest conglomerate. Every year the company holds a celebration honoring innovation accomplishments across its sprawling collection of business units, which range from tea to IT consulting to automobiles. One of the most coveted awards given at that gathering is called Dare to Try. As the name connotes, it goes to a team that failed but in an intelligent way. In the company's words, "Showcasing a growing culture of risk-taking and perseverance across Tata companies. . . . [Dare to Try] recognizes and rewards the most novel, daring and seriously attempted ideas that did not achieve the desired results." Dare to Try is a substantial program, attracting hundreds of applications annually. Promotions for it help nudge innovative behaviors like embracing risk and tolerating failure. The award itself—a trophy—and the highly visible public summary of the event are artifacts that effectively reinforce Tata's innovation culture.

*Questions to consider: How can you condition people for the ambiguity that accompanies innovation? How can you publicly and loudly celebrate learning versus privately and quietly punishing failure?*

EMPOWERMENT. One common complaint from
would-be innovators is the chain of approvals
they need to do *anything*. While that problem can
often be largely perceptual, it also can be a very
real innovation inhibitor. The Adobe Kickbox is
a purpose-built BEAN to empower employees at
the 20,000-person software company. Successful

applications receive a red box that's about the size of an encyclopedia
(if you are reading this and are younger than thirty years old, ask your
parents).[9] Crack open the box and you will see a range of tools designed
to facilitate developing prototypes for ideas. Most critically, the box
contains a $1,000 prepaid debit card that can be spent without asking
for anyone's approval. In its first few years, Adobe granted 1,000 Kick-
boxes. That's $1 million in investment, but it is also 1,000 experiments
that otherwise would not have been run. Many of those experiments
have gone nowhere, but some have informed new product development
or highlighted acquisitions opportunities.

*How can you help people progress an idea? Are there process shortcuts
that can help to more quickly move ideas from paper to reality?*

## One Last Note

The case study that follows will detail a simple process to create a BEAN,
and the next chapter will provide a front-row seat to one organization's
six-week sprint to create the alpha version of a culture of innovation
within their HR community. Before getting there, however, we'd like

---

9. Please note that Adobe employees do have to apply to receive a Kickbox, so there is still
a filter. That was a caveat missed by the CEO of a 10,000-person firm that heard Scott describe the program at a company offsite. Inspired by the story, he followed Scott on stage
to announce that everyone at the company would receive $1,000 to experiment. The CFO,
with whom he had not conferred before making the proclamation, looked on in horror,
as the $10 million commitment would blow a hole in the budget. The firm deftly managed
to keep the essence of the leader's intent while putting up enough guardrails that the program's implementation didn't unintentionally lead to the need to cost cut!

to make one last point: one mistake we see people make sometimes is confusing BEANs (ways to encourage a new behavior) and innovations (something different that creates value).

In September 2019, Scott and Andy were getting ready to share some of the content from this book at a large gathering of HR professionals in Australia. As stimuli for the discussion, they had the US Innosight team create a two-minute video of Innosight new hires describing challenges and opportunities of the onboarding process. For example, one new hire described the stress of trying to quickly remember everyone's name. "One of the things that was a challenge is I am one new person coming in, and there are a hundred people that I am going to meet over the course of a matter of weeks," he said. "This one-hundred-to-one problem is actually really stressful, to try to remember everyone you met. You might run into someone getting a cup of coffee and think to yourself, 'They seem familiar. I think I have met that person before. But I don't remember their name.' So actually, it is quite a lot of stress."

It's not hard to imagine a range of innovative ways to address this "one-time" stress. For example, imagine creating a simple app in which a new hire could tick off employees that they have met, helping them

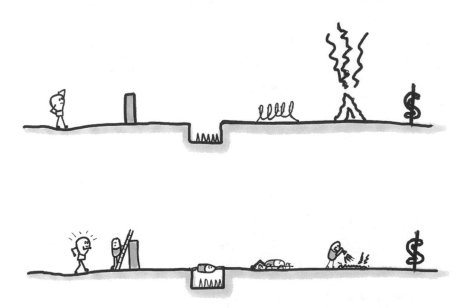

*Innovation solves a problem; BEANs enable innovation.*

keep better track of new faces. Or, to push the imagination a bit, consider an augmented-reality solution that brought up someone's profile on a whiteboard whenever they entered a room. Those kinds of solutions help to solve a single problem. That's innovation—something different that creates value. But there's perhaps a bigger issue at work: what's behind the new hire's angst could also be a lack of deep connection in the community. The recurring behavior to encourage, then, could be to get to know people as humans. Boehringer Ingelheim's Lunch Roulette encourages that behavior. Or consider a suggestion from an Innosight team during an office gathering: Have a table in the café set up as the "Eat with me" table. Ideally this would be a wooden farmhouse table that is larger and more inviting than the normal café tables. It would bear an "Eat with me" sign and possibly include a whiteboard to list topics for discussion. People across the firm would be able to sign up to sit at the table, to ensure there was always someone there for new hires or others who wanted a lunch buddy. There would be reminders of the table in regular company emails, and it could be pointed out on office tours as well. As such, this project has the potential to be a powerful combination of a behavior enabler (the whiteboard with topics and instructions), an artifact (the physical table), and a nudge (reminder emails and tracking).

BEANs and innovations are both valuable things. But they are *different* things. Be clear when you are seeking to solve a problem versus when you are trying to encourage a behavior.

## Chapter Summary

---

- ✓ Fighting against institutionalized inertia requires pulling a page from the habit-change playbook to shape day-to-day behavior. Specifically, hack habits with BEANs: behavior enablers, artifacts, and nudges.

- ✓ Behavior enablers are direct, tangible ways to support behavior change, such as recurring rituals, checklists, and dedicated coaches. Nudges are indirect, intangible ways to make behavior change easy, such as office design and leaderboards. Artifacts, such as prizes, pictures, and stories, connect the two by physically and digitally reinforcing the change.

✓ Successful BEANs are simple, practical, reinforced, organizationally consistent, unique, and trackable.

✓ Our favorite BEANs include DBS's Gandalf Scholarship (which encourages curiosity), Amazon.com's Future Press Release (which reinforces customer-centricity), Boehringer Ingelheim's Lunch Roulette (which aids collaboration), Tata's Dare to Try program (which helps it to be adept in ambiguity), and Adobe's Kickbox (which empowers employees).

✓ An innovation solves a problem, while a BEAN encourages a behavior.

# BEANs in Hyderabad

BEANs are a powerful way to encourage desired behaviors and over-come key blockers. Consider how DBS used BEANs at a purpose-built development center in Hyderabad, India. The new center was taking over previously outsourced operations, such as the design and support of customer-facing mobile applications, and it presented the company with the opportunity to build a more entrepreneurial culture from scratch.

The center's office design mimicked what you'd see at any hot, young tech venture, with open space, snack bars, and, of course, the obligatory foosball table. Its recruitment processes, borrowed from innovative companies like Netflix, were designed to attract distinctive talent. But when the lights went on, it quickly became clear that employees' day-to-day experiences had little of that startup feeling. The engineers fell into well-worn routines, working methodically and avoiding fast-paced experimentation. DBS leaders in Singapore continued to treat Hyderabad like an arm's-length vendor versus a set of colleagues seeking to advance a common mission. While employee engagement scores weren't terrible, they were notably short of DBS's aspiration.

To turn things around, a group of Innosight consultants and DBS Technology & Operations change agents (which we'll call the culture team) decided to develop BEANs that would disrupt the unwanted habits and promote new and better ones. The team followed a four-step process (chapter 4 explores this process in even greater detail).

## 1. Get Granular about Desired Behaviors

The culture team outlined what kind of organizational traits needed to be encouraged at Hyderabad. DBS had already identified the need to be agile, learning-oriented, customer-obsessed, data-driven, and experimental. The culture team went deeper to list more specific behaviors under each of these categories. For example, under "Experimental," were aspirational statements such as "We rapidly test new ideas," "We practice lean experimentation," and "We fail cheap, we fail fast, and we learn even faster."

## 2. Identify Behavioral Blockers

Next the culture team looked for things that were getting in the way of the desired behaviors. To uncover these, members sat in on staff meetings, conducted diagnostic surveys, interviewed center employees confidentially one on one, and reviewed "day in the life" journals that developers kept for a week.

The team was specifically looking for existing habits and behavior patterns that were inhibiting innovation. For example, among other issues, the culture team found that many employees felt that they jumped into work without discussing its context, so they lacked an understanding of how their project fit with the broader strategy, what was expected of each person working on the project, and so on. Some employees also felt that candidly surfacing problems was taboo, so they stewed in silent frustration. Meanwhile, developers reported being stretched so thin that they lacked time to innovate, but deeper exploration revealed the real problem: a lack of clear guidelines for how to prioritize a seemingly never-ending list of requests.

## 3. Design BEANs

The culture team then designed ways to eliminate the blockers. To get things going, it facilitated two two-day workshops with senior leaders, one in Hyderabad and the other in Singapore. After discussing the desired behaviors and their blockers, participants broke into small groups for structured brainstorming. Each group was given examples of BEANs from other organizations for inspiration, and to devise new ones, they used a simple template to specify the behaviors sought, the habits blocking those behaviors, and the behavior enablers and nudges that would help employees break through the blockers (chapter 4 has a sample capture template). All participants then reassembled to review the fifteen ideas for BEANs and voted on a few to implement.

Here are three interventions that were created to tackle lack of context, candor, and prioritization at the center:

LACK OF CONTEXT. This blocker reinforced employees' sense that their business-as-usual approach was good enough. The BEAN targeting it was a Culture Canvas inspired by Alexander Osterwalder and Yves Pigneur's canvas that maps out the  key elements of a business model. The Culture Canvas is, likewise, a simple one-page, poster-size template. On it, project teams articulate their business goals and codify team roles and norms. Filling it out helps them gain a clearer sense of expectations, organizational context, and who does what. Giving teams clarity about their goals and the scope to push boundaries further empowers their entrepreneurial spirit. The resulting physical artifacts, which include photos and signatures from members, serve as a visual reminder of the team members' commitments.

LACK OF CANDOR. A BEAN called Team Temp was devised to liberate employees to speak up when they saw problems. The web-based app, to be used at the first meeting of the week, gauges a project team's mood by inviting members to anonymously describe how they're feeling by entering a score from 1 (highly negative) to 10 (highly positive) and writing a single word that best describes their mood. This quickly reveals if the team has an issue (a string of 1s and 2s is pretty telling) and prompts a discussion—led by the team leader—about what's going on and how it can be addressed. Because the app tracks team sentiment over time, it also gauges whether interventions are working.

LACK OF PRIORITIZATION. To bust this blocker, the culture team created the 70:20:10 BEAN. Inspired by Google's practices, it gives software developers explicit permission to spend 70 percent of their time on day-to-day work, 20 percent on work-improvement ideas, and 10 percent on experiments and pet projects. By formally freeing up chunks of time for unspecified experimentation, 70:20:10 encourages innovative thinking. To reinforce it, the cultural team also created a ritual in which developers share what they've learned from their experimental projects with one another.

## 4. Refine and Implement BEANs

Pilot teams in Hyderabad tested a handful of BEANs, including the three detailed above. Their impact was carefully measured and improvements were made along the way. Ineffective BEANs were discarded, and effective ones were rolled out more broadly and tracked. As a result of the 70:20:10 BEAN, for example, teams automated several previously manual processes, shaving hours off of key tasks, and developed other innovations. (The initial version of the MOJO app described in chapter 3 came out of one developer's experimentation time.) Meanwhile, leaders increased the amount of time they spent walking the halls and modeling the new ways of working.

A year after the interventions began, employee surveys showed that workers' engagement scores at Hyderabad had increased by 20 percent and that customer-centricity had risen significantly. In 2018 LinkedIn named the development center one of the top twenty-five places to work in India, and in 2019 the bank won a prestigious Zinnov award for being "a great place to innovate."

# 4

# Conducting a
# Culture Sprint

Singtel Group is Southeast Asia's largest telecommunications company. Through fully owned operations in Singapore and Australia and substantial investments in operators in markets such as India (Airtel), Indonesia (Telkomsel), Thailand (AIS), and the Philippines (Globe), it has about 700 million mobile subscribers. Over the past few years it has made substantial investments to build a portfolio of digital businesses in new markets like mobile advertising and cybersecurity. In mid-2018 its group chief human resources officer Aileen Tan framed up a different challenge. "I press a button on my phone, and a car appears. I press a different one and food arrives. I can instantaneously initiate a video call with friends around the world. To the consumer, these innovative services are like magic. And we enable that magic," she said. "But inside the organization we have papers and forms and processes and structures and rules. Why can't we be as innovative internally as the market demands externally?"

Remember, it took Destin Sandlin eight months on his own to unlearn how to ride a bike. The DBS story took place over a decade. Was there a way, Tan wondered, to focus and accelerate the culture change journey? She decided to experiment by focusing on the culture of the team closest to her, the Group HR team. Every movement must start somewhere, she posited. What better place to start a culture movement in a large organization than the 150-person-strong Group HR team? After all, this team touches every business unit and employee in the organization.

This chapter borrows the metaphor of a sprint from the agile movement, which originated as an approach to dramatically accelerate software development and has spread as an approach to accelerate a broader set of initiatives. A sprint, performing an integrated set of activities in a tightly defined period of time, follows the agile principles of delivering working software frequently and responding to change over following a plan. At Singtel, that meant developing an alpha version of a culture of innovation within six weeks. The anchor of the sprint was a two-day activation session. People had a chance to follow innovative behaviors on the first day and BEANstorm to encourage those behaviors on the second.[1]

We'll detail the work that preceded and followed the activation session, the session itself, and the key lessons learned. This will be the most detailed chapter in the book, which we hope enables you to execute a similar sprint with your team, group, or department.[2] Figure 4-1 provides a map to guide you through the chapter. At the center is the relationship between the sprint, the activation session, the BEANstorm, and the work after the activation session. The figure references the four steps we followed to create BEANs in Hyderabad and maps how activities in this chapter connect to those steps.[3]

## Preparing for the Activation Session

While it might seem tempting to jump straight into a brainstorming activity, our experience suggests that four activities (summarized in table 4-1) help maximize the impact of a more comprehensive activation session. The first two, determining desired behaviors and diagnosing the current state to identify blockers, match the first two process steps described

1. BEANstorm really wants a trademark on it, doesn't it?

2. "Most detailed" is code for "longest." This clocks in at more than 8,000 words, so grab your beverage of choice and nestle in!

3. Thanks to our favorite reviewer Thomas for suggesting these visuals and helping us to keep all of these pieces straight!

FIGURE 4-1

## Map of activities described in chapter 4

*Numbers in parenthesis connect activities to process steps followed in Hyderabad*

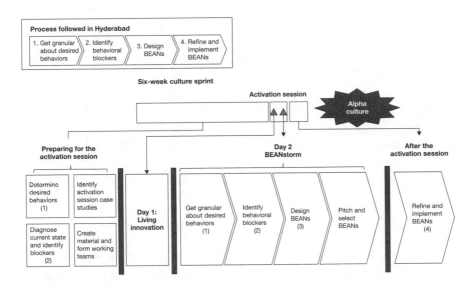

in Hyderabad. The next two, identifying activation-session case studies and preparing for the activation session, set the session up for success.

## Determine Desired Behaviors

Remember, a culture of innovation is one in which the behaviors that drive innovation success come naturally. A critical component of the culture sprint is to determine the specific behaviors you seek to encourage. While there might be some temptation to develop a custom set of desired behaviors, for the purposes of developing an alpha culture, we find it helps to start either with the generic behaviors defined in chapter 1 (be curious, customer-obsessed, collaborative, adept in ambiguity, and empowered) or with other already-agreed-upon desired behaviors.[4] For Singtel we picked the five generic behaviors.

4. For example, one large healthcare company wanted to focus on accountability, agility, and entrepreneurship, which we deemed to be more than good enough to start.

TABLE 4-1

## Prework

| Specific step | Description |
| --- | --- |
| Determine desired behaviors | Pick the desired behaviors you want to encourage, with a default view of the five behaviors from chapter 1. |
| Diagnose the current state and identify blockers | Identify potential blockers that are inhibiting your ability to follow the desired behaviors. |
| Identify day-one activation-session case studies | Identify specific problems to solve to showcase the impact of following the desired behaviors. |
| Create material and form working teams | Create customized stimuli and determine key champions and sponsors for small-group work. |

## Diagnose the Current State and Identify Blockers

The activation session will have the most impact if you come into it with a perspective about the behaviors you currently follow, the ones you do not, and the biggest blockers.

There are three specific ways to diagnose the current state and determine what actually are your organization's day-to-day behaviors. A good starting point is to take either qualitative comments from existing organizational culture surveys or publicly available comments by current or former employees on sites like Glassdoor. Inputting text into one of the many word-cloud generator apps or websites quickly and effectively generates a visual map of employee perceptions about the current culture. Do words related to the desired behaviors appear frequently? Or does it look more like the word cloud in chapter 2, which prominently featured words like "fear," "inertia," and "bureaucracy"?

A second technique is to conduct one-on-one interviews. For Singtel we interviewed a cross section of the HR team. We interviewed those in business partner roles who interacted with the business units and those with more internal functions, such as payroll. We interviewed people with decades of tenure and people who had joined within the last two years. We interviewed Singtel lifers and people with prior experience at multinational companies; those who had worked only in Singapore and those who had significant overseas experience; highly engaged and enthusiastic team members and those more prone to express skepticism. This variety ensured divergent perspectives and helped us avoid the risk of anchoring on the strongly held views of a minority.

We asked interviewees to state a handful of one- to three-word answers to the question, "How would you describe our culture today?" As always, it is good to seek examples and anecdotes to add specificity and richness to the diagnosis. For example, one interviewee described how, when they were dealing with a personal issue, they received a care package from Tan and the leadership team. That is a potential strength to build on, as caring about the team could easily extend to caring about the team *and* the customer.

Finally, you can administer a diagnostic survey. That can be as simple as asking people the degree to which they regularly follow the five innovation behaviors. The appendix has two other surveys you can use: a simple, somewhat tongue-in-cheek way to assess the "status of your relationship with innovation" or a more comprehensive culture-of-innovation survey. The comprehensive survey, which we used both at Singtel and DBS, explores four areas:

1. To what degree do employee perceptions match what you would expect to see in a strong culture of innovation? Perception-related barriers indicate that people think innovative behaviors are not worth their time or effort because, at best, they will have little impact and, at worst, they risk being punished.

2. To what degree are people following specific behaviors? The survey asks questions about the last time people followed behaviors tied to desired ways of working, such as praising someone for taking a risk at work. Have they never done it? Have they done it sometime in their life? Within the last year? Within the last month? Within the last week?

3. To what degree do people have the specific skills to do these behaviors well? While self-reporting has its problems, the survey

asks people to rate themselves on more than a dozen enabling skills, such as experiment design and execution.

4. To what degree are there enablers in place that would help innovative behaviors stick and scale? The survey asks a range of questions that look at the systems and structures that fight against the shadow strategy (some of these systems and structures are detailed in more depth in part II).

Whatever diagnostic tool you use, you should be able to identify clear and obvious areas to address. For example, Singtel has a reputation for expecting very buttoned-up analysis to back up decisions. What do you do, one interviewee wondered, with an innovative idea about which data simply didn't exist? Would it expose the person who submitted the idea to fierce questioning that they couldn't answer? Another issue that emerged was a top-down directive culture that inhibited HR leaders from feeling empowered to deliver the digital future.

## Identify Day-One Activation-Session Case Studies

Culture change and the value it creates can be hard to grasp. At best, it is vague and, at worst, it can be called "woolly," "nebulous," or even "airy-fairy." How can you help people viscerally understand why culture change, and, more specifically, granular changes to ways of working, are worth the time and investment? Nothing substitutes for the firsthand experience of seeing how desired behaviors help to solve real organizational problems. So this step involves identifying case studies—namely, specific problems facing the organization—that will be addressed during the activation session.

As Richard Pascale famously said, "Adults are more likely to act their way into a new way of thinking than to think their way into a new way of acting." As such, we worked with the HR team to identify real problems that people could work on during the first day of the activation session. We wanted people to experience the tomorrow culture where innovative behaviors were second nature. Showing how these behaviors drove tangible progress against real problems—problems they cared about solving—helped them understand the value of adopting new behaviors, making the BEANstorm resonate more deeply.

Ideally, selected problems have three characteristics. First, they should be material. Second, they should be bounded tightly enough to allow teams to make material progress in a short time. Third, they should be open-ended enough that there is space to explore alternative solutions. In Singtel's case, we identified problems statements—questions starting with "how might me"—like the following:

- How might we provide an awesome first-day onboarding experience for any new joiner?

- How might we engage more deeply with alumni?

- How might we maximize the impact of the recently renovated employee collaboration space for which the HR team is responsible?

For each problem, we developed a one-page overview of the problem to share with working teams. We also identified real "customers" that teams could talk to in order to gain deeper insight about the problem (discussed more below).

## Create Material and Form Working Teams

The final piece of prework involves two activities. The first is to create relevant material. For Singtel, we created packs for each participant that detailed the desired innovation behaviors, explained the problem they would be working on, and summarized key lessons from the diagnostic work. We also created "BEAN cards" to serve as stimuli.[5] Finally, we designed detailed instruction guides and capture templates.[6]

---

5. One hundred one BEANs appear in this book. Forty-two are described in depth in parts I and II (MOJO in chapter 2, our five favorite BEANs and two Innosight BEANs in chapter 3, three BEANs in the Hyderabad case study, a Singtel and a DBS BEAN in chapter 4, and twenty-nine BEANs in part II), and the "Bag of BEANs" in the appendix has another fifty-nine. During workshops, we print simple cards that describe the BEANs. We have been amazed at how excited people get about these cards. You can find versions of them at www.eatsleepinnovate.com.

6. Generic versions of all of this material are available at www.eatsleepinnovate.com. Let's be honest: we'd be happy if some of you called Innosight and asked for our help (well,

The second prework activity is to form the working teams for the session. At Singtel, each team had a mix of roles and tenures. We spread Tan's leadership team across the working teams. We told these leaders that they should be team sponsors and would assume responsibility for driving the solutions created on day one of the workshop. Critically, we told them that they should be in "coaching" mode, which fit with the overall theme of shifting toward a more empowered culture. We also identified a small group of "catalysts," who we spread among the teams, to be responsible for carrying the work beyond the activation session.

Our experience suggests that this prework can be done in around a month. As mentioned, that requires agreeing to use the "generic" view of a culture of innovation described in this book. Sometimes, though, it is necessary to take more of an outside-in view of what it will take to succeed in a changing competitive environment, which requires external research and discussions with senior leadership. But however you choose to approach it, keep the metaphor of a sprint in mind—you aren't seeking to create a perfect culture; rather, you are trying to put multiple elements together rapidly, to see what works and what doesn't.

## The Activation Session

The two-day activation session is the central component of a culture-of-innovation sprint. The first day provides a chance to experience a culture of innovation by using the five behaviors (or whatever specific behaviors you chose during the prework) to make tangible progress on real business problems. On the second day, the group BEANstorms to overcome identified blockers and make those ways of working habitual. That's a lot of words, so let's return to Singtel to see and feel a session in action.

---

that matters less to Paul, but he still likes the Innosight team, so he would be happy for his three coauthors), but one of our core values is transparency, so we believe openly sharing our tools and methods is the right thing to do!

## Day One: Living Innovation

Forty-two Singtel Group HR members gathered in August 2018 for a two-day activation session. A design principle was to reinforce the idea of BEANs by using BEANs during the activation session. So Tan kickstarted the session by using an adapted version of Amazon's Future Press Release (described in chapter 3). Tan's future press release outlined how the HR team had led the way in creating the culture now deemed the "secret sauce" to Singtel Group's overall success in digital transformation. This different approach to opening a work-related gathering piqued interest straightaway, as participants realized this would not be "just another workshop."

The group then had a chance to live each of the five innovation behaviors to solve their selected problem, summarized in table 4-2.[7]

LIVING "COLLABORATIVE." Once the teams spent fifteen minutes orienting themselves to their problems, they had a chance to actively experience *collaboration*. It started by defining how they wanted to work together as a team in ways that accentuate collaboration. To surface and subsequently amplify the team's various talents and experiences, each team member shared their unique "superpower." This led to some introspection and humor as people gainfully explained their various powers to their newly acquainted team members. Next, they reflected on how the various superpowers shared could help them collaborate better as a team. The exercise sometimes uncovers surprises, like the lawyer who writes poetry, or hidden skills, like the HR representative who studied finance and has experience in financial modeling.[8]

---

7. Careful readers might wonder why the order of behaviors here differs from that in chapter 1. The list presented in chapter 1 follows the general process of innovation: being curious kicks off the process, being customer-obsessed surfaces the problems to solve, being collaborative aids in developing solutions, being adept in ambiguity refines those solutions, and being empowered helps to launch and scale innovation. However, we have found that it "feels right" to have collaboration come first in a workshop context as it helps groups orient for the day.

8. It also can uncover largely irrelevant but humanizing facts, like one author's (nearly) unblemished track record at Whack-a-Mole. Okay, it's Scott. Bring it on!

TABLE 4-2

## Living innovation

| Behavior | Description |
| --- | --- |
| Collaboration | Set teams up for success by reinforcing the collaborative behaviors needed to solve real organizational problems. |
| Customer obsession | Help teams truly understand what job to be done (problem) they are solving for their customer and why. |
| Curiosity | Help teams tap into their innate curiosity, question the status quo, and ultimately develop great solutions to the problem they have been assigned. |
| Adeptness in ambiguity | Help teams uncover the assumptions behind their solutions so they can navigate and de-risk key uncertainties. |
| Empowerment | Provide ways to accelerate the progress of shortlisted ideas while recognizing the efforts of those that fell short. |

At this point another infused BEAN came into play: DBS's MOJO program (detailed in the DBS case study after chapter 2). Each team appointed a meeting owner (MO) and joyful observer (JO) to ensure more effective discussions and collaborations. The sidebar "Natalie's Favorite Ice Breakers" has additional tips for encouraging session members to enter into "collaborative" and "customer-obsessed" modes.

LIVING "CUSTOMER OBSESSION." To help the teams better understand the problems they were solving they next followed the behavior of customer obsession. We shared the foundational concept of the job to be done: the fundamental problem a customer is trying to solve in a given circumstance (described in more depth in several of Innosight's books). We also shared practical tips to discover jobs to be done during customer discussions, such as:

- Ask why, then ask it again. (This helps get to underlying causality.)

- Start broad to understand the context.

- Ask neutral, nonleading questions.

# Natalie's Favorite Ice Breakers

Natalie has extensive experience designing and executing experiences for Innosight clients and colleagues. In addition to the "playlist" icebreaker described in chapter 3, she likes using the two openers detailed below to help would-be BEANstormers get into collaborative and customer-obsessed modes.

The first icebreaker is a simple way to help participants to get to know each other while also entering into customer-obsessed mode. Have every member of a group write down his or her favorite show, podcast, and book on a whiteboard wall with their name next to it. You don't even need to have a formal debriefing to discuss the list items; people can ask each other during breaks why they like the shows, podcasts, or books they do to learn more about them. You get a surprising amount of energy from this activity and a nice artifact at the end.

Another powerful exercise is called the "river of life." In this exercise, people pair up and spend fifteen minutes jotting down key moments of life, both highs and lows, along a winding river that serves as a more visual way to display a timeline. Then each member spends another fifteen minutes sharing their river with their partner. The listening partner must ask no questions but listen actively to understand what the other person values and feels is important. Once the fifteen minutes is up, the partners swap roles. The activity ends with the partners taking turns sharing what they heard as the other person's values and motivators. This is an effective way to quickly learn about another person and to practice the active-listening skills necessary for effective interviewing.

- Do not provide multiple choices; just pause.

- Be precise: set a limit of ten words to a question.

- Trust actions over statements: encourage stories or ask for a demonstration.

This wasn't abstract instruction. Each team then received a profile of a real customer they would meet, a simple interview guide to help prompt probing questions, and a template to capture the answers.[9] For example, the interview guide for the team solving the onboarding issue prompted them to get the customer to walk them through her own onboarding process, step by step, describing her emotions and digging into specific frustrations to help them identify places to innovate.

Armed with these guides, each team set off to various parts of the building to meet and interview real customers about their real business problems. Alumni came to share their views with the alumni team, the onboarding team interviewed employees who had joined that month, and so on. These customer interviews helped each team to build fundamental insights and to frame the problems they were solving from the perspectives of the customers they were serving—an imperative for the customer-obsessed organization.

LIVING "CURIOSITY." With the job to be done now clear, teams embraced *curiosity* to develop innovative solutions. Each team received prepared stimuli to help them broaden their thinking and question the status quo. The stimuli included HR trends, technologies, and relevant case studies from organizations that had created innovative solutions to similar problems. For example, the onboarding team considered trends such as rising employee expectations and the role that a technology solution—such as one that enabled verified electronic signing of employment contracts—could play in their solution. An inspiring case study outlining how L'Oréal's culture app assists its 11,000 yearly new-

---

9. Again, generic versions of these can be found online. And, of course, there are lots of other good tools and templates out there that overlap with what we did on day one. Use what works for you!

hires to understand, decode, and master their unique company culture supplemented this. Case studies help reinforce the idea that the curious seek inspiration from those who have solved their problems before, whether they are in related fields or in fields as unrelated as cosmetics is to telecommunications.

To develop and prioritize solutions to a customer job to be done, teams referenced the stimuli and followed the same structured "diverge to converge" ideation process that Innosight uses in its innovation consulting work. There is no great secret to this process, but our experience leads to three practical suggestions:

1. Give people a few minutes to think on their own, which helps to avoid groupthink and creates a broad base of different ideas.

2. Give people more than one chance to develop and edit ideas.

3. Keep the timing tight to keep energy high. Better to leave people wanting more than to have them get bored!

Another suggestion is to ask people specific questions that can open up new avenues for exploration. For example, you might ask workshop attendees to consider the following:

- How might we address pain points or frustrations?

- How might we enhance what is currently working?

- What would "awesome" look and feel like?

- How might digital technologies help?

LIVING "ADEPTNESS IN AMBIGUITY." At this stage each team had a solution on paper. But every innovative solution is partially right and partially wrong. The trick to successful innovation is to figure out, as quickly and cheaply as possible, which parts are which. This requires navigating strategic uncertainty through disciplined identification of critical assumptions and rigorous experimentation.

And so, the participants experienced what it was like to experience *adeptness in ambiguity*. They received a quick dose of innovation theory

FIGURE 4-2

## Idea capture template

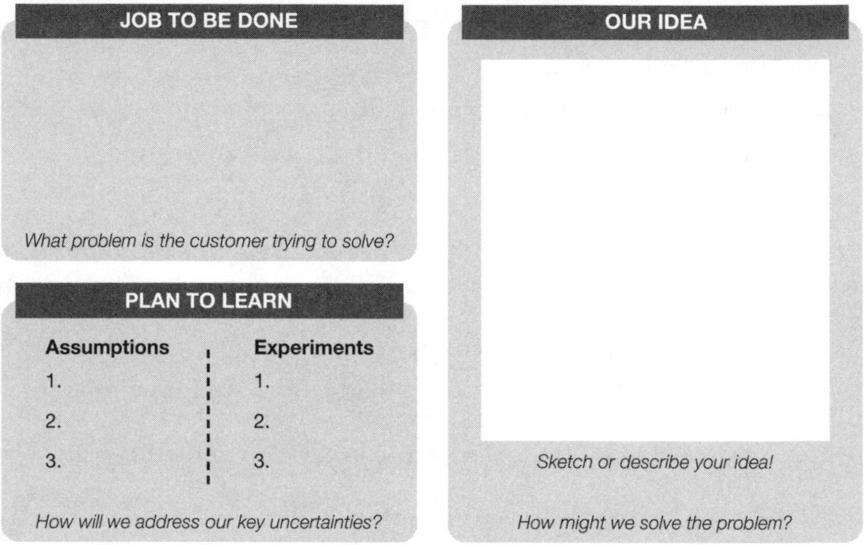

| JOB TO BE DONE | OUR IDEA |
|---|---|
| | |

*What problem is the customer trying to solve?*

| PLAN TO LEARN |
|---|

| Assumptions | Experiments |
|---|---|
| 1. | 1. |
| 2. | 2. |
| 3. | 3. |

*How will we address our key uncertainties?*

*Sketch or describe your idea!*

*How might we solve the problem?*

on assumptions (drawing on content from Scott's book *The First Mile*) and undertook exercises to practice identifying and organizing assumptions. The teams identified their biggest assumptions about their solutions and considered the impact it would have if those assumptions were wrong. High-uncertainty, high-impact assumptions need tackling first, so teams designed experiments that could address those critical assumptions. By the end of this activity, each team had completed a simple template describing their idea, a version of which appears in figure 4-2.

LIVING "EMPOWERMENT." An empowered team exercises initiative to make decisions confidently and takes responsibility for their actions. To reinforce this empowerment, Tan had pre-agreed to implement at least one solution from the group, under the sponsorship and guidance of the selected team's senior leadership representative.

Each team pitched their proposed solutions. Some simple yet highly effective ideas emerged. For example, the team creating an awesome onboarding experience learned that new joiners often arrived early on their first day. Then they sat and waited in the reception area, unclear of what was in front of them. The experience increased the anxiety that naturally accompanies a first day. So the team decided to issue new joiners, before their first day, a coupon for the café located in the reception area. This provided a double benefit, showing hospitality and filling an otherwise nerve-wracking time. This idea could also be expanded to connect several people being onboarded on the same day, so that the first cup of coffee could be a shared experience with someone in the same position. After all, the company's *raison d'être* is to help people connect and communicate!

## Day One Summary

After the applause died down for the teams whose solutions were approved to become projects, it was time for another BEAN. A cool box, previously hidden at the back of the room, emerged, and smaller boxes of popsicles (ice lollies in local vernacular) were taken out of it and handed to the teams selected by Tan. Next, boxes of premium ice creams, made by a well-loved brand, emerged. The twist? The "better" prize went to teams that "failed" the challenge. While popsicles versus premium ice cream runs the risk of being gimmicky, it highlighted an important point. A key environmental component to encourage innovative ways of working is psychological safety, in which intelligent failure is rewarded, not punished (more on this in chapter 7). The joy on the faces of those teams devouring premium ice creams while the winners diligently digested their popsicles admittedly amused the coauthors leading the session.

The first day concluded with two key messages. First, these behaviors are practical and powerful ways to develop and implement solutions to real problems, or—in the language in this book—to do something different that creates value. As such, the group left that day energized and committed to following the new behaviors. Second, these ways of working were *not* everyday habits inside Singtel Group HR. The next day explored why that was the case and what to do about it.

## Day Two: BEANstorming

The second day of the activation session began with an energetic room committed to catalyzing culture change. The same teams that had spent the previous day living innovation to solve real HR business problems now turned their energy to creating BEANs that would hardwire these ways of working into their culture, becoming everyday behaviors and habits and unleashing the group's latent innovation energy.

Each team had a broad way of working that it would focus on during the day (e.g., curiosity). After a quick grounding on the components of a culture of innovation, the teams went through a defined process where they got (even more) specific about desired behaviors, named detailed behavioral blockers, and then brainstormed about and refined their BEANs before pitching them to the group. Table 4-3 summarizes these activities.

A BEANstorm can help to hardwire behaviors into habits.

GET GRANULAR ABOUT DESIRED BEHAVIORS. The first step of the BEANstorm process requires teams to get granular, turning their allocated behavior from a lofty term into specific ways of working that fit their organizational context. For example, the team tasked with the curiosity behavior defined more specific ways of working such as not being complacent, being open to new ideas, and adopting a learning mindset. Each team had a detailed report from the culture of innovation survey to guide the discussion. Teams then got even more specific, describing what it would look like if they followed this behavior on a day-to-day basis in HR. For example, an HR leader adopting a learning mindset would strive for continuous individual improvement and regularly upskill himself.

TABLE 4-3

## Day two activities

| Activity | Description |
|---|---|
| Get granular about desired behaviors | Define and prioritize specific behaviors to encourage ("It would be great if we could . . ."). |
| Identify behavioral blockers | Identify and share what stands in the way of regularly following desired behaviors ("But instead we . . ."), with a particular focus on existing behaviors or habits. |
| Brainstorm and refine BEANs | Complete simple templates and get rapid feedback from other teams about how to encourage the identified behaviors and overcome the selected blockers ("So we should . . ."). |
| Pitch and select winning BEANs | Have each team pitch their BEAN and select winners for implementation. |

If a team got stuck in this activity, they were encouraged to complete the statement, "It would be great if we could . . . ," as precisely as possible. The goal here is to establish a behavior versus a state of mind, so you want verbs, which result from saying, "We will do this," versus nouns, which result from saying, "We are this." The more specific, the better. For example, one group working on collaboration started with "We will break silos" as a desired behavior before going deeper to state, "We will staff project teams with representatives from at least three functions."

Once each team established a long list of both broad and specific behaviors, they prioritized the one behavior they felt would have the greatest impact on their culture if established as an everyday ritual or habit. Prioritization is important. The more specific the behavior, the easier it is to create high-impact BEANs. Trying to solve for multiple behaviors risks overly complicated BEANs. Getting granular helps to maximize impact.

IDENTIFY BEHAVIORAL BLOCKERS. At this point, each team had defined with some specificity ways of working that encapsulated the given behavior and had described what that would look and feel like in practice. They next turned their attention to describing what is currently blocking these behaviors. In other words, why aren't these behaviors happening already? The group brought up and discussed blockers that many readers will likely find familiar, such as being overly metric-oriented (key performance indicators, or KPIs, in the case of Singtel), jumping straight to solutions, and being afraid to make mistakes. Not to be a broken record, but the more granular you make the blocker, the better. We see people frequently start with blockers like "We don't have time" or "We don't have proper training." These kinds of superficial blockers seem easy to fix. For example, if you lack skills, either invest in training, hire new people who have those skills, or form a team of experts to accelerate progress. Our experience shows, however, that blockers are typically more subtle. Culture is complicated and interdependent. If you don't get under the surface, interventions won't work. In other words, if you give people more time, they will often fill it by continuing to do things the wrong way. If you train them in new skills, they often won't use them, because they don't fit existing routines. And so on. What you want to identify is what we call a "behavioral blocker." In other words, your goal is to follow behavior $A$ ("It would be great if we could . . ."). But, instead, you are following behavior B ("But instead we . . .").[10] If you are brainstorming about blockers and you hear someone say something superficial, ask, "Why do we do this?" or "Can you be more specific?" For example, one group we worked with said fear was blocking its desire to be adept in ambiguity. Digging deeper surfaced their fear that a leader might ask for more data on an idea, which would lead to more work. So in meetings, instead of proposing that they test an idea, which they worried would bring extra work, they would sit silently.[11]

Clearly, the more crisply you identify what is blocking the desired behaviors, the easier it is to develop a high-impact way to overcome it. Discussing blockers can be difficult, however, because instead of focusing on positive, affirmative behaviors, participants are looking at the

10. In *Immunity to Change*, professors Robert Kegan and Lisa Laskow Lahey call this a "competing commitment" and note that it is often done for very rational reasons to protect people from shame and guilt. Humans, as always, are complicated.

11. There's a great term in the psychology literature that relates to this: social loafing.

challenges, which means the conversation can easily become despondent and discouraging. It is hard to discuss something that is often subtle or even countercultural. So bring some levity to it. For Singtel, we built a wall. We told each person to pick up a tissue box that had been spray-painted brick-red and yellow. Each person wrote down the biggest blocker to his or her own target behavior on the brick and signed it. Then as Pink Floyd's "Just Another Brick in the Wall" started playing, each person came forward and ceremoniously placed a brick on the ever-rising wall. As you can imagine, forty-two-plus (because several enthusiasts made more!) tissue boxes stacked on the floor creates a reasonably sized wall. And the group physically dismantling the wall at the end of a day of BEANstorming is a powerful moment. Further, the ritual of group construction brought the blockers to life and created the opportunity for another ritual: at the end of the day, people could retrieve their bricks and place them on their desks. There, the bricks would serve not only as a handy source of tissue but as a daily reminder of the blockers they were striving to overcome. (For another approach to surface and describe blockers, see the sidebar "Surfacing Blockers at DBS.")

BRAINSTORM AND REFINE BEANS. Each team now knew what it needed to do: find a way to encourage a specific behavior or overcome one of the blockers in the wall that occupied a significant amount of space in the room. At this point, we formally introduced the idea of a BEAN. Of course, people had used BEANs such as Amazon.com's Future Press Release, DBS's MOJO, and our popsicle and premium ice cream prizes, but we had consciously avoided going deep into BEANs until this moment. We described what BEANs are, why they work, and what the elements of a successful BEAN are, drawing on the material detailed in chapter 3.

Teams then followed the same basic diverge-and-converge process used the day before to create solutions to their business problems. Each team received customized stimuli, including relevant videos and a curated "bag of BEANs." The bag contained cards that showcased examples of organizations from around the world that had created BEANs relevant to behaviors and specific ways of working. For example, the

# Surfacing Blockers at DBS

As part of helping DBS purposefully shape the culture at Hyderabad, Innosight commissioned Tom Fishburne to create customized cartoons. (Tom is a Harvard Business School graduate who runs a boutique agency that develops cartoons for business purposes.) One cartoon he created shows a harried executive addressing a group of people, saying, "Does anyone else have a hypothesis they would like to test?" Meanwhile, the previous responder to his question squats in the corner in shame. This resonated with Singaporeans, in particular, as this is a traditional school punishment for bad behavior in that locale. Another illustration shows an executive assistant at his desk, holding out his phone's receiver to an executive rushing past him toward a full conference room. The assistant says, "The voice of the customer is on line two." The hassled executive responds, "Take a message. We're having a meeting on customer obsession." A meeting on a topic crowds out actually *doing* the topic? Golden.

**Cartoon DBS used to highlight meetings as a blocker to customer obsession.**

*Source:* Tom Fishburne, Marketoonist.

The cartoons themselves were a great way to start discussions about how DBS would really become adept in ambiguity and customer-obsessed, but the *process* of coming up with them was just as important. We had a cross-functional team of DBS leaders who all cared about shaping the bank's culture. Tom led them in conversation to uncover specific stories that showcased DBS's falling short of its aspiration of being a 28,000-person startup. Their discussion time was candid and critical, but it was also filled with laughter as people recounted the day-to-day foibles that are all too typical inside organizations. The team left engaged and eager to solve the problems, and the resulting cartoons made it safe for broader groups to engage in conversations whenever they saw executives clinging to old ways.

In a 2018 TED talk, Fishburne shared his perspective about the power of humor in business contexts. "I think that what gets in the way is fear. I think it is exactly the same fear that keeps us from trying new things, keeps us stuck in the status quo, and holds us back from doing our best work," he said. "And I think that a sense of humor is one of the most important, but completely overlooked, tools in business. If we really want to overcome that fear, we have to learn to laugh at ourselves."

"adeptness in ambiguity" team might consider Spotify's Fail Wall, which publicly shares a team's failure so that others can learn from it. As Pablo Picasso famously said, "Good artists copy, great artist steal."

By the end of a high-energy forty-five-minute session, each team had completed an initial template outlining the behavior they wanted to encourage ("It would be great if we could . . ."), the behavioral blocker they needed to overcome ("But instead we . . ."), a sketch of the BEAN, and a description of how it combined behavior enablers,

FIGURE 4-3

**BEAN capture template**

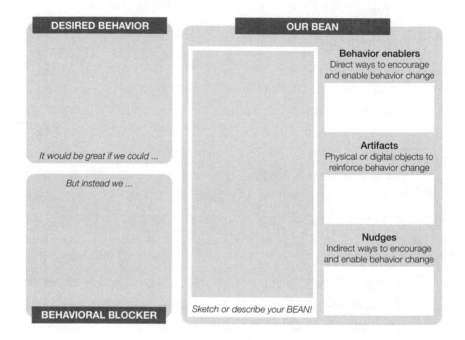

artifacts, and nudges to drive change. A version of the BEAN template appears in figure 4-3.

Armed with their draft BEANs, each team then followed a "speed-dating" process to get rapid feedback. Two "BEANbassadors" were appointed by each team to rotate around the room and showcase their BEANs to receive feedback from their colleagues against five questions:

1. Can we imagine implementing this BEAN within Singtel Group HR?

2. Will people have sufficient incentives to incorporate the BEAN into day-to-day life?

3. Can we imagine using the BEAN repeatedly?

4. Will it be effective in driving behavioral change?

5. How will we define and measure the success of the BEAN?

After digesting the feedback, teams refined the BEANs and developed plans to operationalize them. Teams detailed how they would launch their BEAN and how they would track and measure it.

PITCH AND SELECT WINNING BEANS. Finally, each team pitched their resulting BEAN to their colleagues and Tan. We encouraged the groups to bring energy to the pitch by role-playing a skit that brought their BEAN to life (and brought a bit of levity to a reasonably grueling two days). Singtel Group HR leaders evaluated the most feasible, high-impact BEANs and approved those that met the criteria to progress.

Time for one last BEAN infusion! This time the Innosight team introduced an adapted version of Adobe's Kickbox (described in chapter 3). The "Singtel Group HR Kickbox" that each winning BEANstorming team received contained a half day of leave for each team member, which they could devote to developing the idea further, another half day of paid time off as a reward, and a S$500 credit to fund the BEAN's refinement.

One example BEAN included an idea to reinforce customer obsession. The behavior the team wanted to encourage was to bring the voice of the customer (in this case, Singtel employees) into every HR discussion. The behavioral blocker identified was that Singtel typically started discus-  sions with questions like "What are we planning on doing?" and not "What problem are we trying to solve?" or "For whom are we solving that problem?" As a result, the HR team too frequently succumbed to overly inward thinking. The core behavior enabler was a proposed ritual to make sure that every meeting included discussion around the question, "Who Is The Customer Here?" (which forms the memorable acronym WITCH). In addition, they would seek to answer, "What is the concern?" and "What is the conclusion?" The WITCH acronym lent itself to multiple artifacts to reinforce the idea. A few months after the workshop, employee laptops began to don WITCH stickers that featured a witch's hat as a visible reminder (and a nice nudge) that everyone has a customer and that this customer has jobs to be done that need solving. Around eighteen months after the activation session, Tan told Scott and Andy at a catch-up meeting that she believed the WITCH BEAN was having a significant impact on the HR group, and she shared stories reinforcing its power to focus them on constructive discussions around the customer, the concern, and the conclusion, in turn ensuring more effective and efficient decision-making.

## Keys to Success

The Singtel example shows that there are three key factors to a successful two-day activation session and BEANstorm.

FIRST, PROVE WHY CULTURE MATTERS BEFORE SOLVING CULTURE. People must live new behaviors before they design ways to encourage and enable them. Just because almost everyone intuitively understands the importance of culture does not mean that everyone is willing to dedicate time to progressing culture. Providing firsthand experience about the power of particular behaviors is the best way to convince people of the importance of BEANstorming in order to enable those behaviors.

SECOND, GET GRANULAR. The more specific the behavior, the more specific the blocker, the better the BEAN. BEANs work well when targeting a specific behavior, such as bringing the voice of the customer into meetings, instead of targeting a broader way of working, such as customer obsession.

THIRD, INFUSE BEANS WHEN CREATING BEANS. A great BEANstorm should include BEANs. These not only make the BEANstorm more fun and engaging, but they reinforce the idea that a great BEAN has power to improve the way we work.

# After the Activation Session

It is tempting to declare victory after a great activation session. Recall, however, the fourth step in the process described in the Hyderabad case study: implementation. Even the best preparation and most engaging BEANstorm will leave you with, at best, rough output. That's why we often call the session that contains the BEANstorm an "activation session." A typical BEANstorm creates merely kernels of what might become truly great BEANs. As people reenter the host organization, their enthusiasm for planned interventions can dissipate as the shadow strategy descends and they revert to old habits.

Finishing a culture-of-innovation sprint requires that shortlisted BEANs are refined, tested, modified, and, if successful, launched and scaled. That means that there needs to be a person and, at best, a team accountable for executing and continually improving the BEANs based on data. In addition, this can't be the thirty-fifth responsibility of someone who already has too many things on her plate. It must be someone's top priority.[12]

In Singtel's case, a small team of catalysts iterated and implemented the workshop BEANs, such as WITCH and ideated new BEANs. The team also developed innovative ways to communicate concepts discussed in the workshop to the broader HR community. They engaged a local music artist to create a jingle that made their ways of working more memorable. Finding ways to make new language and concepts easy to remember helped to reinforce understanding and further fuel culture change.

The end of the sprint doesn't end the culture change journey; it simply marks the beginning of the next stage of the journey. The sprint itself starts with generic desired behaviors, surfaces blockers that are typically still somewhat superficial, and develops a handful of BEANs.

---

12. A couple of years ago, Scott was at a conference where someone said the word "priority" had been singular only until about a hundred years ago. Indeed, the dictionary definition of "priority" references "being regarded or treated as more important than others." Of course, today, we all have multiple priorities, including ones that seem to be in conflict. So our rule of thumb here is to designate at least one person to have "Driving BEANs forward" as their most important project.

Interventions focus narrowly on a single team, group, or department, and the constrained time and focus mean avoiding deep work on supporting systems and structures. Therefore, the beta stage of the process moves from being a sprint to executing pilots that expand to more places in the organization. At this stage, people work on customizing behaviors, determining the "blockers behind the blockers," building additional BEANs, and developing an understanding of the supporting infrastructure required to nurture the culture of innovation. Work then becomes more formalized, with people settling into recurring roles. Following the pilot stage is the full launch, where you develop a repeatable playbook that shows how to identify and launch new BEANs, stand up the infrastructure that will be necessary to reinforce identified behavior change (including people formally responsible for setting up the infrastructure and managing culture on an ongoing basis), and bust through key blockers.

DBS used a tool called the Culture Radar to help with its culture change journey. Based on a concept created by the company Thoughtworks to track emerging technology, DBS plotted each BEAN experiment on a paper chart consisting of concentric circles. Each segment on the radar corresponded to a target be-  havior, and each circle represented where the experiment was being run. To use the chart, Paul's team placed each BEAN in a segment with the related target behavior. A BEAN in its experimental stage that was being piloted with a single team would go near the outer edge of the radar. Over time, Paul and his team would review the radar on a regular basis. BEANs moved closer to the center as their adoption increased, until they made it to the bullseye, representing companywide adoption. Unsuccessful BEANs were removed from the chart. This visualization made it easy to track progress, identify gaps, and reinforce the expectation that not all BEANs would succeed. And the Culture Radar is, of course, a BEAN itself.

**TABLE 4-4**

## Culture change stages

| | Alpha/Sprint | Beta/Pilot | Full launch |
|---|---|---|---|
| Implementation focus | Narrow (a single team, department, or function) | Expanding (two to three teams, departments, or functions) | Expansive |
| Behaviors | Broad behaviors taken as given (five innovation behaviors); specific behaviors defined at a rough level | Customized broad behaviors and more-detailed specific behaviors | Codification of behaviors in a culture playbook |
| Blockers | Identification of one to three clear and obvious surface-level blockers | Identification of "blockers behind the blockers" informing supporting infrastructure recommendations | Core blockers removed with interventions now focused on the blockers behind the blockers |
| BEANs | One to three "good enough" BEANs are identified and launched | Initial BEANs are refined and strengthened; new BEANs are launched | BEAN-creation methodology is codified and distributed |
| Infrastructure and environment | None | Recommendations for developing supporting systems and structures | Recommendations for supporting systems and structures in the process of being implemented |
| Supporting resources | One to two ad-hoc catalysts | An emerging catalyst team | A formal catalyst team |
| Supporting documentation | None | A draft of a "culture playbook" (including an inspirational description of the tomorrow culture) | The finalized culture playbook |
| Length | Four to six weeks | Two to three months | Ongoing |

Table 4-4 summarizes the stages of the culture change journey, and tools and inspiration to help with that journey are included in part II. Finally, the appendix describes key themes from the culture change literature.

## Chapter Summary

✓ A sprint is a powerful way to create an alpha version of a culture of innovation within a team, group, or department.

✓ The core of a culture sprint is a two-day activation session. Day one of the session provides an opportunity for attendees to "live" the desired behaviors, while day two focuses on BEANstorming.

✓ The activation session should be preceded by focused activities to define desired behaviors that make sense in a particular context, to identify blockers, and to create customized BEANstorming stimuli.

✓ Driving toward impact after the activation session requires focused resources that cultivate and nurture existing BEANs and create new ones. It also requires a concerted movement to spread, scale, and reinforce the culture change.

Part Two

# TIPS, TRICKS, AND TOOLS

**THE SECOND PART OF** *EAT, SLEEP, INNOVATE* **WILL HELP YOU** drive culture change that sticks and scales. It is organized around the phases of the innovation journey.[1]

- *Chapter 5:* Discover opportunities (by being curious and customer-obsessed).

- *Chapter 6:* Blueprint ideas (by being collaborative and customer-obsessed).

- *Chapter 7:* Assess and test ideas (by being adept in ambiguity and empowered).

- *Chapter 8:* Move ideas forward (by being empowered and collaborative).

For each phase, we'll provide a list of BEANs that include behavior enablers *and* artifacts *and* nudges—we call these full BEANs—and three or four partial BEANs that have one or two of those components but not all of them.[2]

---

1. Of course, innovation isn't a paint-by-numbers linear activity. The innovation process is an integrative, iterative process. But we've found these four phases are a useful way to separate the different activities that help to drive innovation success.

2. Probably not surprisingly, there was significant debate about what to call the partial BEANs. Shoots? Seeds? Fragments? Chopped? We'll take any other great suggestions from readers. If we go paperback, we'll change it and give you full credit!

Second, there are BEAN boosters to help maximize the impact of selected BEANs. At the risk of torturing the metaphor, BEAN boosters help innovation flourish, providing "nutrients" in the form of resources, fertilizing the soil by building supportive infrastructure, and ensuring the environment is hospitable to innovation.

Third, each section will have one or two inspirational case studies. Some show leaders role-modeling new behaviors; others show broad change efforts inside organizations; still others show more grassroots innovation in action.

Finally, each phase has a tool that you can use to help with the journey.

# 5

# Phase 1
## Discover Opportunities

The first phase on the journey toward a culture of innovation is to discover a problem worth solving. Read on to see how Danfoss's Man on the Moon contest spurs curiosity, how P&G's consumer-is-boss movement fundamentally reoriented the company, how a four-star general role-modeled curiosity by going back to school, and how a simple checklist can help you to assess the curiosity of yourself or your team.

## Relevant BEANs

In the beginning of the innovation journey, curiosity and customer obsession are paramount. Let's look at BEANs that encourage those behaviors. Full BEANs appear in table 5-1; partial BEANs appear in table 5-2.

## Danfoss
MAN ON THE MOON

How do you encourage curiosity? The natural inclination is to seek to remove

TABLE 5-1

## Full BEANs for discovering opportunities[1]

| Organization and BEAN name | Description | Behavior enabler | Artifact | Nudge |
|---|---|---|---|---|
| **Danfoss—Man on the Moon** | An innovation competition to encourage expansive thinking | Clear identification of a problem worth solving | Collateral related to an annual competition, including an internal website | Historical stories related to the competition |
| **Google—Bureaucracy Busters** | Organization-wide ideation sessions to source ideas for reducing organizational red tape | Focus on improving internal operations | Web-based voting on ideas | Crowd-sourced approach that encourages ongoing curiosity |
| **MetLife—LumenLab Wall of Customers** | A structured way to help employees better relate to customers | Ritual of drawing the customer at the start of brainstorming sessions | Videos and physical reminders of the lives of regional customers | Large background visuals of customers on the wall; meeting participants who are empowered to "call out" the absence of the customer in discussions |

1. Careful readers will note that about half of the BEANs in part II come not from NO-DETs but from FAANGs, startups, and iconic innovators like Pixar (if the acronyms in that sentence are lost on you, check out the introduction). We certainly think that any organization should be inspired by and take good practices from companies on the cutting edge, but it should also recognize the important contextual differences to make sure what it is doing makes sense in its own context.

constraints so that people can think of new and different things. Paradoxically, research shows that constraints encourage creativity.[3] Danfoss is a Danish industrial company that engineers solutions for food-cooling and for heating and air-conditioning in buildings. Its annual Man on the

3. Chip and Dan Heath gave a great example of this in the book *Made to Stick*: Ask people to brainstorm all of the objects they can think of that are white. Typically, you will get blank stares in response. Then ask people to brainstorm all of the objects they can think of that are white and are in their refrigerator. The floodgates will open and will include nonobvious answers.

TABLE 5-2

## Partial BEANs for discovering opportunities

| Organization and BEAN name | Description |
|---|---|
| **HubSpot—Unlimited Free Books** | A program through which anyone can get any book free of charge |
| **Optus—Close-Ups** | A program where people spend a day in a store with the customer relations team |
| **Qualcomm—My Pain Points** | A ritual where individuals share interesting articles or experiences to spark creativity |
| **Qualcomm—Stumping Google** | A ritual of enabling creativity by trying to design a Google query that returns no results |

Moon competition seeks proposals from all employees for the creation of an entirely new line of business, the creation of a business adjacent to current lines, or the improvement of an existing business, through either a five- to ten-fold performance improvement or a more than 50 percent cost reduction. Taking the time to identify a theme around which the proposals must revolve focuses the creative energies of Danfoss's 28,000 global employees and increases the chances of developing something different that creates value. The collateral that surrounds the contest helps reinforce curiosity, with the prize itself serving as a critical artifact. Winning teams get a three-week trip to MIT plus six months after their return to develop the project. An example idea that emerged from the competition is predictive maintenance, which allows Danfoss to predict a forthcoming breakdown and perform preventive maintenance. Danfoss design manager Michael Qvortrup described the idea as "clever, novel, and easy to implement."

## Google

BUREAUCRACY BUSTERS

In 2009 Google started a program called Bureaucracy Busters. It shares many components with Danfoss's Man on the Moon BEAN but focuses

on day-to-day frustrations. Googlers are asked
to identify areas where unnecessary bureaucracy
hinders performance and then to develop innovative ways to bust that bureaucracy. Google
crowdsources votes and commits to implementing the most popular suggestions. The fact that
the first time Google ran the program, 500 ideas

were submitted that generated more than 50,000 votes suggested that
Google had indeed identified a category of problems worth solving!

## MetLife

### LUMENLAB WALL OF CUSTOMERS

Customer obsession aids in the discovery of innovation opportunities by developing an intimate understanding of
problems that matter (or what we call
"jobs to be done") to current and prospective customers.[4]

In 2014, life insurance company MetLife opened a new innovation
center in Singapore called LumenLab.[5] When you would step off the el-
evator on the twenty-first floor of the Metropolis building in Singapore
and enter the LumenLab, you would immediately enter the world of
regional customers. You would see artifacts reminding of you of day-to-
day life in Asia, such as a rickshaw that remains a popular form of trans-
port in emerging markets. Visual profiles of customers would hang on
the wall, serving as quiet nudges to take a customer-first perspective.
New visitors would often watch short videos to immerse themselves in

4. For nonlinear readers, in chapter 1 we referenced *Competing Against Luck* by Clayton
Christensen (Innosight's cofounder), David Duncan (an Innosight senior partner), and two
other coauthors as a great book-length treatment of the idea of the "job to be done."

5. It chose the word "lumen," which Wikipedia defines as "a measure of the total quantity
of visible light emitted by a source per unit of time," to connote that the lab "lights the
way" for innovation at MetLife. MetLife decided to integrate innovation into its operating
units and shut LumenLab down in 2020.

regional customers' perspectives. For example, one video would show an elderly Japanese man making lunch with his son. The son asks the father to go to the supermarket. The father gets lost and sits on a park bench until the son finds him. The father is very upset, as he does not want his condition to impact his child. MetLife sells insurance, but the vignette shows the importance to aging consumers of avoiding feeling like a burden to their children.

To further drive customer-centricity, LumenLab had a ritual of starting meetings either by projecting a photo of the target customer on the wall or by drawing the customer, with meeting attendees empowered to intervene when the discussion drifts away from the customer. LumenLab also taught team members to use verbs (describing what the customer is doing) versus nouns (describing what the customer is).

## Partial Beans

Up until now, we've generally spoken about BEANs as though they most contain all three components to have impact. While full BEANs are the most robust, partial BEANs can also be powerful. For example,  Optus is a fully owned subsidiary of Singtel, Asia's largest telecommunications company.[6] Its Close-Ups program has had thousands of workers participate in customer close-ups, where they spend an entire day in a store with the customer relations team. The program includes spending time as a shopper, making purchases, shadowing sales reps, and having direct interactions with customers. It helps employees develop deeper empathy with customers and eventually question the underlying assumptions they have about the business.

If you work at HubSpot, a leading digital marketing company, and are curious about a particular book, you are in luck!

---

6. Yes, these are the same heroes who valiantly lived innovative behaviors and BEAN-stormed WITCH in chapter 4.

Any employee can request any book (within reason) by submitting a form, and HubSpot will send them an electronic version or hard copy of the book for free within a week or two. There is no need to seek approval or submit expenses.[7] This is an easy way to encourage continuous learning among employees.

Semiconductor giant Qualcomm has two interesting rituals to help groups open their mind before they brainstorm. The first is a program called My Pain Points. At the start of user-experience meetings, the floor is given to anyone interested in talking about an article they read or a pain point they have, whether it be personal or work related. The second is called Stumping Google. During creative meetings, teams play a game in which they work together to come up with a search engine query that returns limited results.[8]

## BEAN Booster: P&G's Consumer-Is-Boss Movement

Procter & Gamble has a long and proud innovation history. Founded in 1837 in Cincinnati, Ohio, by candlemaker William Procter and soap maker James Gamble, the company built entire product categories

7. Fun fact: Odds are you are reading a physical book. When e-readers came out more than a decade ago, about 30 percent of Scott's reported sales went digital. By 2020 that number had *decreased* to about 20 percent, which is generally true for business books. It makes sense. Business books are given as gifts, people like to take notes in them, and part of the job to be done is to have these books proudly displayed on the bookshelf. Our prediction is that COVID-19 does not fundamentally change these dynamics, but, of course, we will see.

8. During the drafting of this section, the writer Googled "culture of innovation" and received 12,400,000 results (731,000,000 if the quotes were removed). "Behavior enabler, artifacts and nudges" returned 152 results. Adding the Oxford comma added another 24 results. And led the writer to switch music from Of Monsters and Men to Vampire Weekend. This reference confused one of our favorite reviewers. "Oxford Comma" is an excellent song by one of Scott's favorite bands, Vampire Weekend.

based on brands such as Tide laundry detergent (branded Ariel out-side the United States), Pampers disposable diapers, and Swiffer quick-cleaning products. It has also driven industry-changing business-model shifts, such as mass-market advertising, branded television (it created the first "soap opera"), and brand competition within a category. The company is widely considered a paragon of consumer-centricity, where marketers marry fine-grained market understanding with the output of 9,000 scientists to continue to drive growth through innovation.

In the 1990s, however, it seemed the company had drifted away from the consumer. A. G. Lafley, who served as P&G's CEO between 2000 and 2009 and again between 2013 and 2015, played a pivotal role in bringing consumer-centricity back to P&G. Lafley joined P&G after graduating from Harvard Business School in 1977. After a series of suc-cessful roles in North America, he moved to head up P&G's operations in Japan in the mid-1990s before returning to headquarters in 1998. What he saw surprised him.

"What I saw at my company very clearly in 1998 was that we were all so busy every day," he told us. "We had our ears in our cell phones; we had our heads in our BlackBerrys and PDAs; we were consumed in meetings of all kinds. When you thought about it, where was our behind? Our face was internal, and our behind was right facing the customer."

Soon after taking over as CEO in a surprise move in 2000 (predeces-sor Durk Jager lasted less than two years on the job), Lafley and his team launched a multifaceted effort to reorient the company. He introduced the effort using a stump speech that would go something like this:

> Ladies and gentlemen, I would like to introduce you to your new boss. You might think that I, your CEO and chairman, am the boss. I am not. You might think the board of directors, which can hire and fire me, is the boss. They are not. You might think the shareholders, which pick the board of directors, are the boss. They are not. You might think your day-to-day manager is the boss. She is not. We have one and only one boss that matters: the consumer. The consumer is boss. The decisions they make every day to

choose our products, to use our products, or not, are the decisions that will make and break our company. So, we have to invest to understand our boss more deeply than we ever did before.

Consumer is boss. Anne Lilly Cone, an up-and-coming market researcher, was tasked with running a pilot intervention in one of P&G's divisions. "Despite the career benefit to me," Lilly Cone reflected, "I was initially reluctant, as there had been a longstanding culture history of leadership indifference to consumers in that part of the business. But I quickly became convinced of AG's and others' strong support of the work ahead for my team."

The essence of the pilot was to radically increase the amount of time that executives spent in the market with consumers. In classic P&G fashion, it was rigorously organized, with orchestrated (but not staged) market immersions followed by structured debriefs run by a skilled facilitator. The pilot eventually became the cornerstone of a company-wide effort called "Living it. Working it." In this program, everyone at P&G, from Lafley on down, would regularly go out and spend time with consumers in their natural environments, observing them as they went about tasks in their homes, shopping with them, working with them, and, in some cases, even living with them.

Reflecting on the journey, Lilly Cone offered three lessons. First was the management mandate. "Leadership provided a crystalline focus that people had never heard before with such consistency, over a significantly long time." Second was leadership role-modeling, with "no exceptions and no excuses." Finally, was the relentless prioritization of the work: "Monday a.m., not Friday p.m."

Today, if you step into a P&G office anywhere in the world, you are regularly greeted by the consumer, in the form of larger-than-life pictures on walls.[9] You can feel the consumer in each and every discussion. The company, like all companies, has had its ups and downs, but the consumer-is-boss effort certainly left a lasting mark.

---

9. P&G had fun with office design to reinforce the consumer-is-boss idea. At one point, its baby-care division had a room with oversized furniture so that people could look at the world through the eyes of a child.

## Case Study: Sir Chris Goes to School

In the year 2019, when your calendar tells you that you are visiting a military installation, you plan to give yourself extra time to get through the inevitable layers of security.[10] You think carefully about your outfit and how it will fit in with the military garb. But if that military installation is the jHub, prepare to be surprised. Because instead of ending up at the edge of a base, your destination is a coworking space in the middle of a hotbed of startups in London. Lunch is delicious Ethiopian food from a sprawling street market around the corner. The people are dressed utterly normally (although the persistent nicknames and clipped speaking tone does betray the military connection). The tools they use and the processes they follow, rooted in concepts like user-centricity and rapid iteration, would feel familiar to innovation practitioners. And their office looks like, well, the sort of thing you'd see in any innovation outpost.

Team members start rattling off ideas they are working on that have the potential to save taxpayers significant money or save soldiers' lives through the leveraging of some combination of data analytics, visualization, artificial intelligence, machine learning, autonomy and robotics, blockchains, modeling and simulation, quantum computing, and behavioral science. Team members can barely contain their enthusiasm as they describe how, in their short history, they have investigated 585 opportunities, rapidly evaluated 190 specific ideas, deep-dived on 40 of those ideas, piloted 6 of them, and delivered 2 into the hands of end users. One jHub member describes a project in which a technology called Dataminr provides indicators and warnings of major events on social media before the news hits mainstream media. This capability would clearly be valuable for the military. "Dataminr was the most professionally satisfying moment of my life," the project leader said. In a previous role within the military, she found it hard to have similar

10. Yes, it is 2020, or maybe 2021—or, if this book really clicks, it is 2073 and our alien overlords (or Skynet) are contemplating creating a culture of innovation. But Scott visited the jHub in 2019.

impact. The jHub approach allowed her to quickly give dozens of users access to the solution, and, within six months, 360 people were using the system daily.

"This is my dream job," one team member announces. "Ever since discovering it, I have been trying to get into it because it is frigging awesome."

Step back to 2011. That year, the United Kingdom's Ministry of Defence announced plans to add a fourth branch to its military: the Joint Forces Command (JFC). The JFC houses enabling capabilities common to the army, navy, and air force, such as information services, cybersecurity, and medical services. In essence, it leads areas common to all three branches. In 2013 it reached full operating capability with 30,000 military and civilian personnel. Sir Chris Deverell, a four-star general with three decades of military experience, served as the JFC's third head from 2016 to 2019. As he came to grips with the organization and began to formulate his strategy, he decided to make innovation one of its pillars.

Deverell notes that, during his career, he had seen how "increasingly difficult it was to deliver new capability or new functionality into the hands of users," driven by a "system that has evolved to reduce risk and over insures against that problem to the detriment of time, cost, and often performance. The longer you take to do something, the more you have to compromise the performance in order to deliver it. Because time costs money."

The guiding principle of Deverell's strategy was "through innovation, integration, and information, we would deliver advantage for the Joint Forces. Those were the mechanisms we would use to release the latent ability in my organization to deliver benefit to the Joint Forces."

Clearly, the jHub ran against the grain of the military establishment. Fortunately, in Deverell, it had a leader who was willing to draw inspiration from places outside the military.

"My sources of understanding could broadly be characterized in four ways: subordinates, peers, superiors, and external sources," he said. "I think most senior people in defense work on the assumptions that most of their understanding comes from their subordinates and their superiors, and they don't seek to look to the outside to the degree I did in this case. I think it's maybe because people are not convinced that the outside world can tell us very much because we're so different. That's nonsense. Most of the problems and issues we face organizationally, you would find them everywhere. It is just that we don't know what we don't know. The only way you resolve that is by actively looking externally."

As a tangible example of this commitment, in 2013 Deverell enrolled in a program at London Business School. "I believe no one from the defense community had ever done that before," he said. "Of all of the education I have had, this was the most valuable. One of the big things it taught me is there is so much in common between large organizations everywhere. We tend to think in defense that the way to get external insight is to hire consultants. At some level that can be necessary, but it can become a substitute for thinking through what you are trying to achieve and trying to do it yourself."

The core influence for the idea of the jHub came from the 2014 Innosight-authored article "Build an Innovation Engine in 90 Days." Deverell said the article's premise that a small team could rapidly advance innovative ideas was intriguing. "In defense, the notion of trying to do anything without battalions of people was so strange," he recalled. "But generating battalions of people in defense is so hard that I was particularly attracted to the fact that the model claimed it could be done with a small number of people. And, indeed, that's been borne out by how we have operated. We have always had a core of five to six people that we have reinforced with secondees from the business. That model, the small-team approach, has been fundamental to our development."

Deverell retired from the military in 2019. His curiosity and willingness to draw on external perspectives gives the jHub a chance to drive lasting change in the UK military.

## Case Study: Discovering Opportunities in Bangladesh and Philadelphia

The epigraph of lean-startup-godfather Steve Blank's 2013 book *The Startup Owner's Manual* (with Bob Dorf) says it all: "Get out of the building!" Large organizations are used to relying on desk research and consultants to identify market opportunities, but the search for innovative business ideas has to come in or close to the market. As the famous British spy novelist David John Moore Cornwell once quipped, "a desk is a dangerous place from which to view the world."[11]

Imagine a sales rep for an agrichemical company trying to introduce a crop-protection chemical to eradicate weeds in Bangladesh rice farms. Here's the way a typical conversation between a sales rep and a farmer would go:

> Rep: Sir, I'd like to tell you about a new product that can remove weeds from your farm.
>
> Farmer: But I already have a way to remove weeds. When it is harvesting time, I hire day laborers for two weeks. They remove all of weeds. Does your chemical work better than my workers?
>
> Rep: Well, it doesn't take as long. But I can't say that it removes more weeds than your workers.
>
> Farmer: Well, at least I assume it must be cheaper than my workers?
>
> Rep: Well, actually . . . the first use is going to cost more than the laborers. But by the time you get to the fifth season you have paid ba—"
>
> Farmer: Five seasons? Five seasons! Who knows what I will be doing five seasons from now. Bah! This chemical you offer—is it easy to use?

---

11. David John Moore Cornwell is best known by his pen name John le Carré. None of the four of us have pen names. Any suggestions?

Rep: Well, that's another thing. It takes some time to learn how to use it, but we offer a special training program that is free for you and . . .

You can see this conversation isn't going to lead to a sale. However, spending time in the field on the farm led the company to realize there was another way into the market. While the *farmer* himself didn't have a problem that needed to be solved, his *wife* did. She found the harvest period to be brutal. She had to look after a dozen day laborers, which meant waking up at four in the morning to prepare breakfast for them and then cleaning up after them. When the company described something that would remove the need to hire the laborers, she was all for it. And since she managed the household finances, she understood that this also was a positive long-term investment for the family. So the company began organizing "farmer's wife circles" to discuss the benefits of its product. Adoption took off. Curiosity and customer obsession led to a significant innovation opportunity. The moral of the story? *If you don't go, you can't know.*[12]

Let's now move from the farms of Bangladesh to the streets of Philadelphia, and from agrichemicals to music education, to reinforce the power of grassroots market understanding. In 2010, Helen Eaton became chief executive officer of the Settlement Music School. Founded in 1908, Settlement historically provided classes, primarily for children, in classical music and jazz. It had six physical branches in the Philadelphia area. In 2012, Eaton, an accomplished musician who studied at the prestigious Juilliard School, wondered if it was time to change Settlement's tune. Like many arts nonprofits, Settlement found its financial situation had not fully recovered since the 2008 financial crisis and resulting recession. Further, changing demographics and emerging technologies suggested to Eaton that Settlement needed to simultaneously return to its roots *and* rethink its model.

"I was working to uncover what mattered most to our legacy institution—a value I could honor as the new CEO following a leader with

12. A second moral: the customer isn't always who you think it is.

a thirty-year tenure and a value I could build upon. What emerged was authentic to our community, pervasive throughout the institution, and deeply encouraging for me—and that was the concept of service," Eaton said. "There was a core value around service at Settlement Music School—service to our families, service to our teaching artists, and service to our community. At the heart of service is responsiveness to what our constituency really needs from us, and that responsiveness created the foundation for us to innovate."

Eaton formed a small team, engaging faculty and staff at all levels and tenures to explore new areas, such as smart solutions for sustainability and growth and how community arts changes lives. The team received two days of training from a group of Innosight consultants and then went into the field to interview prospective customers about what offerings might enrich their lives. One team member observed a recurrent theme: a desire for adults to reclaim their youth, meet new people, and dust off that guitar they stopped strumming in college. What if, he wondered, they created some way for adults to jam together in a band? The team drafted a three-page brief outlining a rough picture of the idea, which would ultimately become known as the "Adult Rock Band" class. The idea was that a group of likeminded adults would come together and practice under the tutelage of an expert instructor. The class could continue indefinitely, separated into ten-week sessions, at the end of which the band would hold a concert in the school's performance space. As one instructor said, "There's something good for the soul about strapping on the old Fender and banging out a few Jack Bruce lines."[13]

Settlement piloted the idea at a single branch and then expanded to two more, learning in the process that it needed to fine-tune classes to the context of each local community. As it continued to experiment with Adult Rock Band and other ideas—such as a monthly community drumming circle, choirs for seniors at community centers, classes that merged arts and physical or mental therapy, and parenting classes

13. Jack Bruce was a hugely influential guitarist who was the lead vocalist and bass guitarist of British rock band Cream (which featured Eric Clapton). He was the cowriter of the classic "Sunshine of Your Love."

through music at family shelters—a broader strategic shift came into focus. Settlement would reposition its traditional physical locations to become broader community hubs. It would also work with other local providers to bring broader populations in the Philadelphia area access to music instruction. The shift inspired dramatic growth in partnerships, which quintupled over time, dramatically boosting Settlement's revenue and strengthening its balance sheet. The spirit of collaboration and inventiveness led to a first-of-its-kind collaboration with institutions across the city, catalyzed by a grant from the Andrew W. Mellon Foundation.

Eaton's curiosity helped Settlement find new ways to deliver against its mission to provide the highest-quality arts education to everyone. And that mission helped Eaton to secure donors and other key stakeholders who were motivated to continue the innovation journey.

"I keep reminding our donors, our board members, and the foundations that, at the end of the day, it's all about the kids. That seems to have really helped," Eaton said. "I tell them, 'This is what Settlement has traditionally done, but we can have an even greater impact and address much bigger issues that are happening in this city. We can really work towards disrupting the cycle of poverty, and here's how we can do it.' And I give them lots of metrics and ensure they we are partners through the process."

Today students range in age from six months to ninety-five years. In 2016 Eaton was named a "Top 30" innovator by *Musical America Worldwide*, and in 2018 influential blog *Charity Navigator* named Settlement one of the top ten music charities in the country, as it worked to preserve and expand music education and access to the musical arts.

Eaton described the journey as a "rollercoaster ride," with "moments of great highs and lows, moments where you are certain about what you are doing, and moments where you question everything." She traces Settlement's success to rigorously maintaining curiosity and customer obsession. "We understand our audiences better, because we are asking the right questions and responding thoughtfully. This has all led to the organization's capability of doing even greater and more impactful work, and so we become more ambitious, and the journey continues."

Settlement's new capabilities proved vital as COVID-19 crisis unfolded in early 2020. Within two days of local lockdowns, Settlement was ready to provide high-quality virtual learning, with a clear plan and guidelines for families translated into four languages. It trained 170 faculty in distance learning, allowing it to quickly engage with students and launch free classes to raise its local visibility. In essence, Settlement was able to quickly open its seventh branch: a virtual one. Eaton shared the following with her board: "In the face of a global health pandemic, some may wonder—why care about community arts? And we say: Care because it is what lifts our souls. Our shared belief is that the best thing anyone can do in a crisis is to be productive, achieve something. We are the people who believe that the act of doing, of practicing, of reaching goals, will be what gets us through this time with our spirits intact."

Reflecting on her decade at Settlement, Eaton offered the following advice to leaders looking to embrace innovation in their organization:

> Identifying something that is authentic about your institution—in our case, service—and celebrating that in all of its different forms is easy when you are a good listener. Customers (our families), employees, and volunteers want to be heard, and the CEO can be that person if you go into the work with the intent to truly listen and change as a result. That is the easy part. The hard part is when your ability to innovate is so directly tied to people outside your own organization who may not have had their ideas, hopes, and dreams nourished in the same way. At Settlement, we do our most innovative work through community partnerships and collaborations outside our own doors, and those inherently bring in new people with whom we have never worked. The theories, the ideas, the concepts, they all work, no matter how large or small your organization. They are motivating and inspiring. It requires patience and dogged determination coupled with a dose of reality when something is really just not going to take off.

## Tool: Curiosity Quotient

How curious are you or your team? There are seven ways to display curiosity in an organizational context:

1. *Customer intimacy:* Seek to know your customers—not just as numbers but as living, breathing humans.

2. *External orientation:* Take "idea road trips," bring in outside speakers, and use other mechanisms to get external stimuli.[14]

3. *Idea sourcing:* Seek ideas from everywhere, including customers, suppliers, and outside experts.

4. *Collisions:* Bring together diverse groups to break the back of tough problems.

5. *Openness to experimentation:* Experiment regularly, sometimes just to learn.

6. *Idea sharing:* Share rough ideas early to get useful feedback.

7. *Failure tolerance:* Recognize that, in the early stages of innovation, effective learning is more important than commercial success.

Table 5-3, which first appeared in the appendix of *Dual Transformation*, is a simple way to assess your team's "curiosity quotient."[15]

---

14. Scott heard Atari founder Nolan Bushnell use the phrase "idea road trip" at a conference in Australia a few years ago. The idea is that you get out of your normal routine to seek new ideas. That might involve going to a trade show in a disconnected industry, visiting a museum, or even leafing through a magazine.

15. Yes, there are seven items on the list but eight evaluating rows. We split "collisions" into two, given the demonstrated impact that diverse perspectives have on innovation. We said it before, and we will say it again: magic happens at intersections!

TABLE 5-3

## Assessing your curiosity quotient

| Cultural element | Poor fit | Average fit | Clear fit |
|---|---|---|---|
| Customer intimacy | No customer knowledge | Analytical understanding of customers | Intimate, empathetic understanding of customers |
| External orientation | Heavily internal perspective | Occasionally brings in outside speakers and seeks outside stimuli | Regularly brings in outside speakers and seeks outside stimuli |
| Idea sourcing | No mechanisms to source ideas externally | Ideas sourced from customers, employees, or suppliers | Ideas sourced from customers, employees, and suppliers |
| Team diversity | Lacks team diversity | Diversity along one dimension | Diversity along multiple dimensions (industry, education, etc.) |
| Cross-company interaction | Largely operates in silos | Regular interaction between functions or geographies | Regular interaction between functions and geographies |
| Openness to experimentation | No means to design and run experiments | Experiments run with approval from top leaders | Experiments part of day-to-day operations |
| Idea sharing | Ideas shared only when they are "perfect" | Ideas shared when they are well documented | Rough (but well-thought-out) ideas shared to get fast feedback |
| Failure tolerance | Failure carries heavy stigma | No penalties for "intelligent" failure | Learnings from "intelligent" failure celebrated |
| Number of answers | | | |
| Weighting | ×1 | ×3 | ×5 |
| Total score | | | |

Total

| | |
|---|---|
| 8–14 | Hostile to curiosity |
| 15–22 | Pockets of curiosity |
| 23–29 | Foundations of curiosity |
| 30+ | Culture of curiosity |

6

# Phase 2
## Blueprint Compelling Ideas

The next phase of the innovation journey is to come up with a tangible idea to address the problem identified in the previous phase. We call this *blueprinting* because you aren't developing the solution yet; rather, you are developing the plans to come up with the solution.

In this phase, customer obsession continues to be important as it forces you continually check the degree to which the idea solves a real problem for a real person. Collaboration becomes increasingly important, as one of the most time-tested findings in innovation literature is that magic happens at intersections, where different skills and mindsets collide. What follows describes how BNP Paribas makes it easy to draw inspiration from diverse sources, how Pixar's time-tested Braintrust keeps its movies fresh, and how Intuit's leaders role-modeled enabling behaviors. It also shares a cheat sheet of "discovery questions" that helps to shape emerging ideas.

## Relevant BEANs

Our innovation definition consciously uses the word *different* versus *new* to remind would-be innovators that there is no shame in borrowing inspiration. As Steve Jobs once said, "When you ask creative people how they did something, they feel a little guilty because they didn't really do it, they just saw something. It seemed obvious to them after a while. That's because they were able to connect experiences they've had and synthesize new things." Full BEANs that help to foster creativity appear in table 6-1; partial ones appear in table 6-2.

TABLE 6-1

## Full BEANs for blueprinting ideas

| Organization and BEAN name | Description | Behavior enabler | Artifact | Nudge |
|---|---|---|---|---|
| **BNP Paribas— Innovation Book and Awards** | An idea contest where the best ideas are collated into a book | Annual contest with clear definitions and guidelines | Virtual book with summaries of winning ideas | Communications around the awards |
| **Toyota—A3 Report** | A succinct communications tool in which essential information is captured on a single A3-sized page | Self-explanatory categories on form; design forces simple answers | Physical form | Historical legends and supporting infrastructure |

TABLE 6-2

## Partial BEANs for blueprinting opportunities

| Organization and BEAN name | Description |
|---|---|
| **Amazon.com—Empty Chair** | The ritual of leaving an empty chair to remind meeting participants of the importance of the customer |
| **Nordstrom—"Yes, and . . ."** | The practice of having critique come in the form of "Yes, and . . ." |
| **Pixar—intersection- supporting infrastructure** | Office design with open infrastructure that encourages chance meetings and spurs creativity |
| **Pixar—Plussing** | The practice of making sure critique is balanced with constructive suggestions |

## BNP Paribas

### INNOVATION BOOK AND AWARDS

One way to help innovators is to make it easy for them to collaborate, not just with other innovators but with other ideas.

For example, BNP Paribas, a financial services company based in France, has a BEAN to help stoke curiosity and provide stimulation for innovation. Every year, BNP collects innovative and creative projects that have been led by its teams throughout the world. The top ideas are compiled into an innovation book that is distributed to the company—and winning innovators are flown to Paris and awarded in front of the entire company. Imagine you have pinpointed a problem worth solving but are struggling to come up with a solution. No problem! Pick up the innovation book and flip through its pages. Odds are high that you will get some kind of useful stimuli.[1]

## Toyota

### A3 REPORT

One barrier often blocking collaboration is overly complex communication that leads to team members talking past each other. A BEAN that can break this barrier and encourage productive collaboration is

---

1. One of our former colleagues used a similar approach when seeking to develop new ideas. He would flip through historical versions of the Sears catalog. With a good problem on his mind, the catalog often provided surprising inspiration.

inspired by Toyota's A3 Report. The report is named for the single eleven-by-seventeen-inch paper on which it is captured. The report captures the most essential information (the objective, analysis, an action plan, and expected results) to solve a problem on a single sheet that can be disseminated widely. Since it is a single sheet, language must be succinct and clear. And ample communication about and use of the report serves as a corporate-wide nudge to encourage further use. In fact, this BEAN is so embedded in Toyota culture that it passes the basic test of a habit: people do it without conscious thought. Simple ways to capture and communicate ideas helps them to spread and encourages collaboration.[2]

## Partial BEANs

One of Amazon.com's stated goals is to be the world's most customer-centric company. Its Empty Chair ritual helps to reinforce this mission, as it is a powerful reminder that the "most important person in the room"—the customer—isn't physically in the room.[3]

Many ideas get shot down before they ever get blueprinted. Retailer Nordstrom borrows from improv comedy by encouraging the use of "Yes, and . . ." during meetings. In other words, be willing to share what you don't like, but have a solutions mindset where you either

---

2. The companion website to Scott's book *The First Mile* has two such idea-capture forms: a short "idea resume" and a longer "mini-business plan." See www.innosight.com/insight /the-first-mile.

3. One thing we wondered about in the midst of COVID-19-related lockdowns is whether virtual meetings at Amazon have an empty chair, a cardboard cutout of a customer, or some other reminder to reinforce this idea.

highlight other good parts of an idea or seek to improve on the identified deficiency.

Pixar has a number of BEANs to help it continually be creative (one is robust enough to be featured as a BEAN booster on the next page). Its physical infrastructure, with immense open space that connects to individual workspaces, encourages collaboration. Jobs, who was Pixar's chair when the building was constructed, insisted it should encourage employee collisions that bring about unplanned collaborations.[4] Another practice Pixar fol-

lows is called "Plussing." Criticism at its meetings can be brutal. Rather than randomly critique a sketch or shoot down an idea, the general rule is that you may only criticize an idea if you also add a constructive suggestion. Hence the name plussing.

## BEAN Booster: Pixar's Braintrust[5]

In an industry characterized by dizzying swings between blockbusters and busts, Pixar Animation Studios stands out as an anomaly. Since the introduction of *Toy Story* in 1995, the organization has had an uninterrupted string of more than twenty critically acclaimed hits.[6]

What really makes Pixar's story fascinating, however, is what happened in 2006. That was the year Pixar chair Steve Jobs agreed to sell

---

4. Walter Isaacson's biography of Jobs said that Jobs insisted on having a single bathroom for the whole building in the central atrium. Because everyone has to go to the bathroom, he reasoned, this would force chance collisions. The management team raised the practical implications (and limitations) of the suggestion, however, stopping the idea in its tracks.

5. We debated about whether to include this as a BEAN or a BEAN booster. It does appear in the appendix's bag of BEANs, but is profound enough that we thought it worth discussing more extensively.

6. Okay, *Cars 2* did get a 39 percent rating from Rotten Tomatoes (the next lowest score of a Pixar movie is 70 percent). But Happy Harry (see chapter 2) gave it two thumbs up, so there's that!

the company to Disney, whose animation studio had been struggling. Most people assumed that after the sale, Disney would shut down its own studios, whose history traced back to Walt Disney's Mickey Mouse sketches, which launched one of the world's most iconic companies.

But that's not what happened. Pixar CEO and cofounder Ed Catmull and his team believed that they had decoded the formula for managing the process of creativity. They set a goal of reenergizing Disney's animation team by applying a set of principles. If you have seen *Frozen*, *Big Hero 6*, *Zootopia*, *Wreck-it Ralph*, *Tangled*, or *Moana*, you have seen the demonstrated impact of that intervention.

The brilliant book *Creativity, Inc.*, by Catmull and Amy Wallace, details the Pixar approach. While the entire book is worth reading, the appendix beautifully summarizes the approach in thirty-three bullet points. Some of the choice suggestions include the following:

- Give a good idea to a mediocre team, and they will screw it up. Give a mediocre idea to a great team, and they will either fix it or come up with something better. If you get the team right, chances are, they'll get the ideas right.

- It isn't enough merely to be open to ideas from others. Engaging the collective brainpower of the people you work with is an active, ongoing process. As a manager, you must coax ideas out of your staff and constantly push them to contribute.

- The first conclusions we draw from our successes and failures are typically wrong. Measuring the outcome without evaluating the process is deceiving.

- It is not the manager's job to prevent risks. It is the manager's job to make it safe to take them.

- Don't wait for things to be perfect before you share them with others. Show early and show often. It'll be pretty when we get there, but it won't be pretty along the way. And that's as it should be.

- Our job as managers in creative environments is to protect new ideas from those who don't understand that, in order for greatness to emerge, there must be phases of not-so-greatness. Protect the future, not the past.

One of the key mechanisms Pixar has to support these ideas is the "Brain-trust" it forms to guide the develop-ment of a movie. The Braintrust is a small group of some of Pixar's smart-est and most creative people. Direc-tors working on movies show very  early ideas to this group, not to earn praise or platitudes but to experi-ence sharp critique that ultimately results in a much better movie. The Braintrust is not a decision-making body but a mechanism to emphasize candor and to creatively challenge the production team.

One of Catmull's persistent points is that every movie that Pixar has ever made, at one point in the process, "sucks." The Braintrust, Catmull notes, helps Pixar go from suck to non-suck.

"Its premise is simple: Put smart, passionate people in a room to-gether, charge them with identifying and solving problems, and encour-age them to be candid with one another," Catmull explains in *Creativity, Inc.* "The Braintrust is one of the most important traditions at Pixar. It's not foolproof—sometimes its interactions only serve to highlight the difficulties of achieving candor—but when we get it right, the results are phenomenal. The Braintrust sets the tone for everything we do."

As he returned from the wrap party for *Frozen 2*, Catmull, who re-tired in 2019, reflected on the importance of providing candid feedback to directors: "The wrap party for *Frozen 2* was my thirty-second wrap party in my time at Pixar and Disney. One thing I can count on is that every director, including the very best, loses objectivity in their film. They don't particularly want an outside voice hitting them with a two-by-four, but without it, they would not succeed. And, while the directors initially don't want the outside voice, they have learned to value it."

## Case Study: Scott and Brad's Excellent Adventure

Every year since 2007, Innosight has held at least one gathering, bringing together senior leaders from companies it has served and (truth-in-advertising) companies that it hopes to serve in the future. A typical CEO Summit has a social dinner, followed by a full day of facilitated discussions with content from academics (Clayton Christensen, Rita McGrath, and Roger Martin have all appeared as speakers), CEOs, and Innosight's leadership team.[7]

Intuit founder and chairman Scott Cook is the only non-Innosight person to have come to *four* summits. Now a founder-led company might seem to violate the principle laid out in the introduction of focusing on normal organizations doing extraordinary things (NO-DETS), but Intuit is a middle-aged company (founded in 1983) that is publicly traded, Cook is an unusually thoughtful corporate leader who stepped down from his CEO position in 1994, and, let's face it, financial-management software isn't the world's sexiest category.

Soon after Cook and the board appointed Brad Smith as Intuit CEO in 2008, Smith, Cook, and the rest of the leadership team set a goal of building a deep capability around design thinking. Behind the charge was the observation that the number one reason people bought software packages like TurboTax and QuickBooks was their ease of use, and the number one reason people didn't buy the software was . . . their (lack of) ease of use. Cook believed that the principles of design thinking, such as forming deep empathy for customers, developing boundary-pushing solutions, and rapidly testing and iterating ideas, would help Intuit continue to thrive in an increasingly competitive world.[8] The effort worked. Intuit's stock price surged, and, in 2017, *Fast Company* named Intuit as one of the top ten most innovative companies in design.

---

7. 2020 gatherings, not surprisingly, were held virtually.

8. Note those principles mirror the behaviors we detailed in chapter 1. While the words are different, the basic concepts overlap quite tightly.

"The headline of the story makes it sound easier than it was," Cook said during the panel "Culture Change that Sticks and Scales" at Innosight's 2018 event. In 2014, he said, leadership noted that its "Design for Delight" program wasn't having the impact it had hoped. The company had taught its top people the concepts of design thinking and had created a team of coaches and catalysts to augment that teaching (that team is one of the BEANs featured in phase 4), but the behaviors had not yet become habits. So, Scott and Brad set off on their excellent adventure.[9]

Leader role-modeling is a staple of any kind of change management process. That can be a real challenge for leaders seeking to encourage innovation habits, because those habits are probably least familiar to them.

"The top execs have to change," Cook said in the panel discussion. "It is their habits that drive the company, and it is their habits that are the barriers to change."

How can you help seasoned senior leaders learn new skills? Cook's advice: "Learning by doing, by everyone." It is well documented that "lean-back learning" is not an effective way for adults to learn, an idea that calls to mind the Mark Twain quip that a lecture is the quickest way to transfer information from the instructor's notes to the student's notes without passing through the brain of either.

Cook learned that the best way for leaders to make the transition was to get them to experience the new ways of working firsthand. So Intuit's top twenty-five leaders formed groups of three and performed foundational research on predetermined topics such as changes in finance in China, artificial intelligence, and young people's interactions with computing. "The leaders in the case were actively driving the discovery process," Cook noted. "They couldn't delegate it. A number of them *wanted* to delegate to their teams because that's what they do. But not in this case. You had to do it yourself, which means you had to be on the plane to China."

---

9. Yes, that's a reference to *Bill and Ted's Excellent Adventure*, the movie that kickstarted Keanu Reeve's career. The writer that picked the subhead had no idea that a revival was in the works in the midst of the drafting of this book. Crazy times.

Of course, changing twenty-five people doesn't change the culture; hence, the "by everyone" part of Cook's advice. He described how US auto manufacturers struggled for decades to decode the Toyota production system (also described in phase 4). "If you send one guy to see the new process," Cook said, "and that guy gets all excited and comes back and tries to teach the other ten thousand people, it never works." So preceding a major company meeting, Intuit had all 8,000 people "take a day to do our innovation process from the beginning of understanding the customer problem all the way through to designing the experience," Cook said. At the meeting, the teams would then bring in what customer problems they observed and work on developing solutions.

Clearly, having Cook and Smith (and Smith's successor, Sasan Goodarzi, who took over in early 2019) personally participate in these kinds of efforts sent a strong signal that no top leader was above the effort, which helped Intuit achieve its effort of entrenching habits related to design thinking deeper into the organization.

"Learning by doing, by everyone," brings another benefit: It helps to raise collective intuition, which improves the ability to make decisions about uncertain ideas. Rather than sitting in a cushy conference room reviewing PowerPoint slides, leaders should get out and experience the raw data by participating in experiments and joining group problem-solving sessions. Hands-on experience not only demonstrates deep commitment but also allows leaders to observe things that otherwise would be hidden. After all, summary reports always contain biases and interpretations, and sometimes the most important things are the anomalies and surprises that get buried in appendices, if they appear at all.[10]

10. Scott Cook has a lot of quotable quotes about innovation. He told Natalie the idea of "savoring surprises" when she interviewed him in 2008, describing how QuickBooks's growth traced back to a surprising market research insight. Scott Anthony's favorite Scott Cook quote is, "For every one of our failures, we had spreadsheets that looked awesome." Indeed.

## Case Study: Innovation at the Intersections

Once you have found a problem worth solving, the next step is to come up with an idea. This is where it gets hard, right? After all, you have to be a creative genius to "think outside the box." But not if you follow Pablo Picasso's famous mantra: "Good artists copy; great artists steal." You shouldn't literally steal, of course. Rather, you should borrow an idea from one context and bring it to another. Brilliant borrowing is the best way to short-circuit the path to successful innovation.

That's exactly what Fiona Fairhurst did almost twenty years ago when she was tasked by Speedo to come up with a swimsuit that allowed athletes to swim faster. While it would be natural to think that the best way to do this would be to cut down the suit's friction, Fairhurst framed the problem differently. Where in nature, she asked, can I find something that is big but goes through the water quickly? She studied a shark. Sharks are huge but can reach speeds of up to thirty miles per hour in short bursts. And it turns out sharks don't have perfectly smooth skin. They have something called denticles, which essentially propel them through the water. Fairhurst's nature-driven inspiration led to the Speedo Fastskin, and, well, you know the rest.

Alternatively, consider Nick Musyoka. In 2008, Musyoka was hired by Swiss agrichemical giant Syngenta to develop a strategy to crack into the smallholder market; smallholders are small, usually family-owned farms. With 500 million smallholders around the globe, the opportunity looked huge—and hugely challenging. After all, Syngenta's sweet spot was massive, professionally run farms that invested heavily in automation and other tools to boost productivity. Smallholders generally live hand-to-mouth and could rarely think beyond the next growing season. The good news was that Musyoka had already seen the solution to the problem—not at Syngenta but in his previous job working for the global consumer packaged-goods giant Reckitt Benckiser. In the 1980s, shampoo and soap companies pioneered a model where they increased sales in poorer countries by selling affordable single-serve "sachets" and investing in grassroots education. Musyoka incorporated that concept into the Syngenta program launched under the name *Uwezo*, which means "strength" in the native language of Kenya. Instead of buying a big bag of chemicals, farmers could buy a single packet that they could pour into a twenty-liter backpack. Syngenta commissioned close to fifty field agents to travel on motorcycles to teach famers about the benefits of crop-protection chemicals firsthand. Within two years, the program was up to close to $10 million in revenues in just Kenya, which represents a mere 1 percent of the global smallholder market. That's brilliant borrowing!

You can do the same thing that Fairhurst and Musyoka did. Once you have found a problem worth solving, find someone or something that has already solved your problem. Look in different categories and fields and remember the time-tested idea that magic happens at intersections, where different mindsets and skills collide.

## Tool: Discovery Question Cheat Sheet

One of the quickest ways to learn how a company really thinks about innovation is to be a fly on the wall during its budget discussions or project reviews. Those are magic moments where words are given to often unstated assumptions. It happens when leaders draws in their breath and then speak. Do they make declarative statements? That could signal a company suffering from what Google calls the HIPPO problem, where decisions are based on the highest-paid person's opinion.[11] Do they ask thoughtful questions? That could signal an environment that tolerates collective exploration of the unknown.

"A company grows to reflect its leaders. The questions leaders ask are really important," Cook said during the 2018 panel discussion mentioned previously. "We had to make sure we were asking the questions that insisted and evoked the behaviors that we were teaching. Questions

---

11. Another animal Paul has heard exists inside some organizations (but, no longer in DBS!) is a ZEBRA: zero evidence but really arrogant.

like, 'What experiment are you going to run next week?' If they don't have an experiment planned for next week, let's talk about that. If they have a proposal, we'll ask, 'What experiments did you run that prove out the leap of faith assumptions?' These are all the things we teach, but if we're not asking for it, if we're looking at the spread-

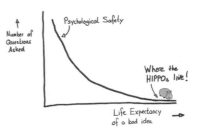

*The questions leaders ask are really important.*

sheet and saying, "That looks good," and are not asking for how they got to the answer, we're not teaching and reinforcing the same behaviors."

The question "What experiment are you going to run next week?" is an example of what we call a *discovery question*, which encourages dialogue and opens possibilities, versus a *delivery question*, which forces a decision and narrows choices. Another way to frame the distinction is that discovery questions *create possibilities*, while delivery questions *demand proof*. You can prove the past, but you need possibility to create the future.

Next time you are in a meeting to discuss an in-process innovation initiative, consider asking one of the following seven questions:

1. *How might we do it differently?* Being curious starts with the belief that there is always a better way to do things. Simple questions like "Why?," "Why not?," and "What if?" function in similar ways.

2. *What is the job to be done?* This question helps to reinforce the notion of being customer-obsessed and avoids the trap of developing a solution to a nonexistent problem.

3. *Who has solved this before?* This question leads you to the intersections, removes the shame of borrowing ideas, and reinforces the idea of smart collaboration.

4. *What would we need to believe?* Uncertain ideas can't be assessed purely analytically. Adeptness in ambiguity involves zeroing in on the key assumptions that would need to prove true for a desired outcome to occur.

5. *What don't we know?*  Another key part of being adept in ambiguity is being humble about the limits of current knowledge. This question role-models humility and accepts that there will always be limits when doing new things.

6. *What did we learn?*  This question further encourages being adept in ambiguity by moving away from a myopic focus on outcomes (which happens when you ask questions such as "Did it work?" or "Did we hit our targets?"). Beyond commercial success, there are three valuable things you can learn from an experiment: you can learn what *won't* work, you can develop a *strategic option* by learning that something will work only when other factors exist, and you can identify the opportunity to *pivot* to a different and better idea.

TABLE 6-3

### Discovery question "cheat sheet"

| When . . . | Instead of asking . . . | Consider asking . . . |
|---|---|---|
| An idea looks like one you have tried before . . . | Why are you proposing something that we know won't work? | What has changed from the last time we tried that? |
| A team suggests exploring a new market space . . . | What does the business case look like? | What evidence suggests that this problem is worth solving? |
| A specific idea is presented . . . | What does the business case look like? | What can we learn from other industries or contexts? |
| A team presents the business case for a new idea . . . | Have you done enough analysis to be confident? Why is cell B4 so low? It needs to be higher. | What would need to be true for this to be interesting? |
| A team makes the case for a big investment . . . | Did McKinsey/Bain/the Boston Consulting Group/ Innosight validate this? Can you go and run some more numbers? | What experiment can we run to learn more? |
| Market research shows that customers like a concept . . . | How quickly can we launch? | How can we test what customers will actually do? |
| Something doesn't work as planned . . . | What did you do wrong? | What can we learn? |

7. *What are our options?* This question helps to reinforce the notion of empowerment, with a leader shifting from asserting the answer to inquiring about possibilities.

In 2009, Natalie and Scott worked with the top leadership company of a $1 billion apparel company seeking to boost innovation. Historically, the company had consciously sought to *avoid* innovation. Rather, it followed a classic fast-follower strategy, waiting for someone else in its category to demonstrate the viability of an innovative idea and then seeking to replicate it at a lower cost. That strategy was running out of steam, however. One fundamental challenge was that leaders had spent years honing the craft of diving into details with probing delivery questions. Early-stage rough ideas crumbled under this kind of scrutiny.

To help them change their behavior, we created a "cheat sheet" that leaders could refer to in meetings about nascent ideas (displayed in table 6-3). Consider giving leaders a version of this as a way to encourage a more discovery-oriented mindset.[12]

12. This is so BEANable. Anyone want to rise to the challenge?

# Phase 3

## Assess and Test Ideas

The next phase in the journey involves picking up the idea, looking at it from multiple angles, separating facts from assumptions, testing rigorously, and adapting quickly.[1] Being adept in ambiguity is a clear key to success. So is being empowered, where you learn through a thoughtful mix of analysis and action. To help with this phase, we'll explore how DBS purposefully brought chaos (and a raccoon!) to meetings, how you can build psychological safety into your organization, and how a CEO brought back a legendary technology company by shifting mindsets—at scale.

## Relevant BEANs

One of the biggest challenges of this phase of the innovation journey is identifying critical assumptions. Part of why this is so hard is that the human brain does not deal well with uncertainty. We *know* that when we are doing new things, what we know decreases and what we assume

1. Scott's 2014 book *The First Mile* deep-dives into this step. The book anchors on two acronyms: DEFT and HOPE. DEFT stands for document, evaluate, focus, and test, and is the core process to help surface and address key strategic uncertainties. HOPE stands for hypothesis, objective, prediction, and execution plan, and it is a reminder about how to experiment with discipline.

increases. But we typically get the slope of the line wrong. We have false confidence and overestimate what we truly know. And we have what former US Defense Secretary Donald Rumsfeld famously dubbed "unknown unknowns," or assumptions lurking deep under the surface. Full BEANs that help to surface and address assumptions appear in table 7-1; partial ones appear in table 7-2.

TABLE 7-1

## Full BEANs for assessing and testing ideas

| Organization and BEAN name | Description | Behavior enabler | Artifact | Nudge |
|---|---|---|---|---|
| Atlassian—Premortem | Team discussions over what factors could lead their projects to fail, helping to anticipate issues before they happen | Checklist to help teams evaluate potential failure modes | Best-practice playbook, available on the company intranet | Health-monitoring tool that reinforces compliance |
| DBS—Wreckoon | A PowerPoint slide randomly appears during meetings, with questions to prompt candid discussions | List of questions to ask to encourage candid discussions about projects | "Wreckoon" avatar; Power-Point slide with key questions | Presence of slide in the template and supporting stories |
| Supercell—Cheers to Failure | The standard process of celebrating success with beer and failure with champagne, with stories shared publicly | Ritual of celebrating when a game-development effort ends | Pictures and memorials from the champagne celebration | Stories of Supercell's past game successes and failures, shared publicly |

TABLE 7-2

## Partial BEANs for assessing and testing ideas

| Organization and BEAN name | Description |
|---|---|
| Airbnb—Live from Day 1 | Direct encouragement to push code to the website on a coder's first day |
| Google—#MonkeyFirst | A mantra and ritual to focus attention on the hardest problem first |
| Innocent—Just Go with It | A practice in which employees who are 70 percent confident in an idea are encouraged to try it out |

## Atlassian

### PREMORTEMS

One way that Atlassian, an Australian software company, deals with the
hidden assumption problem is by rigorously conducting premortems. The
phrase is a play on the term "post-
mortem," which is a medical process
conducted after a patient dies to identify the cause of death. A premortem

is a way to identify potential threats and to take preventative action to
de-risk an idea. Before starting a project, teams conducting an Atlassian Premortem use a checklist to probe the ways a project could fail.
The process identifies critical assumptions and potential threats so that
appropriate preventive actions can be taken to minimize the chances of
failure and mitigate any repercussions. Atlassian supports the program
with an artifact: a team playbook, available online, that contains more
than forty best practices and rituals.[2] It further nudges behavior with
a project-health monitoring tool that uses eight "vital signs" as criteria.
Teams are expected to regularly analyze their health and pick relevant
plays to address vital signs with issues.

## DBS

### WRECKOON

Of course, just identifying the most
critical assumptions isn't enough.
You have to design and execute experiments to address those assumptions.

2. Other plays include Inclusive Meetings (which harkens back to the MOJO BEAN), Get
S#!t Done Day, Disruptive Brainstorming, and Rules of Engagement. The plays are available at https://www.atlassian.com/team-playbook/plays.

You have to make decisions based on the data that result from those experiments. Some assumptions get knocked off; other unstated ones emerge. A key challenge is avoiding problems like confirmation bias, where you see the things you want to see and ignore anything that goes against your hopes and expectations, or like the hierarchy effect, where everyone simply aligns with the leader's opinion. A couple of years ago, DBS wanted to encourage employees to have candid, data-driven discussions about ideas, so it drew inspiration from Netflix's "chaos monkey," a tool to nudge developers to make the platform's movie-streaming infrastructure incredibly stable and robust. The chaos monkey deliberately but seemingly randomly attempts to cause breakdowns, testing the resiliency of Netflix's infrastructure. Inspired by Netflix, DBS created "chaos raccoon" software, which consciously tries to wreck data centers, and gave it the catchy name "Wreckoon."[3] It became the centerpiece for a BEAN that increased DBS's ability to be adept in ambiguity. At any meeting reviewing a major initiative, a slide would appear at some point with a simple but powerful checklist of key questions, such as, "What have we forgotten? What is the riskiest assumption? What is the opposing view? What could go wrong?" Ritually asking these questions in somewhat random spots in meetings showed that what were formerly taboo topics were now fair game. Further, building the slide with a Wreckoon avatar and the question list into basic presentation templates nudged leaders to pick a space in these meetings to pause and ask for dissenting views, challenges, and objections. Leaders were coached to seek out the views of quieter participants, as well, rather than use the space to reinforce their own opinions.

---

3. Inter-author debate (or is that intra-author?): One author thought Wreckoon was an obvious combination of wreck and raccoon and therefore didn't need to be explained. One author thought we needed to do a better job of connecting the dots. If you run into us, tell us what you think!

## Supercell

### CHEERS TO FAILURE

Finally, being adept in ambiguity means recognizing that not every idea is going to work out and that that's okay. A small but growing number of companies visibly celebrate failure to destigmatize it. Finnish mobile gam-  ing company Supercell was founded in 2010, valued at $3 billion three years later and sold to Chinese giant TenCent in 2016 for $8.6 billion. At Supercell, success is celebrated with beer, and failure with champagne. The Cheers to Failure champagne celebration is memorialized with ar- tifacts like pictures and stories on Supercell's website, which nicely sum- marizes the organization's thoughts on the topic:[4]

> We'd like to think that every failure is a unique opportunity to learn, and every lesson will ultimately make us better at what we do. That's why we have a tradition of celebrating these lessons by drinking champagne every time we screw up. For us, it's clear that releasing hit games means having to take big risks. And by definition, taking those risks means that you'll fail more often than you'll succeed. So whenever we realize that we haven't failed in a while, it's a sign that we haven't taken enough risks. And that is truly the biggest possible risk for a creative company like ours.

This champagne ritual signals that failure is acceptable while also ensur- ing that teams know it's time to move onto the next project, allowing them to shift their focus to better ideas. For example, after a year of develop- ment and investment, the company decided to scupper a multiplatform

---

4. There are also rumors that at the celebration there is a champagne bottle with a blank label to capture key lessons from the failure. If Supercell doesn't do this, it should!

approach that fell short of its development targets. In this case, that team went onto develop the massively successful *Clash of Clans* game.

## Partial BEANs

Imagine you wanted to build a monkey to stand on a ten-foot-tall pedestal and recite passages from Shakespeare. What should you do first? Your instinct might be to start build-ing the pedestal to demonstrate progress, but the #MonkeyFirst BEAN from Google X (where Google incubates new "moonshot" ideas) encourages employees to tackle the hardest  problem first. After all, you can be pretty certain that you can build a pedestal; training the monkey to talk, however, is a much bigger chal-lenge, so it should be addressed first. The following example demon-strates why this is important: one team was working on a way to turn seawater into economically friendly fuel. The "monkey" for this team was the economics of the fuel-conversion process, which they tackled first. The team concluded that the odds of the project being econom-ically viable within five years were very low, so they decided to kill the project.

The next two BEANs are ways to encour-age teams to make a habit of not overthink-ing ideas. At Innocent, a beverage company 90 percent owned by The Coca-Cola Com-pany, teams are encouraged to Just Go with It. That is, if they are 70 percent certain about an idea, they are encouraged to actively test it rather than to keep discussing it with management.

Similarly, the Live from Day 1 program at Airbnb encourages engineers to push code di-rectly to the website on the first day of their on-boarding bootcamp.

## BEAN Booster: Psychological Safety

In the 1990s, Amy Edmondson was studying the relationship between the performance levels of medical teams and their reported error rates. Her hypothesis was that high-performing teams would have lower error rates. It turned out the opposite was true: higher-performing teams reported more errors than lower-performing teams. That seemed like a paradox. As Edmondson dug deeper, she realized that the teams didn't actually *make* more errors; they just *reported*

*Not a psychologically safe environment!*

more of them. Edmondson concluded this was because higher-performing medical teams were in an environment that was "psychologically safe," which supported honest conversations, helping them improve and push boundaries. The idea lived at the fringes of academia until a *New York Times* article in 2016 showed that Google's research had identified psychological safety as a key enabler of team success. Edmondson, now a long-tenured Harvard Business School professor, released *The Fearless Organization* in 2018. In 2019 Thinkers50 gave her the Breakthrough idea award, leading her to quip about the irony of winning the award for an idea that is more than twenty years old.

Creating a psychologically safe environment clearly takes work. But we have two suggestions for reasonably simple starting points. First, let's talk about failure. While the academic literature suggests that almost every commercial success has had a failure somewhere in its lineage, inside most companies, working on something that "fails" carries significant stigma, if not outright career risk. Successful innovation often has a lot of false steps that feel like failures. "If I find 10,000 ways something won't work, I haven't failed," Thomas Edison once said. "I am not discouraged, because every wrong attempt discarded is often a step forward." So does that mean a psychologically safe environment supports—and, indeed, even encourages—failure? Not exactly.

It depends on the *type* of failure. When people do something stupid or sloppy or screw up in a way that has negative repercussions—Edmondson calls these preventable failures—they warrant punishment. Can you imagine a doctor performing a routine procedure proudly talking about killing a patient?

A second type of failure is *complex* failure, where a surprise event leads to an unpredictable outcome in an intertwined system.[5] "We couldn't have known or learned about this," you might say. When these failures happen to you, learn from them, strengthen early-warning systems, and reinforce buffers.

The final type of failure is *intelligent* failure. Here, the right answer is unknown and unknowable in advance. When this type of failure happens, you think, "This is good. We smartly learned what we couldn't have known." The only mistake here is taking too long or spending too much money to figure out that you were wrong. This type, and only this type, of failure should be celebrated.

The word *intelligent* here requires extra emphasis. For example, Scott once asked a European bank if they had ever had an intelligent failure. "Boy, did we," said an executive. "We moved fast and launched before we had thought it through or tested it. We bet big. I mean *really* big. Like, billions of euros. We may or may not have broken the law. When we failed, it almost pulled down the global banking system." Again, emphasis on the word *intelligent*.

Edmondson offers a six-point checklist to determine the degree to which a failure truly is intelligent:

1. The opportunity must have had the potential to be material.

2. Assumptions should have been explicitly articulated.

3. There should have been a clear plan to test assumptions.

---

5. A failure triggered by a so-called black-swan event would be an extreme example of a complex failure.

4. Tests should have been bounded within a reasonable cost and scope.

5. Key risks should have been detailed and mitigated where possible.

6. The failure should have created informative and useful learning.

You also need to build a discipline around measuring different ideas differently. As a metaphor (adapted from Michael Mauboussin's great book *The Success Equation*), consider the difference between appraising someone while they are playing roulette as opposed to playing chess or poker. How can you tell whether someone is good at roulette? It feels a bit like a trick question, and it is. There is no such thing as a skilled roulette player, as it is a game of pure luck. If someone is playing a game that looks like roulette in your company, they are taking stupid risks and should be punished, because it will lead to preventable failures. How about chess? What does a good chess player do? Your instinct probably is to look at the player's ability to think several moves ahead of the opponent. Appraising that capability would require carefully watching someone play. There's an easier answer, however. Good chess players *win*. It is a game of almost pure skill. That means you don't need to watch a chess player play to know how good he is; you simply need to look at his results.

In the relative stability that characterizes most companies' core businesses, defining and measuring results is a viable way to appraise talent. Poker, blackjack, hitting a baseball, investing in a stock—and, yes, innovation—blend luck and skill. Over long periods, results are a meaningful guide to capabilities, but in the short run, you can get a good outcome by doing the wrong things and a bad one by doing the right things. Here, instead of appraising the results a player gets, Mauboussin urges you to look at the process or behaviors they follow.[6] That means appraising innovators more on how quickly and efficiently they learn; not on near-term commercial outcomes.

---

6. Consider, as a thought experiment, a blackjack player hitting on eighteen while the dealer is showing a six and drawing a three. Yes, they took a risk and it was rewarded, but it was a stupid risk. They got the right outcome, but they followed the wrong process.

In 2013, Manila Water, a $500 million water utility in the Philippines, built a dedicated team to pursue new growth opportunities. A key lesson it learned is the importance of leaders wearing different "hats." Here is how former CEO Ferdz dela Cruz described it:

> Leaders need to wear two hats. One is for the core business, and the other is for a new venture. The visual of the two hats helps us make sure we are clear what conversation we are having and wear the right hat. Our CFO served as one of the best symbols to the organization on this point. I think we are fortunate that Chito [Manila Water's CFO at the time], in prior roles, was exposed to ventures. Organizationally the CFO is such a strong symbol of how much risk an organization is willing to take. Some companies have problems because the CFO blocks everything. For us, the CFO is a strong symbol of embracing dual tracks.

One final note. People sometimes mistakenly assume that psychological safety requires treating people with kid gloves or glossing over bad performance. That's not the case at all. Psychologically safe environments can be brutally tough. Consider Bridgewater, the world's largest hedge fund founded and led by Ray Dalio. The  company is legendarily transparent. All meetings (except for hypersensitive HR discussions) are recorded. People receive real-time feedback *in the middle of meetings* via an app. Publicly accessible "baseball cards" detail an individual's skills and development areas.[7] This environment

---

7. This is included in our list of BEANs in the appendix. Andy, who is steadfast in his misbegotten notion that cricket is a superior sport to baseball, uses Top Trump cards as a more globally relevant example. After reviewing this footnote, he also noted, "This footnote is scandalous . . . and I have learnt you cannot add a comment to a footnote, which is weird."

is certainly not for everyone! But it is psychologically safe. People can constructively disagree, focusing on underlying assumptions versus personal preferences. They can take well-documented, well-thought-out risks and not face punishment if a hypothesis proves wrong.

## BEAN Booster: Chameleon Leadership

Today, leaders often hear they have to be like the soccer star Cristiano Ronaldo, the cricket legend Sachin Tendulkar, the basketball god Lebron James, or tennis savants Rafael Nadal and Maria Sharapova. No, that doesn't mean they need to endure endless practice hours or be blessed with once-in-a generation genetic gifts. Rather, each of these legends has some degree of *ambidexterity*, which is the ability to use both their left and right hands and feet with dexterity and skill. By analogy, a business leader who is ambidextrous can use her left brain to drill into the details of an Excel spreadsheet when operating her core business and use her right brain to explore the story behind the numbers.

While it is true that leaders increasingly need to learn new skillsets in order to confront different types of challenges, there is a problem with the analogy of ambidexterity. Imagine what would happen if James went onto a cricket pitch or Tendulkar started playing tennis. No doubt they would be better than a layperson, but they wouldn't be world-class. Put another way, ambidexterity helps them to play their chosen sport better but is insufficient to play a very different sport. Execution and innovation are similarly different games. That means executives need more than a range of skill; they need to follow fundamentally different approaches and embrace different mindsets.

A different metaphor is to think about a chameleon leader who can morph his style and approach based on context. Scott Cook, the founder and chairman of Intuit whose story was described in chapter 6, is a prototypical example of chameleon leadership. Cook certainly has discipline in his DNA. After all, he is a graduate of Harvard Business School, a former consultant at Bain & Co, and a former brand manager at Procter & Gamble (he now sits on P&G's board). And his software products have brought financial discipline to millions of people. But Cook also recognizes that he needs to think and act differently when advising teams working on innovation projects. In this capacity, he views his role as the "experimenter-in-chief." He astutely observes that when you innovate, no one knows what the right answer is. And any leader of today's business often lacks intuition about new and uncertain territory. Therefore, the job of the leader isn't to make decisions; rather, in Cook's words, "We teach our leaders that it's your job to put in the systems that enable your people to run your experiments fast and cheap and to keep making them faster and cheaper. Yield as many of your decisions off to the experiment as possible."

It sounds simple, but it isn't. Leaders simultaneously need to think and act in multiple frames that, at best, appear to be in conflict, and, at worst, appear paradoxical. Running today is about working from the present forward, carefully planning, thoughtfully analyzing, and executing with discipline; creating tomorrow involves intuitively working from the future backward, experimenting, and taking prudent risks.[8] Longtime Harvard professor Robert Kegan calls the stage of adult development required to deal with this type of challenge *self-transforming*. In this stage, individuals "can step back from and reflect on the limits of our own ideology or personal authority: see that any one system or self-organization is in some way partial or incomplete; be friendlier toward contradiction and opposites; seek to hold onto multiple systems rather than project all except one onto the other." Unfortunately, research suggests that no more than 5 percent of high-performing managers have achieved this level of leadership. In a stable era, where success requires disciplined execution, that wouldn't matter. But in our turbulent era of nonstop disruption, it does.

It's not surprising that so many leaders lack this capability. After all, most high-performing senior executives developed their skills, intuition, and tacit knowledge in either a today or a tomorrow paradigm,

---

8. *Dual Transformation*, Scott's last book, shorthands those two worlds as Transformation A, where you reinvent today's business to increase its resilience, and Transformation B, where you create tomorrow's growth engine.

but rarely in both and almost never at the same time. And leadership development (with rare exceptions) hasn't caught up with this emerging need. To transform themselves, leaders must focus more on mindset, awareness, and inner capacity both to combat basic biases that make decision-making hard in uncertainty and to toggle between different frames. There are no quick fixes here. But research increasingly suggests that the best starting point is to embrace a practice broadly termed "mindfulness."

To some, that word might sound "squishy" and New Age, but meditation and related practices that use breathing to tune into thoughts and sensations have widely documented health benefits, such as increased energy and decreased stress. For the purposes of this book, it is even more critical to note that mindfulness increases a person's ability to step back, pause, and become aware of not just her habitual thought patterns but also her emotional reactions. A mindful leader can, for example, "see" her own reactivity, giving her the tools to identify and overcome blinding biases and to consciously toggle between different leadership modes.

Some leaders who have successfully managed transformative change have touted the value of mindfulness. Mark Bertolini, who led US health insurance giant Aetna through a bold transformation that resulted in a merger with CVS Caremark, was an early advocate of advancing meditation programs at his company. Bertolini credits mindfulness for easing the chronic pain he suffered after a ski accident and when recovering from a rare form of cancer. He says it also improves his ability to process information and make sharp strategic decisions. "With so many things going on, whether in a small or large organization, you can get frozen by attempting to process it all instead of being present, listening, and focusing on what really matters," he said.

Some companies are seeking to consciously create a cadre of chameleon leaders. For example, SAP has trained more than 10,000 employees to use meditation to improve self-perception, regulation of emotions, resilience, and empathy. Participants report double-digit increases in their personal sense of meaning, their ability to focus, their level of mental clarity, and their creative abilities. Johnson & Johnson has long focused on employee well-being. Its recent efforts focus on energy and performance, with a stated goal to help employees obtain "full engagement in work and life." Participants answer diagnostic questions such as, "Are you present in the moment, focused, and fully aware?" and peer reviewers assess whether "their self-image is keeping them from being the person they wish to be." Leaders serve as active role models for building these capabilities. CEO Alex Gorsky, for example, has long worn a fitness tracker and speaks publicly about the link between mental well-being and productivity.

## Case Study: Satya Refreshes the Code

The first decade of the twenty-first century can charitably be called a lost decade for Microsoft. On January 13, 2000, Steve Ballmer succeeded Bill Gates to become Microsoft's second chief executive officer. Microsoft's market capitalization that day stood at about $400 billion. By the last day of the decade, its value had decreased to about $233 billion, a decline of more than 40 percent. One could turn John Doerr's quip about the emergence of venture capital in the 1980s ("We witnessed [and benefited from] the largest, legal creation of wealth on the planet") on its head and call it one of the largest legal destructions of wealth on the planet. Microsoft clearly had the technological capability to create the Kindle (Amazon), the iPod, the iPhone, and the iPad (Apple), along with search-based advertising (Google). The company's arrogance never diminished, with Ballmer famously quipping that the Apple iPhone would be nothing more than a niche product while ripping one of the devices out of the hands of an employee who had the temerity to . . . well, use a good product . . . and smashing it on the ground. Ballmer would lead an ill-fated effort to accelerate Microsoft's growth in the mobile phone business by buying Nokia's mobile phone arm for more than $7 billion in 2013. Eighteen months later, Microsoft took a write-down on that transaction of, well, more than $7 billion, admitting that it purchased something that was, in essence, worthless.

All the while, important changes were quietly taking place in Microsoft's product portfolio. It moved its core office suite onto the cloud, creating web-delivered models that brought its productivity software to more people in more places on more devices. Its Azure cloud-infrastructure offering established itself as a viable competitor against Amazon's cloud-computing offering. Its Xbox videogame platform built a strong position in the market, with its Kinect motion sensor providing clear differentiation—and room for expansion into new markets. Investments in technologies like augmented reality, haptic computing, and artificial intelligence continued at pace.

On February 4, 2014, Microsoft announced that Satya Nadella would become the company's first non-American-born CEO. The stock market yawned, with Microsoft's stock down a fraction of a point during the day. Over the next five years, Nadella would lead a stunning transformation that led to Microsoft recapturing its seat as the world's most valuable company. Its market capitalization on Nadella's five-year anniversary stood at $810 billion, an almost threefold increase over five years. How did the cerebral, cricket-loving CEO do it? Clearly a lot of the story relates to smart portfolio choices, but Nadella's efforts to drive what is known in academic circles as the *growth mindset* played a central role as well.

The growth mindset is an idea detailed by Stanford professor Carol Dweck in the book *Mindset: The New Psychology of Success.* The essence of a growth mindset is a fundamental belief that an individual is capable of learning and developing. Failure to solve a problem isn't viewed as a character flaw; it is an opportunity to grow and develop. A growth mindset contrasts with a fixed mindset, in which, because an individual perceives his capabilities as fixed, a failure means the lack of a particular capability. Research shows that people with a growth mindset set higher goals, are more comfortable taking risks, have higher levels of motivation and lower levels of stress, form better relationships with colleagues, and achieve increased performance scores. All of this makes it easier to confront ambiguity and to manage the critical third phase of the innovation journey.

Nadella's wife gave him a copy of Dweck's book, not to help with his work but to provide support as the couple dealt with ailments afflicting their children. Soon after being named CEO, Nadella spoke at a large gathering of market-facing Microsoft employees in Orlando to describe his view of the power of a growth mindset and its connection to culture:

> We can have all the bold ambitions. We can have all the bold goals. We can aspire to our new mission. But it's only going to happen if we live our culture, if we teach our culture. And to me that model of culture is not a static thing. It is about a dynamic learning culture. In fact, the phrase we use to describe our emerging culture is "growth mindset," because it's about every individual, every one of us having that attitude—that mindset—of being able to overcome any constraint, stand up to any challenge, making it possible for us to grow and, thereby, for the company to grow.

In essence, Nadella was saying that financial performance was a lagging variable that resulted from pursuing individual growth. "I was not talking bottom-line growth," Nadella wrote in *Hit Refresh*. "I was talking about our individual growth. We will grow as a company if everyone, individually, grows in their roles and in their lives. . . . I had essentially asked employees to identify their innermost passions and to connect them in some way to our new mission and culture."

Nadella's view is that exercising a growth mindset entails being "customer-obsessed, diverse, and inclusive" and moving from being a "know-it-all" to being a "learn-it-all." Sound familiar? Those behaviors overlap closely with the innovative ways of working described in chapter 1. And Nadella doesn't just talk about these behaviors; he regularly models them: "An empathetic leader needs to be out in the world, meeting people where they live and seeing how the technology we create affects their daily activities." He and his team have created programs to help people live out growth-mindset behaviors, such as an annual hackathon called OneWeek. During OneWeek, everyone can be collocated on Microsoft's campus to learn, collaborate and, well, grow. More than 10,000 people participated in the first OneWeek, generating more than 3,000 hacks that ranged from ideas to improve supply chains to ways to make computing more accessible to people with disabilities.

Clear, consistent, and simple communication helped cascade this change throughout Microsoft. It started with an important change in Microsoft's mission—from "A computer on every desktop" to "Empower every person and every organization on the planet to do more." That revision made it clear that Microsoft ought to bring its productivity tools to as many platforms as it could, doing things that once would seem anathema, such as putting full versions of software on the Apple App store or working closely with Linux, an open-source platform. "I knew that Microsoft needed to regain its soul as the company that makes powerful technology accessible to everyone and every organization—democratizing technology," Nadella wrote. He and his team put down Microsoft's (revised) mission, worldview, ambition, and culture on a single page. That approach was highly, dare we say, countercultural, for a company that historically relied on dense PowerPoint presentations to cascade messages. As always, clear communication builds understanding and accelerates change.

"I like to think that the *C* in CEO stands for culture. The CEO is the curator of an organization's culture," Nadella wrote. "As I had told employees in Orlando, anything is possible for a company when its culture is about listening, learning, and harnessing individual passions and talents to the company's mission. . . . An organizational culture is not something that can simply unfreeze, change, and then refreeze in an ideal way. It takes deliberate work, and it takes some specific ideas about what the culture should become."

Nadella recognizes that culture change is necessarily a work in progress. "Because I've made culture change at Microsoft such a high priority, people often ask how it's going. Well, I suppose my response is very Eastern: We're making great progress, but we should never be done. It's not a program with a start and end date. It's a way of being."

## Tool: The Innovator's Checklist

Through our fieldwork on innovation, we developed a simple checklist we can run through to help guide the innovation journey. Note, the checklist doesn't say whether an idea is good or bad—it just says whether a team or group is following an approach that maximizes their chances of learning as quickly as possible, regardless of whether their idea is good or bad. Consider the following ten questions:

1. *Is innovation development being spearheaded by a small, focused team of people who have relevant experience or are prepared to learn as they go?* No idea succeeds without the right dedicated resources. It is very possible for people to contribute in their spare time, but someone has to be on the hook for making things happen, or they simply won't.

2. *Has the team spent enough time directly with prospective customers to develop a deep understanding of them?* However much time you have spent with customers, it is not enough. Steve Jobs famously said, "It is not the customer's job to know what they want." He was right. It is yours. Seek to develop an empathetic connection where you know the customer better than they know themselves.

3. *In considering novel ways to serve these customers, did the team review developments in other industries and countries?* Remember the legendary artist Pablo Picasso's maxim: "Good artists copy; great artists steal." Someone in the world has probably solved the problem you are trying to address. They might not be in your company, industry, or country, but they are out there. Innovators should live at intersections, getting as much stimuli as possible. Adapting existing solutions to solve a problem is one of the best ways to short-circuit the process of doing something different that creates value.

4. *Can the team clearly define the first customer and a path to reaching others?* Good innovators dream big and start small. Be as specific

as you can about your very first customer. What is her name? Where does she live? Why is she going to buy your product or service? At the same time, don't lose sight of what could come next. The more possible paths for expansion, the better!

5. *Is the idea's proposed business model described in detail?* Typically, a lot of things have to come together for innovation success to happen. At a minimum, think about how you will market, distribute, price, produce, supply, sell, support, and profit from your idea. If you aren't thorough, you are likely to miss something critical.

6. *Does the team have a believable hypothesis about how the offering will make money?* Innovation is something different that creates value. If you don't at least have an idea about how you will create value, you aren't really innovating.

7. *Have team members identified all the things that must be true for this hypothesis to work?* Every idea is partially right and partially wrong. Good innovators clearly separate fact from assumption and seek effective ways to turn unknowns to knowns.

8. *Does the team have a plan for testing all those uncertainties, which tackles the most critical ones first?* Does each test have a clear objective, a hypothesis, specific predictions, and a tactical execution plan? Successful innovation always comes from disciplined experimentation. Seek to be scientific as you manage and eliminate the uncertainty that, by necessity, underpins your idea.

9. *Are fixed costs low enough to facilitate course corrections?* The only thing you can be sure about is that you will have to make some changes for your idea to succeed. Even if it costs a little more in the short term, keeping costs variable by engaging contractors and using third-party vendors will save heartache in the long run.

10. *Has the team demonstrated a bias toward action by rapidly prototyping the idea?* One of the most powerful concepts connected to

the so-called lean startup movement is the idea of the minimum viable product ("MVP")—that is, something that is good enough to solve the customer's problem without all the bells and whistles behind it. That doesn't always mean a physical prototype: a mock website, a storyboard that walks you through a new process, or even a skit showing how an idea will work can all serve as vehicles to accelerate learning.

# Phase 4
## Move Ideas Forward

The final phase of the innovation journey involves moving from experimenting and learning to executing and expanding. It's an important switch to flip, because, remember, innovation is something different *that creates value*. If you have found a compelling solution to an important problem and have addressed all of the critical uncertainties, of course you want to create as much value as possible! This is when it is critical to be empowered, as it is too easy for an idea to languish, strangled by the institutionalized inertia that results from the shadow strategy. Read on to see the benefits of pulling the Andon Cord, plugging in your innovation amplifiers, and killing your zombies!

### Relevant BEANs

Acting empowered involves having an ownership mindset, in which you certainly seek guidance but don't wait for permission to act. Full BEANs that help to support these behaviors appear in table 8-1; partial ones appear in table 8-2.

TABLE 8-1

## Full BEANs for moving ideas forward

| Organization and BEAN name | Description | Behavior enabler | Artifact | Nudge |
|---|---|---|---|---|
| Spotify—Bets Board | A centralized database containing all of Spotify's innovation bets that all employees can access | Standard form for ideas, detailing Data, Insights, Beliefs, and the Bet (DIBB) | A Google spreadsheet capturing all of the individual bets | Publicly available information that reinforces Spotify's DIBB framework |
| Tasty Catering—Great Game of Business | A weekly game that associates play to learn more about how the business operates | Checklists and tools to teach business principles | The game itself | Gamification of results |
| Toyota—Andon Cord | A mechanism by which any employee is empowered to stop production when they see a problem | Direct encouragement to think like an owner and take action | A physical cord (or digital version it) | Company history and stories around the value of the Andon Cord |

TABLE 8-2

## Partial BEANs for moving ideas forward

| Organization and BEAN name | Description |
|---|---|
| Asana—No Meeting Wednesday | Guidelines to have one day a week when employees can do "deep work" |
| Intuit—innovation catalysts | Trained employees who act as coaches for up to 10 percent of their time |
| LinkedIn—InDay | A ritual where employees invest one day a month on themselves and their passion projects |

## Toyota

### ANDON CORD

A classic BEAN to encourage empowerment comes from Toyota. The key to Toyota's long-term success is the

well-studied Toyota Production System (TPS). Historically, manufacturers believed there were tradeoffs between quality, speed, and cost. Toyota showed that its approach, with a maniacal focus on continual improvement and waste reduction, could deliver against all three. While there are multiple pieces to the TPS, one key component is the Andon Cord. All Toyota employees are viewed as experts in their respective fields, who can stop the production line when they spot anything perceived to be a threat to vehicle quality. They do so by pulling on the Andon Cord. Not only does this ritual stop problems early, but it also shapes a culture of dispersed empowerment by encouraging employees to take ownership of production processes and to speak up when there is an issue.

## Tasty Catering

### GREAT GAME OF BUSINESS

Two blockers to empowerment are a lack of confidence and a lack of understanding of the full scope of what's required to translate an idea into value. At a conference in 2011, Tasty Catering, a catering company based in Chicago, Illinois, discovered a unique way to help its associates understand more about business: play a game. The catering company had always believed in giving associates full visibility into the organization's financials. Every week, they play a customized version of a game called the Great Game of Business. Each player makes a forecast for a line in the P&L. The projections are then compared with the actual figures. Winners are celebrated and deviations are analyzed, feeding into the organization's overall efforts to identify patterns and to generate ideas for further boosting performance.

## Spotify

BETS BOARD

A third interesting BEAN to help to take ideas forward is the Bets Board that digital music company Spotify uses to track key strategic initiatives at the company, division, and squad levels. Each bet is captured in a short brief that summarizes data around  the bet, interesting insights that come from that data, beliefs spurred by the insights, and the bet itself, a framework that Spotify calls Data, Insights, Beliefs, Bets (DIBB). The bets board is a Google spreadsheet open to everyone in the company. It lists the name of each bet and the bet's sponsor and "road manager." A two-page brief further details the DIBB, stakeholders, and key success metrics. The bets board helps leaders to identify and prioritize projects, helps bets teams to focus on what they need to do to advance their ideas, and helps the broader Spotify community to know the company's key initiatives.

## Partial BEANs

We previously argued that, while people often say a lack of available time or adequate training inhibits innovation, the deeper blocker is typically the inertia of existing habits, which are intertwined with supporting processes and systems. If, however, you have overcome that inertia and have moved an idea forward to this phase of the innovation journey, a lack of time or inadequate training can indeed inhibit progress.

   Making material progress with an idea requires that someone (and, often, many someones) spend significant time on it. However, most people have little slack in their calendars, and few organizations have legions of unallocated employees sitting at their desks twiddling their thumbs. Whether employees are engaged in the right activities can reasonably be debated, but it is generally true that there is not a lot of slack capacity to do different things.

Asana and LinkedIn have BEANs to give the gift of time. Asana, a work-management solution cofounded by Facebook cofounder Dustin Moskovitz, has No Meeting Wednesdays to give employees uninterrupted time to work. LinkedIn has a ritual called InDay, where employees invest one day a month on

themselves and their passion projects. The goal is for employees to have time to "invest, inspire, and innovate." Each InDay has a theme chosen by a member of the executive team, and employees are free to connect their work to the chosen them, aided by "culture champions" distributed throughout the world.

Let's say that people find the time to individually follow innovation behaviors. While innovation is a discipline, doing it well requires practice. To help spread skills through its organization, Intuit has dedicated innovation catalysts. Employees are trained as innovation catalysts and then spend up to 10 percent of their time coaching, mentoring, and inspiring employees in and outside their teams. Employees can ask innovation catalysts for coaching help on their projects and unstructured time. In turn, the catalysts are able to share and draw from the experiences and lessons they receive along the way.

## BEAN Booster: Innoganda Busters

Remember the "inspirational" ideas box, with the rusted lock, from the introduction?[1] BEANs help to fight against what we dubbed *innoganda*. To support those BEANs, particularly in this critical phase of the journey, always remember to connect the dots. Chapter 3 referenced Steve Kerr's management classic, "The Folly of Rewarding A, While Hoping for B." This is the folly that occurs either when what you say you want doesn't match what you reward, or when what you ask people to do doesn't fit with the underlying beliefs of the organization. A simple way to address this issue is to ask a basic question: If we do *this,* what *else* do we need to do to support our goal? Then to answer this question, consider and connect the following five dots.

***If you ask employees to generate ideas, create mechanisms to do something with them.***

Executives often get fooled by inspiring stories of engineers at companies like 3M or Google coming up with germs of ideas in the 15 to 20 percent of their time they allocate to side projects. If your organization does indeed have mechanisms to take idea fragments, process them, and turn them into fully fleshed-out innovations, by all means open up the idea spigot. Too often, however, you create the virtual equivalent of a locked ideas box. You generate a long list of ideas destined to never go anywhere. All this does is create substantial organizational cynicism. You don't have to set up a standing department; you can simply develop a set of criteria by which to judge ideas and predetermine what you will do with the best ones.

***If you ask for answers, define problems worth solving.***

Innovation is something different that creates value. You create value only if you solve a problem that matters. Executives often think that the

---

1. Yes, that was many pages ago. But it was a good story.

best way to spur innovation is to remove constraints and let hundreds or thousands of flowers bloom. Overly fragmented efforts result in nothing more than a lot of undernourished flowers. Constraints and creativity are surprisingly close friends. Problems can range from entering new markets to addressing everyday concerns such as making video conferences more engaging. Whatever they are, the more specific, the better.

*If you want people to experiment, stock the laboratory.*

Innovation success results from disciplined experimentation. Consider how the Wright Brothers developed the first flying machine. Step back in time about 120 years ago. The world was obsessed, the machine age was upon us, and the scientific revolution had passed. Yet we hadn't solved a problem that had perplexed people for eons: birds could fly, but humans couldn't. How did most would-be aviators approach the problem? They designed flying machines, gamely climbed cliffs, and jumped. The best outcome? Back to the drawing board. The worst outcome? No chance to try again.

The Wright Brothers framed the problem differently. Before they built a plane, they flew kites and gliders.[2] The great thing about kites and gliders is that when they crash—and they always do—no one gets hurt. Using a kite or glider is akin to creating a mockup or prototype. It is running a small test market before you launch or trying something yourself before you ask your team to do it. Perhaps even more critically, to optimize their kites and gliders, the Wright Brothers hacked together bicycle-spoke wire, a cardboard box, and a fan to create a wind tunnel that allowed them to simulate flying conditions. Imagine how it felt. Everyone else was working on crazy contraptions that were crashing, and in two exhilarating months, the Wright Brothers ran two hundred experiments testing thirty-eight different types of wing designs. Organizational equivalents of wind tunnels are models, simulations, and

2. Today most innovation practitioners would call this a minimum viable product, or MVP.

test beds—mechanisms to increase the efficiency and effectiveness of experiments.

Of course, your innovators need to have the materials to build kites, the space to fly them, and access to the wind tunnels. If they don't—or if they need to get twelve approvals in order to do so—don't expect to see much experimentation.

### *If you want big impact, allocate real resources.*

Far too many companies create what you might call Potemkin portfolios. In the same way that Russian prince Grigory Potemkin impressed Catherine the Great with villages that were nothing more than facades, companies build beautiful ideas on paper without considering the resources needed to turn them into reality. Innovation is hard work. The vast majority of startup companies fail, and that's with tireless dedication from a team that has everything to lose. If you don't dedicate the right resources to your best ideas, you are consigning them to failure. At the very least, someone must have the idea's advancement among their top three priorities. Otherwise, it is unlikely to happen.

### *If you demand disruption, ring-fence your resources.*

The essence of Harvard Professor and Innosight cofounder Clayton Christensen's famous "innovator's dilemma" is that companies privilege investments made to sustain today's business over those with the potential to create tomorrow's business. Along some dimensions, this is quite rational. After all, a dollar invested in the existing business produces a measurable, near-term return, whereas a dollar invested in a nonexistent business promises ethereal returns at a difficult-to-pin-down future date. Of course, over the long run, that disruptive investment might be a better proposition, but if the company hasn't set aside resources specifically to drive disruption, the short term will always win.

## BEAN Booster: Innovation Amplifiers

Intuit's implementation of innovation catalysts is a BEAN, but it also functions as an innovation amplifier. Below are eight types of amplifiers to consider.

### External Amplifiers

1. *Corporate venture capital:* A corporate venture capital function invests in startups. Corporate investors often seek more than just financial returns; they are looking to learn more about emerging technologies and business models. Intel has a long history of providing capital to companies that might support further developments that, in turn, will grow demand for its core semiconductors.

2. *External incubators and accelerators:* These amplifiers provide a structured way to work with external startups, with the goal of learning more about the startup and creating the potential for future partnerships or acquisitions. Incubators focus more on early-stage startups, and accelerators focus more on growth stage startups. For example, Barclays runs an idea contest for early-stage fintech startups in collaboration with an accelerator called Techstars in New York, London, and Tel Aviv. Winning startups receive funding, accelerator space in Barclays Rise Accelerator in London, and coaching.

3. *Technology and business-model scouting:* This function is typically tasked with systematically exploring new and disruptive business models and their enabling technologies. DZ Bank, for instance, has a "trend-scouting team," which catalogues trends and relevant fintech startups. The team works with internal experts to asses each trend in terms of timing, disruptive risk, and opportunities for new revenue streams. It combines inputs into a "trend radar" that is used for ideation sessions and presentations to product teams.

4. *Strategic business development:* Organizations develop this capability to partner with or acquire external companies or to work with research institutes to drive joint value creation. Cisco Systems is perhaps the best-known example of a company that uses strategic business development as an innovation amplifier. In its history, Cisco has made more than 200 acquisitions to access new capabilities, talented employees, and even business models.

## Internal Amplifiers

1. *Internal incubators:* Incubators house projects generated within the organization by sourcing for internal problems, and then designing, testing, and refining ideas, either through temporary staff secondments or the formation of dedicated "SWAT teams" for more transformational projects. A famous example of an incubator is Lockheed Martin's Skunk Works group. Charles "Kelly" Johnson formed the organization that would later be named Skunk Works in 1943. He and his team developed the XP-80 jet-fighter in a remarkable 143 days. The group (also known as the Advanced Development Programs group) has helped to produce iconic products such as the U-2 spy plane, the SR-71 Blackbird, and the F-22 Raptor.

2. *Innovation catalysts:* Catalysts are experts who coordinate and connect innovation efforts and facilitate skills-transfer and mind-set change within the organization through capability-building initiatives. DBS's "innovation team that doesn't innovate" is an example of an innovation catalyst function.

3. *Idea-sourcing platforms:* These platforms serve as a method of collating internal ideas via crowdsourced activities, such as idea challenges or hackathons. For example, global food giant General Mills has a platform run by a dedicated team called G-WIN. The team works with General Mills's business division to identify important innovation challenges. Employees then can use G-WIN to submit proposed solutions.

4. *Research and development:*  R&D is a formal way to create innovation feedstock. Of course, R&D is core to technology companies, but organizations in many industries can set up similar structures to explore new technology-enabled businesses or operating models. For example, a law firm might create a formal mechanism with dedicated resources who are free to explore and experiment with new models based on smart contracts and artificial intelligence.

Large organizations might have multiple amplifiers working concurrently, while smaller ones might pick a couple that are most appropriate for their environment. Innovation literature (including *Building a Growth Factory* by Scott and Innosight colleague David Duncan) provides additional insight about how to adopt these and related amplifiers.

## Case Study: Scaling Innovation at UNICEF

If necessity is indeed the mother of invention, it should come as no surprise that UNICEF is a hotbed of innovation. The organization was founded in 1946 in the aftermath of World War II with a specific mission to provide food and healthcare to children in war-stricken countries. Today it is one of the world's most global organizations, with more than 19,000 employees operating in more than 190 countries. Its mission is "to save children's lives, to defend their rights, and to help them fulfill their potential, from early childhood through adolescence."

UNICEF has always innovated, but over the past fifteen years, it has sought to innovate more purposefully and with higher impact. This shift traces back to efforts by Dr. Sharad Sapra in UNICEF's Division of Communication in 2007. "We cooked up the opportunity to take a very minimal amount of funding and ring-fence a few people to think about problems differently," recalled Tanya Accone, who was a strategic planner in Sapra's division. "The intent was to carve out space and people to explore ideas. That's where it began."

Sapra moved to Uganda and repositioned innovation by bringing it front and center to UNICEF's operations in that country. Accone described the innovation challenge Sapra gave the organization: "He said, 'We're not going to do anything we have done before, because if we do, we can just extrapolate the trend and things will continue. I want space to see how to create a hockey stick for exponential change.'"

As visitors increasingly came to Uganda to see the results of Sapra's focus, it became clearer that UNICEF should take a more structured approach to innovation. In 2015 it formed the Global Innovation Center (GIC), which Accone now heads. The GIC is a globally connected team that is part of UNICEF's Office of Innovation. The GIC helps to identify and scale promising in-market developments and to strengthen UNICEF's overall innovation capabilities. For example, in early 2020 it released a turnkey innovation toolkit that leverages the services of the International Development Innovation Alliance (a collaborative platform formed in 2015 with the mission of "actively promoting and advancing innovation as a means to help achieve sustainable development"). The toolkit also provides expertise on demand, which can help in-market innovators to shape and scale their ideas both for their own market and, eventually, for others.

The GIC complements other UNICEF innovation enablers. A team in San Francisco, for example, works with startups and venture capitalists to help identify promising technologies that could help UNICEF deliver against its mission. Another team in New York acts more like a venture capitalist, giving grants to startup companies to help them further develop their ideas and execute in-market pilots that fit UNICEF's mission, such as drone-based delivery of medicines in rural areas. Other groups develop innovative approaches to fundraising (clearly core to UNICEF's mission) and supply-chain management.[3] UNICEF firmly believes it is at its best when it collaborates actively with its ecosystem, where it seeks to "maximize shared-value partnerships with businesses while leveraging our core assets."

Accone's group has a global advisory committee that permanently includes its donors (the Government of the Republic of Korea; the Philips

---

3. Fun fact: UNICEF is the world's largest purchaser of pencils and vaccines!

Foundation; and the UNICEF National Committees of Canada, the United Kingdom, and the United States) as well as handpicked subject-matter experts, depending on the location and topic of a meeting. UNICEF's convening power allows it to access leading experts, and its innovation infrastructure helps to ensure expertise flows to the right locations.

UNICEF's innovation infrastructure is intentionally staffed with people who have diverse backgrounds. Of course, team members need to have experience in developing economies, but they mix relevant skills for their respective roles with new-to-UNICEF capabilities, such as data analytics, human-centric design, and business modeling.

Accone also noted the importance of having the right mindset. "There is a proverb that you can go fast alone but you can go far together. Our team needs to be humble, have a learner's mind, and professional maturity," she said. "You are going to deal with a range of pushback. You have to be the ultimate professional and take it."

The GIC helps to strengthen in-country execution while also looking for opportunities to refine and scale programs that could work across multiple countries. "We can see actual programmatic problems that are being solved. Is that solution showing potential to be relevant and scalable because it solves the same or similar problems in many places?" Accone said. "What are the few things we put into the portfolio that we will then nurture to scale to dozens of countries?"

The foundational tenets below connect UNICEF's innovation efforts and map very nicely to the behaviors that form the backbone of a culture of innovation.

1.  We speak tech, design, and international development (curiosity and collaboration).

2.  We believe that no one gets there alone (collaboration).

3.  We've been doing this since 2007 and have a proven and ongoing track record of success and failure (adeptness in ambiguity).

4.  We move quickly and take calculated risks on ideas that could change the game for children (empowerment).

5. Our work is driven by children's needs in over 190 countries, especially the most marginalized (customer obsession).

6. We start small but scale proven solutions globally (adeptness in ambiguity).

Of course, driving innovation across a large, dispersed organization presents its challenges. As such, many at UNICEF conflate innovation and technology, (unintentionally) underinvesting in low-technology solutions that could go on to create tremendous value. In early 2020, UNICEF announced a revised innovation strategy with an intent to focus on digital innovations, physical product innovations, innovative financing, and program innovations to advance against identified social goals, such as providing access to clean water and education. There also can be a perception that if you didn't come up with it yourself, it can't be innovative, meaning there can be bias toward being the first country to do something small versus the twenty-third country to do something big. To combat this challenge, as part of its 2020 strategy, UNICEF announced a goal to have 80 percent of its innovation efforts focused on scaling and spreading ideas and 20 percent on ideating and shaping ideas. It also shared an "innovation ambition matrix," which it would use to help categorize and manage the effort, and outlined the criteria it would use to "scrutinize and prioritize" innovation activities.[4]

These systematic and structural upgrades can only help advance UNICEF's innovation efforts, which have already created tremendous value for children and constituencies. As noted in the GIC's 2019 annual report, "Applying a demand-driven, centre-of-excellence model, the GIC has supported 85 countries to identify, adopt and adapt innovative solutions. To date, these new technologies and approaches have affected the lives of 115 million people across these 85 countries: directly used by 18 million young people, frontline workers and women, and bringing indirect benefits to a further 97 million children and their communities."

---

4. The specific criteria set is called "3S MI": 3S refers to the three *S*-words solutionable (solves problems and does no harm), sustainable (has a life cycle and is upgradeable), and scalable (is easy to use and understand). MI stands for measurable (defines milestones and objectives) and inclusive (involves multiple stakeholders).

## Case Study: DBS's Systemic Support

The companion case study to chapter 2 described how DBS fought the shadow strategy and transformed its culture. As we near the end of part II, let's return to DBS to further explore the thorough and thoughtful way in which it has engaged in that fight. Yes, there have been catchy slogans and highly effective BEANs, but DBS has supported those efforts with the following:

CHANGED ITS OFFICE DESIGN. Paul took over the real-estate portfolio in 2013. He admits that he completely underestimated the power of space in driving change. If you think about it, your behavior is heavily influenced by the space around you. For example, you behave differently in a  library than in a supermarket. So DBS started to use the design of space as a powerful tool to encourage cross-team collaboration. DBS's former office design had been based on the longstanding belief that people like to have their own desks, as it gives them a sense of belonging. But its hypothesis for its new space was that to create a sense of belonging, you needed to feel like part of a community—not feel attached to a piece of furniture. And a real community would lend itself to more collaboration. So, DBS designed a new kind of work environment. The resulting space became known as Joy Space, as a nod to DBS's vision of making banking joyful. The space is open-plan with no fixed seating, and zones, ranging from the "Library" to the "Pub," were developed based on type of work. The new space proved to be hugely popular.[5] Team members started to invite colleagues and even families to tour the new space. But most importantly, DBS saw better collaboration across teams. Other

---

5. Joy Space is a BEAN you can borrow and appears in the bag of BEANs in the appendix.

departments began to request similar designs, so DBS began to roll the concept out across the company.

CHANGED ITS PERFORMANCE METRICS. DBS sets the direction of the company through a balanced scorecard. Historically this scorecard was split over two sections: traditional output measures across financials, customers, and employee engagement and a series of the most important initiatives for the given year. Some years ago, DBS introduced a third section, in which it set transformative goals aligned to its 28,000-person startup aspiration. One year, it targeted running 150 customer-journey projects; another year it introduced targets around capturing tangible economic value from its digital transformation; and a third year it focused on making decisions based on data derived from well-designed experiments. These goals get cascaded through the company and are taken very seriously.

CHANGED CONSTRAINING POLICIES. DBS has learned that relaxing policy can be a powerful way to send signals across the company and encourage empowerment. For instance, when it opened its new technology and innovation center in Hyderabad, its dress code policy was "You can wear anything you want, as long as it would not embarrass your parents." The underlying message was "We have guardrails, but you decide." DBS analyzed its corporate purchases and learned that most were for small amounts. Inspired by Netflix's famous "Freedom and Responsibility" culture document that cascaded around the internet in 2009, DBS removed the requirement to get expenses preapproved.

It also developed a new approach to root out processes and policies that might have made sense at some point in history but outgrew their usefulness. DBS set up a special committee named after a self-deprecating Singaporean slang word, *kiasu*, which roughly translates to "behaving in a selfish manner due to fear of  missing out." The head of Legal and Compliance chairs the Kiasu Committee, which takes the form of a mock courtroom where any employee can "sue" the owner of a policy or process that they feel is getting in the way.[6] The "jury" is made up of some senior executives but also some of the most junior people in the bank. They collectively deliberate over whether a change should be made. One of the first decisions was to remove the need for physical signatures for approval. The approach caused quite a ripple through the company and gave DBS employees confidence that their issues would be heard and addressed.

CHANGED ITS ORGANIZATIONAL STRUCTURE. Probably the single biggest advantage that "born digital" companies have is that they recognize technology *is* the business. In contrast, many legacy companies see IT as a necessary but largely unwelcome cost. A 1979 *Harvard Business Review* article, for example, suggested forming a "banking back office" to drive IT efficiencies and allow the "real business" to focus on what mattered: engaging with customers and making money. This shift created unhealthy tensions between revenue-hungry frontline leaders and IT departments charged with injecting huge amounts of software change into ever-increasingly critical systems while still keeping them stable. A master-and-servant relationship evolved, in which the front office held the purse strings and prioritized new revenue-generating functionalities over necessary improvements to stability.

As DBS progressed along its digital transformation journey, the sharp increase in digital interactions challenged the conventional model. System stability, scalability, and security are business issues that require close collaboration between the business and IT functions. After all, if a customer-facing system is down, there is no business at all. It was clear that digital leaders needed the business acumen and tech savviness to be able to make tradeoffs and priorities. DBS set out to solve the problem of fusing the business and tech teams together by creating a new organizational and operating model.

---

6. The Kiasu Committee appears in the bag of BEANs in the appendix. One Innosight team member (who is Singaporean) expressed confusion over the name, however, saying *kiasu* is better used for instances such as when Singaporeans stocked up on instant noodles and toilet paper anytime there was a government announcement about COVID-19 in early 2020. For what it is worth.

After researching how companies like Spotify, ING, and Google operate, DBS landed on a "platform operating model," by which 600 or so applications and their associated teams were logically grouped into 33 "platforms." The groupings were carefully considered, with some aligned to business functions (e.g., lending), others aligned to support functions (e.g., HR, finance), and still others spanning the company (e.g., data and payments). DBS appointed two leaders to each platform: one from business and one from IT. Each platform had a single budget, roadmap, and set of objectives, shared by the joint platform leaders. This change had a profound effect on the relationships between the two departments. Healthy debates about the tradeoffs between new functionalities and stability improvements ensued. And there was an immediate halt to the finger-pointing that typically followed an unplanned IT outage.

CHANGED HOW IT HIRES. The companion case study to chapter 3 described how DBS used BEANs to help to shape the day-to-day culture of its recently opened facility in Hyderabad. Of course, that culture drives the creation of value only with the right people. This presented a challenge, as DBS did not have a visible brand in India, and to make matters worse, the best software engineering talent was opting to work for Google, Apple, or Microsoft, all of whom had centers in Hyderabad. After conventional hiring approaches sputtered, DBS tried something different. DBS, by this time, had firsthand experience with the energy generated by "hackathons," where people would come together for a constrained period of time to crack a tough challenge. So DBS designed a "Hack2Hire" process. The hiring team used digital channels to reach out to a large number of potential candidates across India. Candidates who signed up competed a coding test. DBS invited the best candidates to participate in a forty-eight-hour hackathon in Hyderabad. For the hackathon, participants were put into small teams, and a DBS software engineer was assigned to each. The team picked from a set of challenges and spent forty-eight hours developing working prototypes, which culminated in a pitch session. Candidates that demonstrated the highest level of engineering ability and, more importantly, the ability to be an effective team player under stressful conditions, received a job offer on the spot. The first hackathon attracted 12,000 applicants, from which only 50 hackers were hired. DBS repeated the program several times and adapted it based on specific needs. For example, it held one "Hack2Hire" specifically for female candidates, designed to help address the industry's gender imbalance.

## Tool: Zombie Amnesty

Do you feel like you don't have sufficient resources to take promising ideas forward? It is possible that you have succumbed to a pernicious plague that can kill innovation energy: the plague of the zombie project. Do you have efforts that, if you are honest, will never have material impact but still shuffle and linger on, sucking the innovation energy out of your organization? If so, then a zombie amnesty, where you kill projects but pardon people, may be for you! Innosight's fieldwork and the work of like-minded academics—most notably Rita Gunther McGrath of Columbia University (a certified zombie killer if ever one existed)—suggests six keys to success:

1. *Predetermine criteria.* Shutting a project down can be very emotional. Setting and sharing a shortlist of criteria before the process begins can help participants to view the process as being as rational as possible. These criteria will be guidelines, not rules, as final decisions will always require subjective judgment.

2. *Involve outsiders.* Parents can attest to how hard it is to be objective about something you played a part in conceiving.[7] An uninvolved outsider can bring important impartiality to the process.

3. *Codify reusable learning.* McGrath teaches that any time a company innovates, two good things can happen. Successfully commercializing an idea is clearly a good outcome. So too, however, is learning something that sets you up for future success. As seminal research into product failure notes, "knowledge gained from failures [is] often instrumental in achieving subsequent successes."

---

7. For example, Scott will attest his four kids are the cutest kids in the world. An outsider might point out flaws in Happy Harry. They would be wrong, of course.

So capture knowledge to maximize the return on your investments in innovation.

4.  *Celebrate success.* Any time you innovate, future success is un-known. Therefore, learning that an idea is not viable is a success-ful outcome—as long as that learning happened in a reasonably resource-efficient way. Prospect theory holds that people hate losses more than they enjoy equivalent gains. Add this to a culture in which taking well-thought-out risks carries the potential for punishment, and it is no surprise that people hesitate to take risks.

5.  *Communicate widely.* Innovation happens most naturally at com-panies that "dare to try," a conscious reference to the BEAN at Tata that celebrates failed projects (see chapter 3). Shining a spotlight on purged zombies naturally makes it safer for people to push the innovation boundaries.[8] After all, if you don't dare to try, how can you hope to succeed?

6.  *Provide closure.* This idea is ripped straight from McGrath's excellent 2011 *Harvard Business Review* article "Failing by De-sign": "Have a symbolic event—a wake, a play, a memorial—to give people closure." Without closure, it is too easy for someone, somewhere to revive the zombie. The Supercell Cheers to Failure BEAN (see chapter 7) fits perfectly here.

Our experience is that, typically, almost 50 percent of a company's in-novation portfolio can be safely killed. Find and put the zombies down, reallocate resources to your most promising projects, and you will sud-denly see your innovation efforts become bigger, better, and faster.

---

8. On the phrases "zombie killer" and "purged zombies," one organization that Innosight worked with preferred to talk about transforming zombies into angels. It certainly sounds more pleasant than purging or killing zombies! We do purposefully call this a zombie amnesty to highlight the fact that the *people* working on zombie projects should be safe from punishment.

# Starting a Movement

Picture the scene: A jerky video shows a grassy hill at what appears to be a music festival. You can't see a band, but you can hear the rhythmic beat of music. On this grassy hill stands a man. He starts dancing without a care in the world. Those around him sit passively on rugs. Before long, someone stands up and joins the dancing man. This person is the first follower willing to brave ridicule, and he transforms this dancing man, this "lone nut," into a leader. A second follower joins. A small crowd forms. A crowd is news, so two more people join, and then three more. Momentum builds. And then in the blink of an eye, this small group of dancers has become a crowd of close to a hundred enthusiastic dancers, reveling in the spontaneity of their collective efforts. It is a movement, as eloquently described by Derek Sivers in a 2010 TED Talk.

Culture change in organizations that consist of tens of thousands of employees cannot be mandated. A top-down directive is insufficient. Organizational culture change requires a movement that goes beyond a "lone nut." It requires followers fed by behavior enablers, artifacts, and nudges (BEANs), boosted by appropriate programs, systems, and structures, and led thoroughly and carefully.

*Eat, Sleep, Innovate*'s conclusion provides cross-cutting lessons from the NO-DETs (normal organizations doing extraordinary things) profiled here before ending with a call to action from each of the four authors.

## Lessons from NO-DETs

DBS, The Salvation Army's Eastern Territory, Intuit, the UK Joint Forces Command, Microsoft, P&G, the Settlement Music School, Singtel, and UNICEF are very different organizations. They are in different sectors, headquartered in different locations, and organized in fundamentally different ways. Their culture-change efforts focused on different levels of the organization and progressed at different paces. But despite their disparity, there are six clear commonalities.

### Lesson 1: Innovation Can Happen Anywhere

Remember our definition of innovation? Something different that creates value. The intentional vagueness of the word "something" is a reminder that innovation can happen anywhere. DBS, The Salvation Army, and UNICEF clearly show this in action. Yes, DBS has introduced bold new products, such as the digital bank that has allowed it to enter new markets, but innovation has also helped it solve day-to-day problems, such as shortening ATM lines and helping customers who have lost cards. The dispersed nature of UNICEF and The Salvation Army's Eastern Territory and the close connection to end markets has helped both to drive improvements ranging from mobile coffee dispensers to communications tools to use during disasters. So remember, no matter where you are or what you, do there is room for you to innovate!

### Lesson 2: Innovation DOES Happen Everywhere

Every organization has at least some pockets of innovation. Following Steve Bussey's cooking analogy from the case study that followed chapter 1, every organization has some intuitive "innovation chefs." Organizations that desire to build a culture of innovation should follow the lead of The Salvation Army's Eastern Territory and ask themselves, "What is working?," "What's possible?," and "How do we do it better?," rather than "What's wrong?" and "How do we fix it?" These questions are based on appreciative inquiry, an approach aimed at encouraging and motivating change by focusing on positive experiences. A metaphor for appreciative inquiry is that organizations are "mysteries to be embraced" rather than "problems to be solved." Research shows that following appreciative inquiry leads people to have more confidence and comfort in journeying to the unknown future by carrying forward parts of the past. So follow the light and find ways to make it shine more brightly.

## Lesson 3: Incumbency Has Its Advantages

Where is the best home for someone who wants to innovate for impact? Ask most groups that question, and the typical response is a startup company. It is easy to get entranced by enthralling stories of legendary entrepreneurs who hustle and scrape to create world-changing enterprises. It is also easy to forget that these stories are extremely rare exceptions. The overwhelming majority of startup companies fail, even with smart, dedicated people pouring every ounce of effort into building the business. The NO-DETs are far from scrappy garage-based startups. They show, however, that incumbency has its advantages. Today, entrepreneurs can start a business spending basically nothing. But that means those businesses can be immediately copied, making success brutally difficult. The good news is, innovators inside large companies can access the same tools as entrepreneurs. They can combine those tools with hard-earned assets of scale. And that combination can be absolutely magical.[1]

## Lesson 4: Culture Change Takes Time

Scott Cook from Intuit would say that Intuit's change has been a decade in the making; Satya Nadella from Microsoft says culture change is never done. An organization's culture is complicated, and purposefully

---

1. This was the thesis of Scott's 2012 *Harvard Business Review* article "The New Corporate Garage," which profiled Nick Musyoka (from chapter 6) and other "corporate catalysts."

changing that culture takes time. While every culture-change movement follows its own unique rhythm, it is helpful to consider the following general steps:

1. *Define the desired culture.* Create an evocative story and detail specific behaviors that define the "tomorrow culture."

2. *Diagnose key blockers.* Zero in on the systems, behaviors, and norms that power the shadow strategy and stand in the way of success.

3. *Implement BEANs.* Drive habit change with well thought out behavior enablers, artifacts, and nudges.

4. *Hardwire supporting systems.* Reinforce the desired behaviors in formal systems (e.g., KPIs, budgets) and key processes (e.g. recruiting, training).

5. *Role-model the desired behaviors.* Have leaders show the way, particularly during highly visible moments like project-review meetings.

6. *Track and measure progress.* Use data to iterate toward the desired future state of culture.

This is hard work. Clever campaigns or snappy slogans have no impact without hard work to shape day-to-day behaviors, change the underlying environment, celebrate success stories, carefully handle failures along the way, and more.

## Lesson 5: Use Specific Language

Clarity in language is a step that is often skipped in change efforts. That's a problem, as a lack of common language can kill well-intentioned change efforts. People *think* that because they have picked a default language for meeting, whether it be English, Mandarin, Tagalog, or a particular regional dialect, they all understand each other. But often, people ascribe different meanings to the specific words they use, which means they end up talking past each other. For example, a cynic would view the phrase "culture of innovation" as a meaningless combination of business buzzwords strung together to cover the fact that the speaker *wants* to sound smart but doesn't actually have anything to offer to the conversation. And there's some truth to that. Don't believe us? Next time you hear someone say "culture of innovation" in a meeting, stop the meeting. Ask everyone to take out a pen and paper and silently write down what "culture" and "innovation" both mean. We are willing to bet the price of this book that there will be substantial deviations in even very small teams that work together closely. Those two words are used frequently but rarely defined clearly; and the problem is compounded when they are combined. Whether you use the definitions in this book or definitions derived from elsewhere is irrelevant. What is relevant is to make sure you and your team use the same words and think the same thing when you say them. Get specific. Here is one way to test the specificity and clarity of your thinking. Imagine you are going to announce your culture change agenda. Think about how you will answer the following questions:

- To what? What are the specific behaviors that will characterize the tomorrow culture?

- Why haven't we already done this? What blockers need to be addressed that we haven't addressed?

- By whom? What are the specific resources that will head up the culture-change effort?

- How are we going to do it? What is our culture-change plan? What time and additional resources are behind it?

If your leadership team answers these questions differently, keep working until you have a clear, consistent view. Then think about a simple catch phrase that captures the essence of your efforts. Can you come up with (or borrow!) something as memorable as "28,000-person startup," "consumer is boss," and "learn-it-all?"

## Lesson 6: Leaders Need to Lead, but Carefully

It is no accident that senior titles appear frequently in our stories. Culture change that sticks and scales requires active participation from senior leaders. P&G's consumer-is-boss movement, for example, would likely fail if not for CEO A. G. Lafley's stump speech and in-the-field role-modeling. Intuit's design thinking movement fails too without Scott Cook's carefully considered interventions. Settlement Music School doesn't boldly embrace the idea of using music education to combat poverty without Helen Eaton's leadership. Culture change can be localized, of course. A team, group, or department, such as the Singtel HR community, can have its own identifiable culture, which differs in significant ways from the overall organizational culture. Nonetheless, the leader of the locus of change needs to be willing to commit the time and energy to drive cultural transformation.

## Starting a Movement: Our Parting Thoughts

While we've written this work using the royal "we," the four authors are, of course, distinct individuals with their own perspectives on the topics. So, to end *Eat, Sleep, Innovate,* "we" will give way to "I," as each of us provides our parting thoughts about how to spark a culture-change movement.[2]

## Scott's Parting Thoughts

The writing of this book started with a 2019 experiment we did with *Harvard Business Review* called IdeaLab. As the name connotes, the intent was to create a laboratory for an idea. We had been thinking about how to purposefully shape a culture of innovation for some time, and the IdeaLab provided the opportunity to get a curated community to

---

2. If you are still with us, stick around for the appendix. There are more good things in there!

react to and strengthen what was essentially the alpha version of this book. So I thought it fitting to have my call to action come from my IdeaLab post from March 28, 2019, which follows (with slight alterations and additional footnotes).

\* \* \*

All good things must come to an end. This is the last post that I, on behalf of a team that has included Innosight colleagues Rahul Nair,[3] Cathy Olofson, Natalie Painchaud, Andy Parker, Elliot Tan,[4] TY Tang, and DBS friend Paul Cobban, will introduce to the culture of innovation IdeaLab.

It has been a fun journey. As an artifact memorializing it, we have created a short document of "postcards" from the IdeaLab, including a few summary slides from our culture of innovation toolkit and a single page with links to each of our posts. Feel free to use the images in presentations and share profligately.[5]

Way back in mid-February[6] I described how my Happy Harry got slapped on the wrist by our condo association in Singapore after expressing himself creatively. Harry is one of my four children. Our oldest son Charlie is thirteen and, this week, is

*Bring back Happy Harry!*

representing Singapore in a big regional baseball tournament (Dad is serving as an assistant coach).[7] Holly is eleven, currently doing an end-of-term research project on how video games affect the brain (when I

---

3. We miss you, Rahul!

4. We miss you, Elliot!

5. The postcards can be accessed at https://innosight.app.box.com/v/COIPostcards.

6. This is chapter 2 of this book—which maybe you, dear reader, read in February?

7. The team lost a tough game to Perth, which took them out of the running for the championship, and ended up losing the third-place game against a scrappy Doha squad. Why Doha, who flew almost 4,000 miles to get to Singapore, was in a "regional" tournament is a different discussion topic.

was eleven, my brain was being affected by video games without my asking any questions about it!). Happy Harry is seven, and, if we're honest, he does whine on occasion, but he also brings glorious curiosity and creativity to everything he does. And our little two-year-old Teddy just is a babbling brook of cuteness.[8]

The parallel experience of watching my children grow up while I have advised large organizations around the globe on how to confront the dilemmas of disruption has crystallized a belief within me, turning it into a conviction. The world's biggest untapped source of energy isn't in the wind, water, or sun. It's inside established organizations. These organizations—companies, governments, hospitals, schools, and more—are populated with people who, like all people, entered the world naturally curious and creative. That curiosity and creativity has been blunted and constrained, but it is there. And organizations are only scratching the surface of their innovation potential.

My job as a father is to make sure my children never lose their love of learning. My job as an adviser to organizations is to help them release, harness, and amplify this same kind of latent energy. Imagine a world where the Curious Charlies, Hopeful Hollys, Happy Harrys, and Thoughtful Teddys break free of their shackles. Imagine a world where your employees show up to work every day in an environment where people feel like they are doing more than they thought possible. Imagine they go home with a spring in their step and the feeling that they have the best of both worlds.[9] They can fuse the unique assets their organizations have built over decades—or, in some cases, centuries— together with the entrepreneurial energy that emboldens would-be disruptors around the world, and in doing so they can have a massive impact on the problems that matter to them. That world is different and better than today's world. And it is within our grasp.

8. A note on Teddy. His obsession in February 2020 was the traditional lion dances done to celebrate the Chinese New Year. The best $30 his parents ever spent got him a lion-dance costume. Much hilarity ensued.

9. Whether, it must be noted, in a post-COVID world, going home is a physical or virtual act.

Good luck to each of you in your respective efforts to help the organizations that matter to you develop cultures in which the behaviors that drive innovation success come naturally.

## Paul's Parting Thoughts

Many factors have contributed to the successful transformation at DBS, not least of which has been the sustained supportive leadership of our CEO and executive team, and an enthusiastic workforce. However, it has been our sustained programmatic and inclusive approach that has set us apart from other transformations. Despite a widely held belief that bankers do not make good innovators, we made an early decision to bring all our people along for the journey, because we needed everyone to become an innovator if we were to realize our ambitions. We did set up a small innovation team but, as you have read, we gave the team instructions not to innovate. The team's role was, and continues to be, to teach the rest of the company to innovate. Over the past ten years, we have executed a series of innovation programs, each building on the success of the previous one. Our key lesson was that, by creating a low barrier to participation, we saw our people grow in confidence, and they delivered results at scale. As Steve Jobs said, you "can only join the dots by looking back" and it was through reflection that we understood that we had unconsciously been creating counter-measures to some of our most persistent cultural blockers—interventions we would later call BEANs—and they were driving the behavioral shifts that were moving us steadily toward a culture of innovation. In working with my coauthors, we realized that BEANs were helping to "shrink the challenge" into micro shifts of change. The thoughtful introduction of BEANs into our way of working has fundamentally changed our approach to innovation and beyond.

As you embark on your own transformation journeys, remember that nothing will change unless the behavior of your people changes. Vision statements, knowledge, and logical arguments are not enough, yet we see many companies expecting people to be motivated into action based on leadership rhetoric alone. I would encourage you to embrace the ideas in this book to build creative confidence in your people and to gradually shift to the new behaviors required to unleash innovation throughout your company. Most people agree with Peter Drucker that "culture eats strategy for breakfast," but very few companies have figured out how to systematically change a culture. This book sets out a powerful and proven approach. Just add tenacity, adaptability, and enthusiasm, and you, too, can succeed.

## Natalie's Parting Thoughts

I have the distinct privilege to both advise clients (including Patsy Quek from Paul's team at DBS) and to be responsible for implementing culture initiatives at Innosight (with chief talent officer Kady O'Grady's unwavering support and openness to new ideas). Because of my dual role, I have a deep sense of empathy for how much work it is to shift a culture. I continue to be impressed on a daily basis by how inspirational my colleagues and clients are and how many ideas they have. That said, they do cautiously hold back these ideas. This is where unleashing innovation and coaching comes in to set goals, identify what's getting in the way—real or imagined—and put a plan into action. I am excited for people to get started on this work to unleash innovation in themselves, their teams, and their organizations. And I bet you have done more than you give yourself credit for. This is what my colleague Annie Garofalo and I discovered about most people when we captured the innovation stories of The Salvation Army Eastern Territory and the Innovation Factory.

So my advice is to take stock of what you've done and give yourself credit. Get started with the practical advice in this book, whether it is a BEANstorming session or even something smaller. Immerse yourself, bring others along with you, and have fun. This is important and highly enjoyable work that positively impacts how you and your colleagues spend your days together. It is estimated we spend 90,000 hours over the course of our lifetime at work, so why not make the most of them?

## Andy's Parting Thoughts

I have been fortunate in my career to have spent a significant time working on every continent except for Antarctica. I have also been fortunate on these travels to serve clients across myriad industries. The human connections this has afforded me, and the exposure to different organizations and their cultures, has been a great source of professional energy. Contributing to this book has prompted me to consider what a culture of innovation really feels like and to reflect on the different organizational cultures my travels have allowed me to experience. Above all, I have seen that the behaviors we outline in this book are universally applicable—across geographies, industries, and types of organizations. I have seen that the approaches described in this book really do enable high-performing teams to deliver better outcomes in all corners of the world, including the corner I currently call home—Singapore. My primary contribution to this book has been to summarize the work Scott and I undertook for Innosight's Singapore-based client, the Singtel Group. That effort helped me to understand that a culture of innovation is not verbiage we use to describe ourselves, our department, or our institution, but it is, more fundamentally, the way we get things done every day and the reasons we choose to do them that way.

Creating a culture of innovation does not have to be an aspirational and esoteric thing; it is eminently practical. I encourage anyone with a passion for improving the way your institution creates value to take a practical approach and start by removing culture blockers. If you start with blockers, the people around you will more readily agree they exist and, more than that, will thank you for removing them! Start by identifying the top two or three culture blockers in your team or department and design practical ways to remove them using BEANs, as described in these chapters. Don't stop there. Make sure you go further to engage colleagues to create, test, and refine your BEANs using the tools in this book. And remember, by engaging your colleagues, you will flush out those first followers who will transform you from a lone nut into the leader of a culture movement that will make creativity an everyday habit in your organization. Once you have had some success removing blockers, turn your attention to BEANs that encourage the specific be-haviors you believe will have the greatest impact in your organization. This will ensure your movement gets momentum. And who knows? One day you may end up the hero of a culture change story that others will readily study and write books about, as we have done here with Paul and DBS. Good luck to all the lone nuts. But, remember, it is the first followers who create a movement, and that is a role everyone, in all organizations, should aspire to take on.

# Appendix

*Eat, Sleep, Innovate*'s appendix provides the following reference materials and tools:

- *Culture of Innovation Bookshelf:* Indispensable sources for learning more about creating a culture in which the behaviors that drive innovation success come naturally

- *Culture Change Literature Review:* A summary of our study of recent research and writing about culture change

- *Culture of Innovation Diagnostic:* A detailed diagnostic to help you assess the degree to which your organization has a culture of innovation

- *What's the Status of Your Innovation Relationship?:* A quick diagnostic to assess the degree to which your organization is committed to innovation

- *Bag of 101 BEANs:* Brief descriptions of 101 BEANs, including the 42 that appeared in the main part of this book along with 59 additional ones

## Culture of Innovation Bookshelf

The following "bookshelf" contains the authors' favorite literature related to the topics in *Eat, Sleep, Innovate*.

### Innovation

*Innovation and Entrepreneurship* by Peter Drucker (1985). Rereading Drucker is always amazing. He was way ahead of his time.

*The Four Steps to the Epiphany* by Steven Gary Blank (2005). Not as widely known as Eric Ries's 2011 book *The Lean Startup*, but Blank served as Ries's mentor and serves as the originator of the translation of academic research by Rita McGrath, Henry Mintzberg, and others into the world of startups.

*Change by Design* by Tim Brown (2009). A very useful overview of the principles and practices of design thinking by IDEO's longtime CEO.

*Business Model Generation* by Alexander Osterwalder and Yves Pigneur (2010). A practical, visual guide to business models and a great companion to *Reinvent Your Business Model* by Innosight's Mark Johnson (2018).

*How Will You Measure Your Life?* by Clayton Christensen et al. (2012). Clearly, many Christensen books could make this list, but this is the most accessible guide to his core research.

*Seeing Around Corners* by Rita McGrath (2019). Many McGrath books and articles could make this list as well. This is her most recent feature-length book and provides a good overview of her other work.

### Behavior Change

*The Power of Full Engagement* by Jim Loehr and Tony Schwartz (2003). This book showcases the concept that, by focusing on energy and not on time, one can achieve peak performance and get more done by doing less.

*Mindset* by Carol Dweck (2006). Dweck's research and cogent writing on fixed-versus-growth mindsets has influenced everything from organizational design to school curriculums.

*Nudge* by Richard H. Thaler and Cass R. Sunstein (2007). This book is academically rich while also driving real practical impact; it helped, for instance, to inform the formation of the "nudge unit" (formally known as the Behavioural Insights Team) in the UK government.

*Switch* by Chip and Dan Heath (2010). Like all the books by the Heath brothers, this is very accessible, providing a practical guide to behavior change.

*Thinking, Fast and Slow* by Daniel Kahneman (2011). The seminal work by the person who many consider the intellectual founder of behavioral psychology.

## Culture

*Organizational Culture and Leadership* by Edgar H. Schein (first published in 1985). Schein's work—particularly that on breaking culture down into artifacts, espoused values, and shared assumptions—has defined the field for two generations.

*Change the Culture, Change the Game* by Roger Connors and Tom Smith (2011). This book details how organizations can build and then sustain a new culture by fostering accountability across all levels and by considering the relationships between experiences, beliefs, actions, and results.

*Collective Genius* by Linda A. Hill, Greg Brandeau, Emily Truelove, and Kent Lineback (2014). A powerful book that details how "creative abrasion" can unleash innovation.

*Creativity, Inc.* by Ed Catmull with Amy Wallace (2014). The Pixar story told in this book is compelling and serves as a practical guide to creating a culture that spurs creativity.

*The Fearless Organization* by Amy Edmondson (2018). This is a great book that showcases how psychological safety encourages risk-taking and innovation.

## Organizational Capabilities

*Out of the Crisis* by W. Edwards Deming (1982). A timeless classic that shaped the quality movement, which informed agile development, the lean startup, and more.

*Managing to Learn* by John Shook (2008). One of Paul's nominees, this book goes deep into "A3 thinking," one of the pillars of lean management. Paul's review: "Amazing."

*Building a Growth Factory* by Scott D. Anthony and David S. Duncan (2012). This is the shortest of the eleven books written by members of Innosight's leadership team, and, dare we say, the dullest. But it provides (in our view!) a clear, cogent overview of how to think systematically about innovation.

*Scaling Up Excellence* by Robert Sutton and Huggy Rao (2014). A useful, scientifically grounded guide to what it takes to scale and spread good ideas in established organizations.

*Measuring What Matters* by John Doerr (2018). This recent book is an accessible guide to the ideas that longtime Intel CEO detailed in the classic book *High Output Management*, most notably the power of OKRs (objectives and key results).

## Culture Change Literature Review

There is no shortage of advice for the culture-change-seeking leader. The word cloud that follows (shaped like a butterfly to indicate "change") resulted from an Innosight team analyzing twenty-two articles on culture change. The articles were published between 2014 and 2019 in the *Harvard Business Review*, the *Sloan Management Review*, and the *McKinsey Quarterly*, and in literature by design consulting company IDEO. Ten of the articles had some variant of the word "innovation" in the title. Ten themes appeared across multiple articles and stand as reasonable principles for driving culture change:

**Culture change literature review word cloud.**

1. *Align strategy with culture:* Too often a company's strategy is at odds with the ingrained practices and attitudes of its culture. A strategy's effectiveness depends on cultural alignment, and leaders must clearly connect their desired culture with their strategy and business objectives.

2. *Communicate effectively:* Leaders must make sure the target culture is clearly articulated and communicated throughout the organization. Effective communication links to challenges that matter with employees and provides opportunities to help people better understand and connect to the change imperative.

3. *Secure buy-in:* Culture change requires strong senior-leadership support. Unless there is vocal and consistent support from the top of the company, managers tend to default to doing what is easy, which is to keep doing what they are currently doing.

4. *Focus on the customer:* Leaders should remain customer-centric and put the customer's point of view among their top considerations.

Customer needs should be understood at the outset and their feedback sought continually.

5. *Value teamwork and openness:* Today's problems are far too complex to be solved by a lone genius working in isolation and require people who can collaborate, listen, and build strong networks. Unnecessarily narrowing the backgrounds, experiences, and outlooks of the people on a team limits the solution space and risks creating an echo chamber that normalizes and reinforces inherent biases. Unvarnished candor ensures that ideas evolve and improve. If people are afraid to criticize, openly challenge superiors' views, debate the ideas of others, and raise counter-perspectives, change can be crushed.

6. *Encourage experimentation:* Culture change struggles in a risk-averse environment that punishes failure. Small experiments that allow people to fail quickly and cheaply and to share their learning helps accelerate change.

7. *Give people autonomy:* While senior leaders can set a broad direction for employees to set their sights on, they must provide autonomy to enable those deeper in the organization to localize the culture change to their specific context.

8. *Walk the talk:* Leaders should make sure they are setting the kind of behavioral example they want the organization to emulate. In particular, they should show a sense of inquiry and curiosity, in which they accept new ideas and avoid being dismissive of change.

9. *Celebrate quick wins:* The easiest way to quash criticism is to demonstrate success. Quick wins build momentum for broader change.

10. *Measure and monitor:* Culture is ephemeral enough to begin with. Finding ways to measure and monitor change helps employees understand how their contributions are being evaluated, developed, or deployed. This encourages accountability at all levels.

# Culture of Innovation Diagnostic

Are your Happy Harrys fearful of expressing themselves? Have they broken through their individual shackles but lack the skills to successfully innovate? Or is there yet another barrier standing in the way of creating a culture where the behaviors that drive innovation success come naturally? The culture of innovation diagnostic goes through five areas to help you answer these questions.

## 1. Perceptions

The perception battery has twelve items:

1. I feel confident that I understand how to innovate.

2. Our leaders regularly "act as innovators."

3. I believe that our organization truly puts the customer first when making strategic decisions.

4. We are expected to voice our opinions.

5. We are empowered to make decisions.

6. I feel that teams take ownership of their actions.

7. Decision-making in our organization is guided by data.

8. Our organization makes it "safe" to take well-thought-out risks, even if we might fail.

9. I am confident that the ideas I work on will move forward and help the organization.

10. I get energized and excited by being in this organization.

11. When I think about innovation, I get energized and excited.

12. I am allowed to be creative with a job I have to accomplish.

Respondents are given seven answer choices for the above questions:

- Completely disagree (1 point)

- Mostly disagree (2 points)

- Somewhat disagree (3 points)

- Neither agree nor disagree (4 points)

- Somewhat agree (5 points)

- Mostly agree (6 points)

- Completely agree (7 points)

The total score for this section ranges from 12 to 84.

## 2. Proficiencies

This battery asks respondents about the degree to which they individually possess fourteen specific skills that help to drive innovation success.

1. Ethnographic research (the process of spending time in the field to develop a rich, nuanced understanding of customers and stakeholders)

2. Ideation (developing innovative ideas to address identified problems)

3. User experience design (designing products and services in ways that help prospective customers adopt and use them)

4. Business and technology scouting (looking externally to identify interesting companies or technological developments before they become mainstream)

5. Business model design (developing ways to support compelling products with methods for delivering and capturing value at scale)

6. Entrepreneurial finance (capably using mechanisms, such as Eric Ries's idea of "innovation accounting" or Rita McGrath's

concept of "reverse income statements," to gain financial insight into early-stage ideas without getting lost in overly detailed, and surely incorrect, financial forecasts)

7. Assumption identification (being able to separate out the few things you truly know about an idea from the greater number of explicit and implicit assumptions you have about it)

8. Data analytics (designing, executing, and interpreting numerical analyses to inform strategic decisions)

9. Prototyping (creating a "good enough" version of an idea; this could be a physical prototype of a product, a mockup of a digital service, or a test market of a business model)

10. Experiment design and execution (designing and executing robust tests to learn about critical assumptions)

11. Summarizing and acting on learning from experiments (comparing results of tests against initial hypotheses and determining whether to keep exploring, change course, or stop the effort)

12. Pitching ideas (summarizing and sharing an innovative idea in a way that quickly captures its essence and motivates action)

13. Launching ideas (moving from testing and prototyping to implementation)

14. Scaling ideas (creating a robust, repeatable idea that delivers sustainable value)

For more information on these skills, see *The First Mile*, *The Lean Startup*, *Discovery-Driven Growth*, and *The Innovator's DNA*.

Respondents are given four answer choices to use for the questions above:

- Not aware of the skill (0 points)

- Can describe what the skill is (3 points)

- Can do it on my own (4.5 points)

- Can teach others how to do it (5 points)

The total score for this section ranges from 0 to 70.

## 3. Practices

This section asks respondents about the last time they engaged in twelve specific innovation practices.

1. Spent time with a customer (external or internal) without a formal agenda to better understand "what makes them tick"

2. Went to an external trade show or conference

3. Visited a startup

4. Had a supplier, customer, or partner share an innovative idea with them

5. Shared a rough idea for a new product, service, or process/internal improvement with a work colleague

6. Talked to someone at their organization about their interesting habit or background

7. Worked on a cross-functional project team with colleagues outside of their function, division, or geography

8. Used an innovative product or service launched by a competitor

9. Ran an experiment at work

10. Received praise for taking a risk at work

11. Read a book, watched a movie/video, or listened to a podcast to learn more about innovation

12. Had hands-on experience designing or launching a new product, service, or process/internal improvement

Respondents are given four answer choices:

- Never (0 points)

- At some point in my life (3 points)

- Within the last year (4 points)

- Within the last month (5 points)

The total score for this section ranges from 0 to 60.

## 4. Enablers

This section asks respondents about their work experiences to gauge the presence of fifteen specific innovation enablers.

1. I have a clear understanding of my organization's vision.

2. I know how my role helps achieve my organization's vision.

3. I have a clear understanding of how my work impacts the business functions and customers.

4. We have a common understanding of what we mean by "innovation" in this organization.

5. There are formal structures or groups in my organization to help identify new ideas and develop solutions.

6. I have a clear understanding of why innovation ideas are accepted or rejected by leaders.

7. I can get the resources I need to innovate.

8. I have sufficient time and space on my calendar to innovate.

9. The way in which I am appraised (e.g., KPIs) supports the vision and culture we want to create.

10. I can easily access tools to help with experimentation and innovation.

11. We have good tools to assess the value of, and make decisions about, uncertain ideas.

12. We have a formal mechanism that seeks to extract lessons from failures.

13. I know where to find support and coaching to help with innovation-related activities.

14. I have a clear understanding of the reporting structures in my organization.

15. Our office space and environment is conducive to collaboration.

The answer choices are the same as those in the perceptions section. The total score for this section ranges from 15 to 105.

## 5. Innovation Performance

The section asks five questions about the degree to which a company's innovation efforts are creating value.

1. We are better than our industry peers at driving growth through innovation.

2. We are a global leader (across industries) at driving growth through innovation.

3. We are responding to marketplace changes faster than our competition.

4. Our innovation efforts are delivering meaningful commercial results.

5. We are ahead of our peers at driving transformation.

The answer choices are the same as those in the perceptions section. The total score for this section ranges from 5 to 25.

## Calculating the Culture of Innovation Score

Our culture of innovation score gives equal weight to perception, skills, behaviors, and enablers. Performance is not part of the score. To calculate the score, we divide each section by its maximum score, and multiply by 25. See the table below for an example calculation.

| | Section score | Max section score | Percent of max score | Weighted score (out of 25) |
|---|---|---|---|---|
| **Perception** | 50 | 84 | 59.5% | 14.9 |
| **Proficiencies** | 35.5 | 70 | 50.7% | 12.7 |
| **Practices** | 49 | 60 | 81.7% | 20.4 |
| **Enablers** | 48 | 105 | 45.7% | 11.4 |

The resulting score in this case is a 59.4 out of 100.

The full survey also asks basic demographic questions around an individual's geographic base and job role. Adding on customized choices, such as a division or home office, allows an analysis of how culture-of-innovation scores vary across an organization.

The survey is available on this book's companion website (www.eatsleepinnovate.com). Fill it in yourself to get an individual score. Send it to a few of your colleagues. If you can get ten or more people to take the survey (and you contact us to let us know), we'll send you a customized report showing how your organization scored.

The culture of innovation diagnostic is still an emergent instrument and not the result of rigorous academic research. As such, the results, particularly if the survey is self-administered, should be viewed as directional and illustrative.

## What's the Status of Your Innovation Relationship?

The culture of innovation diagnostic is a serious instrument. And innovation—something different that creates value—requires a serious ongoing commitment. But many leaders who think they are seriously committed to innovation are really just flirting with it. There's nothing wrong with flirting—or even with taking the next step and having an innovation fling—as long as leaders recognize that they aren't likely to get significant returns without making a more serious commitment.

Unfortunately, because innovation is so frequently confused with creativity or the generation of ideas, many companies dramatically overestimate their commitment to innovation. That leads to disappointment when creative ideas don't translate into impact. The short quiz below, inspired by the somewhat tongue-in-cheek quizzes that populate fashion magazines, is a simple way to assess your organization's commitment level to innovation.

|  | Flirting | A Fling | Committed |
| --- | --- | --- | --- |
| **Who is working on innovation?** | What's innovation? (If this is your answer, you might want to stop the quiz now!) | Some people spend bounded time on innovation (like on Free Thinking Fridays). | We have dedicated resources who eat and sleep innovation. |
| **What are the backgrounds of the people working on it?** | Some of our best performers. | Internal employees who have demonstrated a history of successful innovation. | A blend of internal talent and external hires who have a proven track record. |
| **What are they working on?** | Nothing specific—it takes a thousand flowers, right? | All hands are on deck for a single make-or-break "bet the company" initiative. | We have a portfolio of efforts ranging from day-to-day improvements to more strategic opportunities. |
| **Where does the money come from?** | Our budget is focused on operating priorities, so there isn't any money for it. | We don't have a budget for innovation, but we find money when we need it. | We have a dedicated budget for innovation. |
| **What's in it for them?** | Suffering—it's their job. If they screw up, they'll feel it. | Glory—the spotlight shines bright when they succeed. | Riches—we have specific incentive programs for innovation. |

| What is leadership's role? | Get out of the way—we don't want to constrain it. | We have a special quarterly meeting where senior leaders talk about it. | We have a member of the executive committee or board who owns it. |
|---|---|---|---|
| **Word association: "Innovation is . . ."** | Random! We just hope for the best. | Fun! We support it but don't constrain it. | A discipline! We approach it systematically. |

Give yourself a point for every answer in the left column, three points for every answer in the middle column, and five for every answer in the right column. Use your total score find where you stand on the scale below.

- *Fewer than 10 points:* You tease! You are still just flirting with innovation.

- *Between 10 and 25 points:* All right, you've had your innovation fling. Are you ready to get serious?

- *More than 26 points:* Congratulations! You have made the lifelong commitment to innovation.

# Bag of 101 BEANs

BEANs are behavior enablers, artifacts, and nudges that hack habits, encourage innovative ways of working, and drive cultural change that sticks and scales. This book included detailed writeups of these forty-two BEANs.

| Organization and BEAN name | Description |
|---|---|
| **Adobe—Kickbox (chapter 3)** | A physical box with step-by-step experiment guides and a prepaid $1,000 debit card |
| **Airbnb—Live from Day 1 (chapter 7)** | Direct encouragement to push code to the website on a coder's first day |
| **Amazon.com—Empty Chair (chapter 6)** | The ritual of leaving an empty chair to remind meeting participants of the importance of the customer |

| | |
|---|---|
| **Amazon.com—Future Press Release (chapter 3)** | The practice of describing ideas via "future press releases" from a customer perspective |
| **Asana—No Meeting Wednesday (chapter 8)** | Guidelines to have one day a week where employees can do "deep work" |
| **Atlassian—Premortem (chapter 7)** | Team discussions over what factors could lead projects to fail, helping them to anticipate issues before they happen |
| **BNP Paribas—Innovation Book and Awards (chapter 6)** | An idea contest where the best ideas are collated into a book |
| **Boehringer Ingelheim—Lunch Roulette (chapter 3)** | An easy-to-use website to set up "lunch dates" with new people |
| **Bridgewater—transparent employee ratings (chapter 7)** | An employee-rating mechanism to publicly determine each employee's strengths and weakness and to share ratings on virtual "baseball cards" |
| **Danfoss—Man on the Moon (chapter 5)** | An innovation competition to encourage expansive thinking |
| **DBS—Culture Canvas (case study after chapter 3)** | A ritual where a team fills in and then signs a poster-sized template with business goals, team roles, and norms |
| **DBS—Culture Radar (chapter 7)** | A mechanism to visualize and track experiments related to culture change. |
| **DBS—Gandalf Scholarship (chapter 3)** | Employees can receive S$1,000 (US$740) to study any topic of interest, as long as they teach it back to the organization |
| **DBS—Joy Space (chapter 8)** | An open infrastructure to encourage agile ways of working and to spark collaboration |
| **DBS—*Kiasu* Committee (chapter 8)** | A mock courtroom in which any employee can "sue" the owner of a policy or process that is unnecessarily standing in the way of getting things done |
| **DBS—MOJO (case study after chapter 2)** | A way to bring greater discipline and inclusivity to meetings by routinely designating a Meeting Owner ("MO"), who sets the agenda and ensures wide participation, and a Joyful Observer ("JO"), who intervenes if people are distracted and provides public feedback to the MO |
| **DBS—70:20:10 (case study after chapter 3)** | A framework borrowed from a similar program at Google suggesting that developers spend 70 percent of their time on day-to-day work, 20 percent on work-improvement ideas, and 10 percent on experiments and pet projects |
| **DBS—Team Temp (case study after chapter 3)** | Teams use a web-based app to gauge a project team's mood, both quantitatively and qualitatively |
| **DBS—Wreckoon (chapter 7)** | A PowerPoint slide randomly appears during meetings, with questions to prompt candid discussions |
| **Google—Bureaucracy Busters (chapter 5)** | Organization-wide ideation sessions to source ideas for reducing organizational red tape |
| **Google—#MonkeyFirst (chapter 7)** | A mantra and ritual to focus attention on the hardest problem first |
| **HubSpot—Unlimited Free Books (chapter 5)** | A program through which anyone can get any book free of charge |

| | |
|---|---|
| **Innocent—Just Go with It** (chapter 7) | A practice in which employees who are 70 percent confident in an idea are encouraged to try it out |
| **Innosight—Innosight Different (chapter 3)** | Visible cartoons and an annual award to reinforce following values like humility and collaboration, supported by a regular survey that nudges leader role-modeling |
| **Innosight—First Friday** (chapter 3) | A monthly ritual where the organization gathers, thoughtfully designed and supported to spur collaboration |
| **Intuit—innovation catalysts** (chapter 8) | Trained employees who act as coaches for up to 10 percent of their time |
| **LinkedIn—InDay (chapter 8)** | A ritual where employees invest one day a month on themselves and their passion projects |
| **MetLife—LumenLab Wall of Customers (chapter 5)** | A structured way to help employees better relate to customers |
| **Nordstrom—"Yes, and . . ."** (chapter 6) | The practice of having critique come in the form of "Yes, and . . ." |
| **Optus—Close-Ups** (chapter 5) | A program where people spend a day in a store with the customer relations team |
| **Pixar—Braintrust** (chapter 6) | A group of diverse thinkers who ritualistically provide honest critiques on work-in-progress movies |
| **Pixar—intersection-supporting infrastructure** (chapter 6) | Office design with open infrastructure that encourages chance meetings and spurs creativity |
| **Pixar—Plussing** (chapter 6) | The practice of making sure critique is balanced with constructive suggestions |
| **Qualcomm—My Pain Points (chapter 5)** | A ritual where individuals share interesting articles or experiences to spark creativity |
| **Qualcomm—Stumping Google (chapter 5)** | A ritual of enabling creativity by trying to design a Google query that returns no results |
| **Singtel—WITCH (chapter 4)** | The ritual of regularly asking, "Who is the customer here?" "What is their concern?" and "What is the conclusion?" to reinforce customer-centricity |
| **Spotify—Bets Board** (chapter 8) | A centralized database containing all of Spotify's innovation bets that all employees can access |
| **Supercell—Cheers to Failure (chapter 7)** | The standard process of celebrating success with beer and failure with champagne, with stories shared publicly |
| **Tasty Catering—Great Game of Business** (chapter 8) | A weekly game that associates play to learn more about how the business operates |
| **Tata—Dare to Try** (chapter 3) | An annual prize and public recognition for teams that failed but learned something valuable |
| **Toyota—A3 Report** (chapter 6) | A succinct communications tool in which essential information is captured on a single A3-sized page |
| **Toyota—Andon Cord** (chapter 8) | A mechanism by which employees are empowered to stop production when they see a problem |

Innosight has collated another fifty-nine BEANs, which are detailed
below.

| Organization and BEAN name | Description |
| --- | --- |
| 3M—Thou Shall Not Kill a New Product Idea | A management policy never to immediately reject new ideas proposed by employees |
| Airbnb—Elephants, Dead Fish, and Vomit | A common vocabulary to catalyze honest two-way conversations ("elephants" are big things no one is talking about, "dead fish" are incidents from a few years back that people can't get over, and "vomit" represents issues that people just need to get out of their systems) |
| Alibaba Group—Aliway | An internal, rewards-based communications platform to solicit honest firmwide feedback on ideas |
| Alibaba Group—Kung Fu Nicknames | The practice of giving employees kung fu nicknames (founder Jack Ma's was *Feng Qingyang*) to break down barriers and encourage collaboration[1] |
| Amazon.com—Disagree and Commit | A principle to encourage debates during decision-making but to give 100 percent commitment to the decisions made |
| Amazon.com—Institutional Yes | Formal mechanisms to discourage rejection of ideas without an explanation or suggestions to improve it |
| Amazon.com—memos over slides | The practice of sending memos for prereading instead of using PowerPoints during meetings to encourage focused discussions |
| Amazon.com—The "?" Email | A process in which CEO Jeff Bezos forwards customer complaints to relevant employees with a simple "?" as the subject line, with an expectation that a response will come in a few hours |
| Amazon.com—Two-Pizza Rule | A mantra and principle to keep teams small enough to be fed by two pizzas, in order to encourage collaboration and agility |
| Amazon.com—WOCAS Reports | An automated process to extract customer insights ("What our customers are saying?") from contact centers and share them with the relevant departments |
| Apple—Monday is Review Day | A ritual to ensure an efficient and lean decision-making process during time-critical product-development cycles |
| Asana—Polish Week and Grease Week | A practice where employees spend a week each to improve customer experiences (polish) and back-end processes (grease) |
| Atlassian—Innovation Week | A weeklong hackathon to create a feature or prototype for a bounded strategic area |

1. We're not sure this counts as a kung fu nickname, but a team once gave Scott a bobblehead with his head on the body of Yoda from the *Star Wars* movies, leading to the nickname . . . wait for it . . . Scoda.

| | |
|---|---|
| **Atlassian—Shipit** | A dedicated twenty-four-hour hackathon to question the status quo and create something new |
| **Bank of America—data-based employee experience design** | A program to collect behavior data using wearable devices and use that data to create better employee experiences, such as common lunch hours to facilitate knowledge sharing |
| **Conductrics—Best Case, Worst Case** | The practice of accelerating decision-making by articulating the best and worst outcomes for each idea |
| **DBS—3S 1R** | People presenting ideas need to have three suggestions (3S) and one recommendation (1R), which encourages divergent thinking and empowerment |
| **Evernote—The Dialogue Box** | A weekly ritual where senior leaders dedicate an hour to chat with employees |
| **Facebook—Faceversary** | An annual ritual of celebrating employee anniversaries |
| **Google—café for interactions** | An infrastructure to encourage interactions and collaboration |
| **Google—Fixit Sprints** | A twenty-four-hour sprint dedicated to fixing a specific problem |
| **Google—Googlegeist** | An annual firmwide survey to solicit feedback on a range of topics |
| **Google—GUTS** | A mechanism by which employees raise issues using the Google Unified Tracking System (GUTS) and leaders prioritize issues worth solving |
| **Google—Noogler Hat** | The ritual of making new employees feel welcome and at ease during their first firmwide meeting by having them wear a funny hat saying they are a new Googler, or "Noogler" |
| **Google—Nooglers, Xooglers, and Spooglers** | Standard terms used to refer to employees and their families: a Noogler is a new employee, a Xoogler is a former employee, and an employee's spouse or significant other is a Spoogler |
| **Google—OKR sharing** | Product-development teams publicly share objectives and key results to create alignment and accountability |
| **Google—Tech Talks** | A series of talks on diverse topics to infuse diversity in thinking and curiosity |
| **Google—10X Thinking** | A guiding principle and ritual that encourages people to think about what it would take to come up with something ten times better than current solutions |
| **HubSpot—JEDI: "Just Effing Does It"** | An award to recognize an ownership mindset and proactive actions |
| **HubSpot—Unlimited Free Meals Program** | A fully sponsored lunch program to encourage curiosity and collaboration |
| **HubSpot—SFTC: "Solve for the Customer"** | A mantra and guiding principle to encourage customer-centricity |

| | |
|---|---|
| **IBM—Innovation Jam** | A large-scale online platform to solicit opinions and suggestions on varied topics |
| **IDEO—Tea Time** | The ritual of sharing knowledge and exchanging ideas over sponsored tea and snacks |
| **Jobvite—Rookie Cookies** | A ritual in which new-hires bring cookies on their first day to share with colleagues and encourage introductory conversations |
| **Johnson & Johnson—Creative Engagement Community** | A community program and tools to encourage employees to develop themselves and their ideas |
| **Kraft—Foodii** | A online employee community for conducting market research, generating ideas, and testing new concepts |
| **LinkedIn—company all-hands** | Biweekly full-company meetings to encourage open communication and collaboration |
| **LinkedIn—Space Lift** | An annual workplace decoration competition to encourage humor and a sense of belonging |
| **Nestlé—reverse mentoring** | A reverse mentoring program, where insights and business concepts are exchanged between young and senior executives |
| **OOG Rotterdam Eye Hospital—Team-Start Huddles** | A daily team huddle to encourage open communication and collaboration |
| **OXO—Glove Wall** | Lost gloves, signifying the different hands that touch OXO's products, are displayed on the wall to nudge customer-centricity |
| **P&G—Heroic Failure Awards** | An award ceremony to recognize intelligent risk-taking and failures |
| **Pixar—effective postmortems** | Data-informed after-action review sessions to capture learnings |
| **Pixar—Failure Gallery** | Artifacts from failed projects that are displayed in a gallery to celebrate failures and nudge experimentation |
| **Pixar—Incomplete Works** | The ritual of sharing unfinished work at team meetings to catalyze creativity |
| **Pixar—Notes Day** | An all-hands-on-deck day dedicated to improving operational efficiency |
| **Porch—Around-the-Porch** | A weekly ritual of discussing experiments and their outcomes |
| **Porch—Mr. Sparkles** | A ritual in which employees who try something big and bold but spectacularly fail proudly display a stuffed animal, named Mr. Sparkles, on their desks for a week |
| **Qualcomm—Flux** | An employee-driven ideation ritual where diverse groups spend ninety minutes every two weeks to discuss user needs worth solving |

| | |
|---|---|
| **Rite-Solutions—Mutual Fun** | A gamified employee upvoting system to prioritize projects and make investment decisions via an internal ideas stock market |
| **Spotify—experimentation weeks** | Weeklong "unbounded" hackathon events to drive experimentation and risk-taking |
| **Spotify—Fail Wall** | The ritual of showcasing and discussing failures to capture learning and encourage risk-taking |
| **SWA—Culture Wall** | A physical wall with photos of people, inspirational ideas, trends, news stories, and current work projects to remind employees of the world beyond their desks and office |
| **Toyota—5 Whys** | A ritual of arriving at the root cause of the problem by asking "Why?" five times |
| **Toyota—TCISS** | A platform called Toyota's Creative Idea and Suggestion System (TCISS) to collect ideas augmented by an award ceremony to recognize the best ones |
| **Toyota—Impossible Goals** | The practice of setting audacious goals to inspire employees and encourage expansive thinking |
| **Twitch—new-employee videos** | An employee onboarding process in which new-hires share a video about themselves at companywide events |
| **Twitter—weekly launch meetings** | Weekly team meetings where experiment data is used to drive launch decisions |
| **Vivint—full-scale model home** | A large-scale physical replica of a customer's home to support customer-centricity |

You can see more complete descriptions of the 101 BEANs listed here and download BEANstorming cards from our companion website at www.eatsleepinnovate.com.

# Notes

## Introduction

*Market capitalization data for BAT (Baidu, Alibaba, and Tencent) and FAANG (Facebook, Apple, Amazon.com, Netflix, and Google):* finance.yahoo.com, accessed May 5, 2020.

## Chapter 1

*UNICEF's U-Report:* Victoria Maskell, "Hurricane Irma: U-Report Works to Protect Children," UNICEF Connect, September 7, 2017, https://blogs.unicef.org/blog /hurricane-irma-u-report-works-protect-children/; "UNICEF + Trello | Tips & Tools for Extreme Remote Teamwork," Youtube.com, November 27, 2017, https://www .youtube.com/watch?v=bSToAcRHahY; "U-Report," UNICEF, https://www.unicef.org /innovation/U-Report; email exchange with Victoria Maskell, June 4, 2019.

*Edison history and quote:* Randall E. Stross, *The Wizard of Menlo Park: How Thomas Alva Edison Invented the Modern World* (New York: Crown, 2007).

*Definition of culture:* Edgar H. Schein, *Organizational Culture and Leadership* (San Francisco: Jossey-Bass Publishers, 1985).

*UNICEF UPSHIFT case study:* Lisar Morina, "Youth Engagement for a Better World: Sejnur Veshall's Road to Social Change-Making," Innovations Lab Kosovo, June 13, 2017, http://kosovoinnovations.org/youth-engagement-for-a-better-world -sejnur-veshalls-road-to-social-change-making/; "UPSHIFT," UNICEF, https://www .unicef.org/innovation/UPSHIFT; "Story for Golden Hands," YouTube, August 29, 2017, https://www.youtube.com/watch?v=ZZXr3uzu6oc; emails from Tanya Accone and Katherine Crisp, June 13, 2019, and June 19, 2019.

*Benefits of a culture of innovation:* "Creativity Pays. Here's How Much," *Bloomberg Businessweek*, April 24, 2016; "Glassdoor & MIT Sloan Management Review Launch Culture 500," Glassdoor, https://www.glassdoor.com/research/studies/mit-culture -500/; "Gallup Q12 Meta-Analysis Report," Gallup, https://news.gallup.com/reports /191489/q12-meta-analysis-report-2016.aspx; Paul van Keeken, "How Creativity Impacts Business Results," Adobe.com, April 23, 2015, https://blogs.adobe.com/creative /how-creativity-impacts-business-results/; "How Customer Experience Impacts Company Stock Performance," *Forrester*, February 22, 2018; "The Business Impact of Investing in Experience," *Forrester Consulting Thought Leadership*, April 2018; Adi Gaskell, "New Study Finds That Collaboration Drives Workplace Performance," *Forbes*, June 22, 2017; Darrell K. Rigby, Steve Berez, Greg Caimi, and Andrew Noble, "Agile Innovation," *Bain & Company*, April 19, 2016; Charles Duhigg, "What Google

Learned from Its Quest to Build the Perfect Team," *New York Times*, February 25, 2016; Sergio Fernandez and Tima Moldogaziev, "Employee Empowerment, Employee Attitudes, and Performance: Testing a Causal Model," *Public Administration Review* 73, no. 3 (April 13, 2013).

## The Salvation Army Case Study

*The Salvation Army brings supplies to Gander:* Ken Ramstead, "Memories of 9/11," *Salvationist*, September 8, 2016, https://salvationist.ca/articles/2016/09/911-gander-salvation-army/.

*History and overview of The Salvation Army:* "Transforming Lives Since 1865," https://story.salvationarmy.org/; Elisha Fieldstadt, "Salvation Army Red Kettles by the Numbers," NBC News, December 24, 2015, https://www.nbcnews.com/feature/season-of-kindness/salvation-army-red-kettles-numbers-n472246; Drew Lindsay, "Who's Raising the Most: the 100 Charities That Are America's Favorites," *Chronicle of Philanthropy*, October 30, 2018, https://www.philanthropy.com/article/Who-s-Raising-the-Most-The/244933.

*Mobile Joes story:* Robert Mitchell, "Brew Something!" *SA Connects*, https://saconnects.org/brew-something/.

*Apple Pay story:* Kathleen Foody and The Associated Press, "No Cash? Now You Can Donate to the Salvation Army Using Apple Pay or Google Pay," *Fortune.com*, November 30, 2019, https://fortune.com/2019/11/30/salvation-army-mobile-donations/.

*Strike Point grant program:* https://easternusa.salvationarmy.org/use/news/event-strikepoint; interview with Lt. Col. Jim LaBossiere, April 15, 2019.

*The Salvation Factory's purpose and mission:* "Who We Are," The Salvation Factory, https://www.salvationfactory.org/about/who-we-are/; interview with Steve and Sharon Bussey, April 15, 2019.

## Chapter 2

*Kindergarten graduates outperform MBAs on the marshmallow challenge:* Tom Wujec, "Build a Tower, Build a Team," TED, February 2010, https://www.ted.com/talks/tom_wujec_build_a_tower_build_a_team.

*Microsoft's miss:* Robert A. Guth, "Microsoft Bid to Beat Google Builds on a History of Misses," *Wall Street Journal*, January 16, 2009.

*Bower and Gilbert on strategy:* Joseph L. Bower and Clark G. Gilbert, *From Resource Allocation to Strategy* (New York: Oxford University Press, 2005).

*Data from Innosight survey:* "The Strategy Confidence Gap," Innosight, Winter 2014, https://www.innosight.com/insight/the-strategy-confidence-gap/.

*Rita McGrath story:* Rita Gunther McGrath, *Seeing Around Corners* (New York: Houghton Mifflin Harcourt, 2019).

## DBS Case Study

*"It is demonstrably the case . . .":* "World's Best Digital Bank 2016: DBS," Euromoney, July 6, 2016, https://www.euromoney.com/article/b12kq6p8mv5rh3/world39s-best-digital-bank-2016-dbs.

*UK Design Council 4D model:* "The Design Process: What Is the Double Diamond?" Design Council, https://www.designcouncil.org.uk/news-opinion/design-process-what-double-diamond.

*MOJO effort:* Scott D. Anthony, Paul Cobban, Rahul Nair, and Natalie Painchaud, "Breaking Down the Barriers to Innovation," *Harvard Business Review,* November–December 2019.

## Chapter 3

*Learning to ride a bike backward:* "It's Like Riding a Backwards Bicycle," The Arbinger Institute, February 13, 2018, www.arbingerinstitute.com/BlogDetail?id=91.

*Lessons from habit-change literature:* See the Culture of Innovation Bookshelf in the appendix.

*History of Alcoholics Anonymous:* "Historical Data: The Birth of AA and Its Growth in the US/Canada," Alcoholics Anonymous, https://www.aa.org/pages/en_US /historical-data-the-birth-of-aa-and-its-growth-in-the-uscanada.

*History of WW:* "WW International," Wikipedia, https://en.wikipedia.org/wiki /WW_International.

*Steve Kerr's management classic:* Steven Kerr, "On the Folly of Rewarding A, While Hoping for B," *Academy of Management Journal,* December 1975, http://www.csus.edu /indiv/s/sablynskic/documents/rewardinga.pdf.

*Amazon.com Future Press Release:* John Rossman, "Innovate Like Amazon with the Future Press Release," The Amazon Way, May 24, 2019, http://the-amazon-way.com /blog/future-press-release/.

*Lunch Roulette BEAN:* Sylvia Ann Hewlett, "A New Way to Network inside Your Company," *Harvard Business Review Online,* January 8, 2013, https://hbr.org/2013/01 /a-new-way-to-network-inside-yo.

*Dare to Try:* Amrita Nair Ghaswalla, "Daring to Fail: A Programme That Lauds the Unsuccessful," *Hindustan Business Line,* September 24, 2014, https://www .thehindubusinessline.com/companies/Daring-to-fail-a-programme-that-lauds-the -unsuccessful/article20872449.ece.

*Adobe Kickbox program:* David Burkus, "Inside Adobe's Innovation Kit," *Harvard Business Review Online,* February 23, 2015, https://hbr.org/2015/02/inside-adobes -innovation-kit.

### Hyderabad Case Study

*BEANs in Hyderabad:* Anthony et al., "Breaking Down the Barriers Innovation."

## Chapter 4

*Richard Pascale quote:* Richard Tanner Pascale, Jerry Sternin, and Monique Sternin, *The Power of Positive Deviance: How Unlikely Innovators Solve the World's Toughest Problems* (Boston: Harvard Business Review Press, 2010).

*"Jobs to be done" theory:* Clayton M. Christensen, Taddy Hall, Karen Dillon, and David S. Duncan, *Competing Against Luck: The Story of Innovation and Customer Choice* (New York: HarperCollins, 2016).

*Tools to manage ambiguity:* Scott D. Anthony, *The First Mile: A Launch Manual for Getting Great Ideas into the Market* (Boston: Harvard Business Review Press, 2014).

*Tom Fishburne on the power of humor:* "The Power of Laughing at Ourselves at Work," TED, October 2018, https://www.ted.com/talks/tom_fishburne_the_power_of _laughing_at_ourselves_at_work#t-143675.

## Chapter 5

*Danfoss's Man on the Moon:* Astrid Stokholm, "Danfoss: We Design the Full Experience," Danish Design Award, October 31, 2018, http://danishdesignaward.com/en/2018/10/we-design-the-full-experience/.

*Google's bureaucracy buster program:* Laszlo Bock, *Work Rules!: Insights from inside Google That Will Transform How You Live and Lead* (New York: Hachette Book Group, 2015).

*MetLife's LumenLab Wall of Customers:* Interview with MetLife Asia-Pacific chief innovation officer Zia Zaman, January 20, 2020.

*Optus Customer Close-Ups:* "Innovating for a Better Tomorrow: 2016 Optus Sustainability Report," Optus, https://www.optus.com.au/content/dam/optus/documents/about-us/sustainability/Sustainability-Report-2016.pdf.

*HubSpot's Unlimited Free Books:* Riley Stefano, "HubSpot Named a Best Company for Happiness, Perks & Benefits, and Work-Life Balance by Employees Comparably," Hubspot, October 3, 2019, https://www.hubspot.com/company-news/comparablyawards.

*Qualcomm's My Pain Point:* Jorge Barba, "Q&A: Babak Forutanpour on How to Start a Grass Roots Innovation Program in a Big Company," Game-Changer, October 7, 2013, http://www.game-changer.net/2013/10/07/qa-babak-forutanpour-start-grass-roots-innovation-program-big-company/#.XkpDdGgzZ3j.

*Qualcomm's Stump Google Search:* Babak Forutanpour, "Don't Dream Alone: Story of an Employee-Run Innovation Program in a Fortune 500 (Part XI–Final)," LinkedIn, October 12, 2017, https://www.linkedin.com/pulse/dont-dream-alone-story-employee-run-innovation-500-part-forutanpour-2/.

*Lafley's "our behind was right facing the customer":* Discussion with Scott Anthony at the May 2008 PDMA and IIR Front End of Innovation conference in Boston. A summary of this conversation appears in Scott D. Anthony, "Game-Changing at Procter & Gamble," *Strategy & Innovation* 6, no. 4 (2008).

*Lilly Cone's reflections:* Email from Anne Lilly Cone, July 1, 2015.

*Joint Forces Command:* Interview with Sir Chris Deverell, May 13, 2019; site visit to the jHub, April 10, 2019.

*Settlement Music School story:* Scott D. Anthony, David S. Duncan, and Pontus M. A. Siren, "Build an Innovation Engine in 90 Days," *Harvard Business Review*, December 2014; Scott D. Anthony, Clark G. Gilbert, and Mark W. Johnson, *Dual Transformation: How to Reposition Today's Business While Creating the Future* (Boston: Harvard Business Review Press, 2017); "Dual Transformation in Action: Reinventing Today While Creating Tomorrow," Innosight CEO Summit Report 2017, https://www.innosight.com/wp-content/uploads/2017/10/CEO-Summit-2017-Chapter-Two-Dual-Transformation-in-Action.pdf; email with Helen Eaton, May 8, 2020.

*Curiosity quotient tool:* This tool first appeared in the appendix of Anthony et al., *Dual Transformation.*

## Chapter 6

*Steve Jobs quote on connecting things:* Gary Wolf, "Steve Jobs: The Next Insanely Great Thing," *Wired*, February 1, 1996, https://www.wired.com/1996/02/jobs-2/.

*BNP Paribas's Innovation Book and Awards:* Constance Chalchat, "BNP Paribas CIB Celebrates Innovation with the CIB Innovation Awards 2015," LinkedIn, February 2, 2016, https://www.linkedin.com/pulse/bnp-paribas-cib-celebrates-innovation-awards-2015-constance-chalchat/.

*Toyota A3 report:* Hirotaka Takeuchi, Emi Osono, and Norihiko Shimizu, "The Contradictions That Drive Toyota's Success," *Harvard Business Review,* June 2008.

*Amazon.com empty chair:* John Koetsier, "Why Every Amazon Meeting Has at Least 1 Empty Chair," *Inc.,* April 5, 2018, https://www.inc.com/john-koetsier/why -every-amazon-meeting-has-at-least-one-empty-chair.html.

*Nordstrom's "Yes, and . . .":* "Nordstrom Technology NorDNA Culture Deck," Slideshare, January 15, 2015, https://www.slideshare.net/NordstromPeopleLab /nordstrom-technology-nordna-culture-deck.

*Pixar BEANs:* Ed Catmull with Amy Wallace, *Creativity, Inc.: Overcoming the Unseen Forces That Stand in the Way of Creativity* (New York: Random House, 2014).

*Ed Catmull reflecting on* Frozen 2: Email from Ed Catmull, November 4, 2019.

*Intuit's design-driven transformation:* "Why Intuit founder Scott Cook Wants You to Stop Listening to Your Boss," interview with Drake Baer, *Fast Company,* October 28, 2013, http://www.fastcompany.com/3020699/bottom-line/why-intuit -founder-scott-cook-wants-you-to-stop-listening-to-your-boss; Brad Smith, "Intuit's CEO on Building a Design-Driven Company," *Harvard Business Review,* January– February 2015, https://hbr.org/2015/01/intuits-ceo-on-building-a-design-driven -company; "Intuit Founder and Chairman of the Executive Committee Scott Cook on Culture Change That Sticks," panel discussion at Innosight 2018 CEO event, August 7, 2018, https://vimeo.com/291177163.

*Fiona Fairhurst story:* "A Revolutionary Swimsuit," 2009 European Inventor Awards, https://www.epo.org/learning-events/european-inventor/finalists/2009 /fairhurst.html.

*Nick Musyoka story:* Scott D. Anthony, "The New Corporate Garage," *Harvard Business Review,* September 2012.

# Chapter 7

*Atlassian's premortem:* "Premortem," Atlassian Team Playbook, https://www .atlassian.com/team-playbook/plays/pre-mortem.

*Supercell's beer and champagne ritual:* "The Best Teams Make the Best Games," Supercell, https://supercell.com/en/our-story/.

*Google's #MonkeyFirst:* Astro Teller, "Tackle the Monkey First," Blog.x.company, December 8, 2016, https://blog.x.company/tackle-the-monkey-first-90fd6223e04d.

*Innocent's Just Go With It:* "Innocent Employee Innovation," Engage for Success 2012, https://engageforsuccess.org/wp-content/uploads/2015/11/Innocent-Employee -Innovation.pdf.

*Airbnb's Live from Day 1:* Alice Truong, "The Oddball Ways Tech Companies Welcome You on Your First Day of Work," *Quartz,* March 8, 2015, https://qz.com/346035 /the-oddball-ways-tech-companies-welcome-you-on-your-first-day-of-work/.

*Intelligent failure:* Amy C. Edmondson, *The Fearless Organization: Creating Psychological Safety in the Workplace for Learning, Innovation, and Growth* (Hoboken, NJ: John Wiley & Sons, 2019).

*Metaphor of roulette, blackjack, and chess:* Michael J. Mauboussin, *The Success Equation: Untangling Luck and Skill in Business, Sports, and Investing* (Boston: Harvard Business Review Press, 2012); Scott D. Anthony, *The Little Black Book of Innovation: How It Works, How to Do It* (Boston: Harvard Business Review Press, 2012).

*Two-hat leadership:* Anthony et al., *Dual Transformation.*

*Scott Cook on experimentation:* Scott Cook, as told to Drake Baer, "Why Intuit Founder Scott Cook Wants You To Stop Listening To Your Boss," *FastCompany,*

October 28, 2013, https://www.fastcompany.com/3020699/why-intuit-founder-scott
-cook-wants-you-to-stop-listening-to-your-boss.

*Robert Kegan's quote on self-transforming leaders:* Robert Kegan and Lisa Laskow
Lahey, *An Everyone Culture: Becoming a Deliberately Developmental Organization* (Boston: Harvard Business School Publishing, 2016).

*Self-transforming leadership and mindfulness:* Scott D. Anthony and Michael Putz,
"The Deceptions of Disruption," *Sloan Management Review*, March 2020.

*"Largest legal creation of wealth":* "Done Deals: Venture Capitalists Tell Their
Story: Featured HBS John Doerr," Harvard Business School Working Knowledge,
December 4, 2000, https://hbswk.hbs.edu/archive/done-deals-venture-capitalists-tell
-their-story-featured-hbs-john-doerr.

*Quotes from Satya Nadella:* Satya Nadella, Greg Shaw, and Jill Tracie Nichols, *Hit
Refresh: The Quest to Rediscover Microsoft's Soul and Imagine a Better Future for Everyone*
(New York: HarperCollins, 2017).

*The Innovator's Checklist:* A version of this first appeared in Anthony et al., "Build
an Innovation Engine in 90 Days."

## Chapter 8

*Spotify's bets board:* Henrik Kniberg, "Spotify Rhythm; How We Create Focus,"
June 1, 2016, https://blog.crisp.se/2016/06/08/henrikkniberg/spotify-rhythm.

*Tasty Catering's Great Game of Business:* "All-Star Case Studies," Greatgame.com,
https://www.greatgame.com/resources/case-studies/case/tasty-catering.

*Toyota's Andon Cord:* "Andon—Toyota Production System Guide," Toyota.co.uk,
May 31, 2016, https://blog.toyota.co.uk/andon-toyota-production-system.

*Asana's No Meeting Wednesday:* Dustin Moskovitz, "No Meeting Wednesdays,"
Asana blog, February 14, 2013, https://blog.asana.com/2013/02/no-meeting
-wednesdays/.

*LinkedIn's InDay:* Andie Burjek, "Employees Use InDays to Improve the World
around Them," Workforce, November 9, 2017, https://www.workforce.com/news
/employees-use-indays-improve-world-around.

*Intuit's innovation catalysts:* Roger L. Martin, "The Innovation Catalysts," *Harvard
Business Review*, June 2011, https://hbr.org/2011/06/the-innovation-catalysts; https://
hbr.org/2011/06/the-innovation-catalysts; Thomas Lockwood and Edgar Papke,
"How Intuit Used Design Thinking to Boost Sales By $10M in a Year," *FastCompany*,
October 31, 2017, https://www.fastcompany.com/90147434/how-intuit-used-design
-thinking-to-boost-sales-by-10m-in-a-year.

*Connect the dots:* Scott D. Anthony, "How to Tell If a Company Is Good at Innovating or Just Good at PR," *Harvard Business Review Online*, December 18, 2015,
https://hbr.org/2015/12/how-to-tell-if-a-company-is-good-at-innovating-or-just-good
-at-pr.

*Wright Brothers story:* Scott D. Anthony, *The First Mile*; "Wright Brothers Wind
Tunnel," http://www.solarnavigator.net/inventors/wright_brothers_wind_tunnel.htm.

*UNICEF's efforts to scale innovation:* Interview with Tanya Accone, May 22, 2019.

*International Development Innovation Alliance Mission:* "About IDIA," IDIA, https://
www.idiainnovation.org/about-idia.

*UNICEF's Office of Innovation principles:* "About the Office of Innovation," UNI-
CEF, https://www.unicef.org/innovation/about-us.

*Summary of UNICEF's innovation impact:* "Pathways to Scale, Pathways to Results
for Every Child," UNICEF Global Innovation Centre Annual Report, Novem-

ber 2018, https://www.unicef.org/innovation/reports/pathways-scale-pathways-results
-every-child.

*UNICEF's 2020 strategy:* "Matching Today's Challenges with Tomorrow's Solutions," UNICEF, January 2020, https://www.unicef.org/innovation/GlobalStrategy.

*Netflix freedom and responsibility culture:* "Netflix Culture," Netflix, https://jobs
.netflix.com/culture.

*Article backing the idea of a banking back office:* Richard J. Matteis, "The New Back Office Focuses on Customer Service," *Harvard Business Review,* March 1979, https://hbr.org/1979/03/the-new-back-office-focuses-on-customer-service.

*Addressing zombies:* Scott D. Anthony, David S. Duncan, and Pontus M. A. Siren, "Zombie Projects: How to Find Them and Kill Them," *Harvard Business Review Online,* March 4, 2015; Modesto A. Maidique and Billie Jo Zirger, "The New Product Learning Cycle," *Research Policy* 14, no. 6, December 1985; Rita Gunter McGrath, "Failing By Design," *Harvard Business Review,* April 2011.

## Conclusion

*Derek Sivers TED Talk:* Derek Sivers, "How to Start a Movement," TED, February 2010, https://www.ted.com/talks/derek_sivers_how_to_start_a_movement.

*Anthony's IdeaLab call to action:* Scott D. Anthony, "Postcards and Parting Thoughts," HBR IdeaLab, March 28, 2019, https://idealab.hbr.org/groups/building
-a-culture-of-innovation/forum/topic/22-our-gift-to-you-postcards-and-parting
-thoughts/. (You must be subscribed to HBR.org to see the content.)

## Appendix

*Innovation's relationship status:* Scott D. Anthony, "What's the Status of Your Relationship with Innovation?" *Harvard Business Review Online,* September 11, 2013, https://hbr.org/2013/09/whats-the-status-of-your-relationship-with-innovation.

*Curated BEANs:* see www.eatsleepinnovate.com for more details.

# Index

A3 Report, 138*t*, 139–40
Accone, Tanya, 183–85
Adobe, 31, 74*t*, 78, 109
Adult Rock Band, 132–33
agile movement, 88
agility, 53
Airbnb, 154*t*, 158
Alcoholics Anonymous, 65, 66
Amazon.com, 74*t*, 75–76, 138*t*, 140
ambidexterity, 163
ambiguity, adeptness in
  as behavior of innovators, 24*t*,
    28–29
  benefits of, 31
  and culture sprint activation session,
    96*t*, 99–100
  and DBS Wreckoon, 156
  discovery questions for, 149–51
  and Supercell's Cheers to Failure,
    157–58
  and Tata's Dare to Try, 74*t*, 77
Andon Cord, 174–75
Anthony, Robert N., Sr., 17–18
Apple Pay, 37
artifacts
  copying those in innovative
    companies, 5–6
  and culture of innovation, 20, 22
  defined, 66, 68, 81
  as part of BEANs at Innosight,
    69–70
  *See also* BEANs (behavior enablers,
    artifacts, and nudges)
Asana, 174*t*, 177
Atlassian, 154*t*, 155
autonomy, 210

Ballmer, Steve, 166
bananas, at McDonald's, 45–46
Barclay's, 181
BEAN boosters, 118
  for blueprinting ideas, 141–43
  for discovering opportunities, 124–26
  for idea testing and assessment,
    159–66
  for moving ideas forward, 178–83
BEANs (behavior enablers, artifacts,
    and nudges)
  authors' favorites, 73–78
  for blueprinting ideas, 137–38
  brainstorming and refining, 103*t*,
    106–9
  capture template, 107–8
  at DBS development center, 82–86
  defined, 9
  for discovering opportunities,
    119–24
  elements of successful, 71–73
  full, 117
  for idea testing and assessment,
    153–58
  impact of, 201
  implementation of, 85–86, 111–12, 114
  at Innosight, 68–71
  and lessons from habit-change litera-
    ture, 64–68
  list of, 219*t*–25*t*
  for moving ideas forward, 171–77
  partial, 117
  pitching and selecting winning, 103*t*,
    109–10
  process for creating, 78–80
  refining and implementing, 85–86

BEANstorming, 102–10
behavioral blockers
  eliminating, 83–85
  identifying, 83, 90–92, 103–5
  surfacing, at DBS, 106–9
behavior enablers, 66, 67, 69, 80–81.
    *See also* BEANs (behavior enablers,
    artifacts, and nudges)
behaviors
  getting granular about desired, 102–3
  identifying desired, 83, 88–89
Bertolini, Mark, 165
Bets Board, 174*t*, 176
beverage-dispensing backpacks, 35–36
bike riding, unlearning, 63–64
Blank, Steve, 130
BNP Paribas, 138*t*, 139
Boehringer Ingelheim, 74*t*, 76–77, 80
Booth, Catherine, 33–34
Booth, William, 33–34, 38
Bower, Joseph, 48
Braintrust, 141–43
Bridgewater, 162–63
Brooks, Christopher, 16
Bureaucracy Busters, 120*t*, 121–22
Bushnell, Nolan, 65
Bussey, Sharon, 38
Bussey, Steve, 35, 36, 37–38, 39

candor, lack of, 84–85
catalysts, innovation, 174*t*, 177, 182
Catmull, Ed, 142–43
chameleon leadership, 163–66
chaos monkey, 156
Cheers to Failure, 154*t*, 157–58
choice architecture, 67
Christensen, Clayton, 26n7, 180
Cisco Systems, 182
Close-Ups, 121*t*, 123
closure, 192
Cockcroft, Adrian, 3
collaboration
  as behavior of innovators, 24*t*, 26–28
  benefits of, 31
  and blueprinting ideas, 137, 139–40
  and Boehringer Ingelheim's Lunch
    Roulette, 74*t*, 76–77
  and culture sprint activation session,
    95–96, 97

discovery question for, 149
comment cards, 5–6
communication, effective, 209
competing commitment, 104
competition, reframing, 52
complex failure, 160
confirmation bias, 156
constraint, creativity and, 178–79
Cook, Scott, 144–46, 148–49, 163–64
corporate incubators and accelerators,
    181
corporate venture capital, 181
COVID-19, 4, 16, 60–62, 134
creativity
  benefits of fostering, 31
  and constraint, 178–79
  Pixar and formula for, 142–43
  risks of, 42–45
culture
  defined, 32
  and strategy, 47–50, 209
culture blockers, 203–4
Culture Canvas, 84
culture change, 6–8
  at DBS, 187–91, 201
  effecting, 169, 201–2
  measuring and monitoring, 210
  principles for driving, 208–10
  showing value of, 92
  stages of, 113*t*
  time required to change, 195–96
culture of innovation
  additional resources for learning
    about, 206–8
  benefits of creating, 30–32
  and clarity in language, 197
  creating, 1–2, 6–8, 203
  defined, 8, 19–23, 32
  diagnostic for, 211–17
  survey, 91–92
Culture Radar, 112
culture sprint, 87–88
  activation session, 94–110, 114
  following activation session, 111–12
  preparation for activation session,
    88–94
curiosity
  assessing curiosity quotient, 135–36
  as behavior of innovators, 23–25
  benefits of fostering, 31

and culture sprint activation session, 98–100

and DBS's Gandalf Scholarship, 74t, 75

encouraging, 119–20

impediments to, 44

current state, diagnosing, 90–92

customer obsession

   and Amazon.com's Future Press Release, 74t, 75–76

   as behavior of innovators, 24t, 26

   benefits of, 31

   and blueprinting ideas, 137

   and culture sprint activation session, 96–98

   at DBS, 53

   and discovery of innovation opportunities, 122–23

   discovery question for, 149

   and P&G's Consumer-Is-Boss Movement, 124–26

   as principle for driving culture change, 209–10

   reinforcing, 109–10


Danfoss, 119–21

Dare to Try, 74t, 77

Dataminr, 127–28

DBS Bank

   culture change at, 2–3, 51–62, 187–91, 201

   Culture Radar at, 112

   Gandalf Scholarship, 74t, 75

   MOJO, 73

   surfacing blockers at, 106–9

   uses BEANs at development center, 82–86

   Wreckoon, 154t, 155–56

dela Cruz, Ferdz, 162

delivery question, 149

Deming, W. Edwards, 50

Development Bank of Singapore. See DBS Bank

Deverell, Sir Chris, 128–29

disciplined experimentation, 179–80

discovery question cheat sheet, 148–51

Disney, 141–42

"diverge to converge" ideation, 99

Dlugose, Dave, 35

Doerr, John, 166

double diamond model, 56–57

Drucker, Peter, 33, 202

Duncan, Dave, 17n3

DZ Bank, 181


Eaton, Helen, 131–34, 198

Edison, Thomas, 18–19, 159–60

Edmondson, Amy, 31, 159, 160–61

empowerment

   and Adobe's Kickbox, 74t, 78

   as behavior of innovators, 25t, 29–30

   benefits of, 31

   and culture sprint activation session, 100–101

   discovery question for, 151

   and moving ideas forward, 174–75

Empty Chair, 138t, 140

*Essentials of Accounting* (Anthony), 17–18

experimentation

   at DBS, 53

   disciplined, 179–80

   encouraging, 210

external innovation amplifiers, 181–82


failure

   celebrating, 157–58

   preventable, 160, 161

   and psychological safety, 159–61

   rewarding intelligent, 101

Fairhurst, Fiona, 147

fear

   as behavioral blocker, 104, 107

   as impediment to innovation, 42

First Friday BEAN, 70–71

Fishburne, Tom, 106–7

4D model, 56–57

Future Press Release, 74t, 76, 95


Gandalf Scholarship, 74t, 75

Gander, 33

General Mills, 182

Gilbert, Clark, 48

Global Innovation Center (GIC), 184–85

Golden Hands, 27–28, 29–30

Google
  AdWords, 47
  Bureaucracy Busters, 120*t*, 121–22
  #MonkeyFirst, 154*t*, 158
  Pay, 37
Gorsky, Alex, 165–66
Great Game of Business, 174*t*, 175
growth mindset, 167–69
Gulley, Rich, 35
Gupta, Piyush, 2, 51–52, 59
Guth, Robert A., 47
G-WIN, 182


habits, 21
  and authors' favorite BEANs, 73–78
  and BEAN creation process, 78–80
  and BEANs at DBS development
    center, 82–86
  and BEANs at Innosight, 68–71
  changing, 63–64, 66
  and elements of successful BEANs,
    71–73
  engrained, 47–50
  lessons from habit-change literature,
    64–68
hackathons, 190–91
Harper, Mike, 35–36
hats, importance of leaders wearing
  different, 162
Heath, Chip and Dan, 67, 120n3
hierarchy effect, 156
HIPPO problem, 148
Hoffmann, Dave, 45–46
HubSpot, 121*t*, 123–24
Hurricane Irma, 15–16


ice breakers, 97
idea capture template, 100
ideas, blueprinting
  BEAN boosters for, 141–43
  discovery question cheat sheet for,
    148–51
  Intuit case study, 144–46
  and problem solving at intersections,
    147–48
  relevant BEANs for, 137–38
IdeaLab, 198–99
Ideas Box, 5–6

idea-sourcing platforms, 182
idea testing and assessment
  BEAN booster for, 159–66
  innovator's checklist for, 170–72
  Microsoft case study for, 166–69
  relevant BEANs for, 153–58
incubators, internal, 182
incubators and accelerators, corporate,
  181
InDay, 174*t*, 177
inertia, 42, 66, 176
Innocent, 154*t*, 158
innoganda, 6, 22, 178–80
Innosight, 48–49, 66, 68–71, 99
innovation
  in action, 19
  assessing relationship with, 217–18
  barriers to, 41–42, 49
  and conflation of technology, 184
  confusion of BEANs with, 79–80
  defined, 17–19, 32
  as discipline, 23
  as happening everywhere, 194–95
  in large companies versus startups, 195
  room for and possibility of, 194
  at The Salvation Army, 33–40
  teaching, 60
  uncertainty and need for, 4
  *See also* culture of innovation
innovation amplifiers, 181–83
Innovation Book and Awards, 138*t*, 139
innovation catalysts, 174*t*, 177, 182
innovators
  behavior of and support for, 23–30, 53
  integration of, 59–60
innovator's checklist, 170–72
InnoVision, 40
institutionalized inertia, 47–50, 66
intelligent failure, 160–61
internal incubators, 182
internal innovation amplifiers, 182–83
International Development Innovation
  Alliance, 184
intersection-supporting infrastructure,
  138*t*
interviews, and diagnosing current
  state, 90–91
Intuit, 144–46, 163–64, 174*t*, 177
Irma (hurricane), 15–16
IT, at DBS, 52, 189–90

jHub, 127–29
Jobs, Steve, 138, 141–42, 170, 201
"job to be done," 26n7
Johnson, Charles "Kelly," 182
Johnson & Johnson, 165–66
Joint Forces Command (JFC), 128
Joy Space, 187–88
Just Go with It, 154t, 158

Kegan, Robert, 104n10, 164
Kerr, Steven, 72, 178
Kiasu Committee, 188–89
Kickbox, 74t, 78, 109

LaBossiere, Dan, 35–36
LaBossiere, Jim, 38–39
Lafley, A. G., 125–26, 198
Lahey, Lisa Laskow, 104n10
language, clarity in, 196–97
leadership
  careful, 198
  chameleon, 163–66
  Cook, Scott at Intuit, 144–46,
    148–49, 163–64
  Deverell, Sir Chris at Joint Forces
    Command, 128–29
  Eaton, Helen at Settlement Music
    School, 131–34
  Lafley, A. G. at P&G, 125–26
  Nadella, Satya at Microsoft, 167–69
  and setting behavioral example, 210
  wearing different hats, 162
learned helplessness, 44
learning organization, DBS as, 53, 75
light bulb, development of, 18–19
Lilly Cone, Anne, 126
LinkedIn, 174t, 177
Live from Day 1, 154t, 158
"Living it. Working it" program, 126
Lockheed Martin, 182
LumenLab Wall of Customers, 120t,
  122–23
Lunch Roulette, 74t, 76–77, 80

Manila Water, 162
Manirakiz, Jamie, 39
Man on the Moon, 119–21

markets, breaking into new, 54
Maskell, Victoria, 15–16
McDonald's, 45–46
McGrath, Rita Gunther, 49, 191–92
meetings, 57–59, 62, 64, 72, 73
MetLife, 120t, 122–23
Microsoft, 47, 166–69
mindfulness, 165
minimum viable product (MVP), 171–72
Mobile Joes, 35–36
MOJO, 58, 62, 64, 72, 73, 96
#MonkeyFirst, 154t, 158
movement, starting, 193
  authors' parting thoughts on, 198–204
  lessons from NO-DETs, 194–98
moving ideas forward
  BEAN boosters for, 178–83
  DBS case study for, 187–91
  relevant BEANs for, 171–77
  UNICEF case study for, 183–86
  and zombie amnesty, 191–92
Musyoka, Nick, 147–48
My Pain Points, 121t, 124

Nadella, Satya, 167–69
Netflix, 3, 156
NO-DETs (normal organizations doing
  extraordinary things), 2, 33
  lessons from, 194–98
No Meeting Wednesday, 174t, 177
Nordstrom, 138t, 140–41
nudges
  defined, 66, 67–68, 81
  at Innosight, 70–71
  See also BEANs (behavior enablers,
    artifacts, and nudges)

office design, 187–88
OneWeek, 168–69
opportunities, discovering
  and assessing curiosity quotient,
    135–36
  and grassroots market understand-
    ing, 130–34
  jHub case study on, 127–29
  and P&G's Consumer-Is-Boss
    Movement, 124–26
  relevant BEANs for, 119–24

Optus, 121*t*, 123
organizational consistency, as element
    of successful BEAN, 72–73
organizational structure, changing,
    189–90

Pascale, Richard, 92
Picasso, Pablo, 107, 147, 170
Pixar, 138*t*, 141–43
platform operating model, 190
Plussing, 138*t*, 141
policies, relaxing, 188–89
Powell, James, 16
practicality, as element of successful
    BEAN, 72
premortems, 154*t*, 155
preventable failures, 160, 161
prioritization
    of BEAN implementation, 111
    lack of, 85
problem-solving, success through, 47
Procter & Gamble, 124–26, 198
Project Lemonade, 61
psychological safety, 101, 157–58, 159–63

Qualcomm, 121*t*, 124
quick wins, celebrating, 210
Qvortrup, Michael, 121

reinforcement, as element of successful
    BEAN, 72
research & development, 183
resource allocation, 45–46, 180
"river of life" exercise, 97
Roma community, 26, 27–28
Ronn, Karl, 41n1
routines, 21, 72

Salvation Army, The, 33–40
Salvation Factory, 38–40
Sandlin, Destin, 63–64
SAP, 165
Sapra, Sharad, 183–84
Schein, Edgar, 20–21
scouting, technology and business-
    model, 181

self-transforming, 164
September 11 terrorist attacks, 33
Settlement Music School, 131–34, 198
70:20:10 BEAN, 85
shadow strategy, 41–42
    acknowledging and defeating, 7
    and changing habits, 64
    and culture, 47–50
    and resource allocation, 45–46
    and risks of creative expression, 42–45
Singtel Group, 87–88, 90–91, 93–94,
    95–110, 198
Skunk Works, 182
SmartBuddy, 56–57
Smith, Brad, 144, 145, 146
songs, favorite as icebreaker, 71
Speedo, 147
Spotify, 174*t*, 176
sprint, 88. *See also* culture sprint
strategic business development, 182
strategy, culture and, 47–50, 209
Strikepoint grant program, 38–39
Stumping Google, 121*t*, 124
Supercell, 154*t*, 157–58
superpowers, as icebreaker, 95
surveys, diagnostic, 91–92, 211–17
Syngenta, 147–48

talent, appraising, 161
Tan, Aileen, 87–88, 95, 100, 110
Tasty Catering, 174*t*, 175
Tata Group, 74*t*, 77
Team Temp, 84–85
technology, conflation of innovation
    and, 184
technology and business-model
    scouting, 181
technology operations, at DBS, 52,
    189–90
Thompson, David, 76–77
Toyota
    A3 Report, 138*t*, 139–40
    Andon Cord, 174–75
Toyota Production System (TPS), 146,
    174–75
trackability, as element of successful
    BEAN, 73
trend scouting, 181
Twain, Mark, 145

uncertainty, 4, 153–54
UNICEF
    as case study for moving ideas
        forward, 183–86
    and U-Report for disaster prepared-
        ness, 15–16
    and youth empowerment, 25, 28
    *See also* UPSHIFT
uniqueness, as element of successful
    BEAN, 73
Unlimited Free Books, 121*t*, 123–24
UPSHIFT, 25, 26, 27–28, 29–30
UPSHIFT 2.0 conference, 28
U-Report, 15–16


venture capital, corporate, 181
Veshall, Sejnur, 26, 27–28, 29–30
video games, lessons from, 65–66

Wallace, Amy, 142–43
"wallow in the problem," 56–57
Watson, Chaz, 37
Weight Watchers (WW), 65, 66
WITCH ("Who Is The Customer
    Here?"), 109–10
working teams, forming, 94
Wreckoon, 154*t*, 155–56
Wright Brothers, 179–80
WW (Weight Watchers),
    65, 66


"Yes, and . . . ," 138*t*, 140–41
youth, empowering, 25


zombie projects and amnesty,
    191–92

# Acknowledgments

Every book goes through its journey, but this one has been a particularly winding one. I and my colleagues at Innosight have been thinking hard about some of the themes in the book for more than a decade. A client moment in 2015 crystallized how important it was to synthesize and share those thoughts. Pontus Siren and I were facilitating a session with the top leadership team of a big global logistics company. We started the session by sharing our usual thoughts around disruptive change and competitive threats. The CEO politely (but brusquely) responded by saying, "We understand all of this and have set up a separate group to pioneer new business models. My question is, What do I do with the other 20,000 people we have?" The question motivated me to collaborate with my friend and longtime colleague Dave Duncan to create a mash-up of 55,000 words on the topic and give it the title *Everyday Innovation: A Practical Guide to Creating a Culture of Innovation.* As we stepped back from what we had created, however, it became clear that we didn't yet have the right answer to the CEO's question. So, we shelved the book and moved onto other ideas. Not long after, coauthor Paul Cobban did a thing that has kept me hooked on consulting for far longer than I expected: he asked a question to which I not only did not know the answer but also did not know how to come up with the answer. That question, in essence, was this: Can you purposefully design and change a culture? That led to a yearlong project through which we pushed the experimental envelope and ultimately came up with the central idea in this book: BEANs. (In parallel with this project, Dave coauthored *Competing Against Luck* with Innosight cofounder

Clayton Christensen and is currently working on two exciting streams of research and writing).

There are, as always, many people to thank. I'll start with collective thanks on behalf of the writing team before offering personal thanks. First, we'd like to thank the DBS project team and our colleagues at Innosight who have continued to advance the thinking around innovation culture. The core DBS team at Innosight was Rahul Nair, Elliot Tan, and TY Tang. Innosight colleagues Dave Duncan and Pontus Siren helped to stress-test our thinking, intern Xun Yang Tay did yeoman's work to put together the first set of BEANs, Kit Lee was a masterful coordinator during the DBS project and beyond, Crystal Spanakos helped make the ideas sparkle, Cathy Olofson and Kristen Blake supported efforts to spread the key ideas that emerged from the project, Craig Deao of the Studer Group provided valuable insight, and Amantha Imber and Michelle Le Poidevin from Inventium pressure-tested our emerging framework. Beyond Paul, Dave Gledhill, Melissa Heng, Mohit Kapoor, Jimmy Ng, Patsy Quek, Asnaa Sabzposh, Nina Santana, Constance Soh, Tammy Tsang, Sonia Wedrychowicz, and Angie Yeo from DBS all played vital roles in our work together. Sadly, one of the DBS team members, Paul Tan, unexpectedly passed away in the middle of the project. His dedication and creativity inspired us through both the project and the process of developing this book.

We would also like to thank the great team at Harvard Business Review Press. The conclusion notes that the book's writing was tied to an experiment in early 2019 called IdeaLab. We'd like to thank Adi Ignatius for having the idea and Walter Frick for making it happen. Kevin Evers has been a tireless advocate whose deft editorial hand helped us bring out the book we were trying to write. Stephani Finks did her usual magic in the design of the book's vibrant cover. Finally, thanks to Jennifer Waring, Kim Giambattisto, and Lynn Everett for their great support shaping and refining the final manuscript. We'd also like to thank Tanya Accone from UNICEF, Steven and Sharon Bussey from The Salvation Army, Sir Chris Deverell from the UK Joint Forces Command, Helen Eaton from Settlement Music School, and Aileen Tan and Chee Keat Koh from Singtel, who generously shared their stories with us, showing that innovation can flourish in unexpected places.

On the personal side, I'd like to start by publicly thanking my collaborators, each of whom brought important energy to the book. Paul, thanks for sharing the DBS story with clarity and humility and for your surprising doodling superpower, which makes the work more accessible and approachable. Andy, thanks for doing such a great job bringing the Singtel story to life and for your consistent and diligent willingness to offer thoughtful perspectives throughout the editing process (which includes listening to my occasional rants). Natalie, thanks for your great work helping to build the core toolkit during the DBS project and for your passion and enthusiasm in bringing the ideas of this book to Innosight and beyond. You have brought a warm humanity to the book and, indeed, to our organization! I'd next like to thank my children: Charlie (age fourteen as I write this), Holly (twelve), Harry (eight), and Teddy (three). You are great kids who teach me more than you know. I can't wait to see what you will do as you continue to grow up, and I hope you never lose your curiosity, creativity, kindness, and love for each other. I am truly grateful to my wife, Joanne. She has an unbeatable combination of patience, competence, and generosity. Jo, I couldn't do what I do without you. Every day I thank God that you and our wonderful children are part of my life.

Finally, I would like to acknowledge my mentor and Innosight's co-founder Clayton Christensen. Clay sadly passed away as we were working on the final draft of this book in January 2020. Without him I would be neither where I am today nor who I am today. I am honored and privileged to play a part in carrying the torch that he helped light when he and my colleague Mark Johnson started Innosight in 2000. This book is dedicated above all to his memory.

—Scott Anthony
*Singapore*

I owe a deep debt of gratitude to the amazing people of DBS whose open-mindedness and creativity over the last ten years has proved boundless. Ultimately, it was these wonderful colleagues who delivered an incredible corporate transformation. I am truly thankful to my long-term bosses and mentors Piyush Gupta and Dave Gledhill, who set the ambitious direction of the company and who gave me the space to try new things and the support to scale. Thanks also to the DBS transformation team, past and present, who made it so much fun along the way (how we laughed!): Andrew Sidwell, Tim Kyle, Arin Basu, Kelvin Chow, Michelle Lay, Raju Nair, Rajdeep Ghai, Patsy Quek, Jurgen Meerschaege, Rachael Straiton, Mohit Kapoor, Cade Tan, Melissa Wong, Neal Cross, Bidyut Dumra, Mark Evans, Linda Lee, Constance Soh, Sameer Gupta, Lim Choon Heong, Phillipa McNaughton Smith, and Angie Yeo.

Special thanks to Scott and the talented team at Innosight who not only pushed our "Culture by Design" thinking at DBS to a new level while steering the journey that resulted in this book, but who also—and especially—let me know that I give away my age every time I leave two spaces after a period.

But most of all, thank you to my wife, Fiona, and our two boys, Ross and Ewan, who continually remind me of the most important things in life. Without your loving support, endless patience, and willingness to try new experiences, I would not have been able to enjoy this incredible journey.

—Paul Cobban
*Singapore*

I am very thankful for my coauthors, Innosight colleagues, and clients who I learn from every day. My officemate Sharon Wilson reminds me that we build on the last best answer, and we have been fortunate to have been able to build on the great work of so many people. I'd like to express a special thank-you to coauthor Scott Anthony for being a mentor and friend for the last sixteen years and for inviting me to join him to support DBS in its transformation. I had the very good fortune to work with Paul Cobban, Patsy Quek, Melissa Heng, Constance Geok, Shaun Ang, and Nina Santana for a month in Singapore, together with TY Tang. There I learned about DBS, life, and the amazing food culture in Singapore. In my dual consulting and internal role, I've been able to bring the culture of innovation practices to the talent team at Innosight.

Thank you to Kady O'Grady and Patrick Viguerie for being open to trying new things and for helping to create our desired culture at Innosight. I'm grateful for the opportunity to have interviewed Sharon and Steve Bussey at The Salvation Army, together with Annie Garofalo, to understand what innovation looks like at a normal organization doing extraordinary things (NO-DET). I am also very grateful to Innosight's cofounder Clayton Christensen, who taught me the importance and value of helping individuals and organizations view the world through different lenses. I'd like to acknowledge and say a special thank-you to my family and my husband, Jonathan, who encourages me and always makes a point to remind me how proud he is of me. The love, support, and delicious meals he provides enable me to do work that I love.

—Natalie Painchaud
*Bartlett, New Hampshire*


I am grateful to my collaborators on this book. Their dedication to helping organizations improve the way they work to unleash innovation and creativity inspires me deeply. I am grateful to my Innosight colleagues who, with their questions and ideas, make me smarter every day. I owe a special thanks to Scott Anthony, my coauthor, mentor, and friend. Scott has tirelessly helped me innovate (and sometimes eat and remind me to sleep too!) during my time at Innosight by making sure we never stop striving to find better ways to help our clients solve their toughest growth problems. I am grateful to Innosight's client Singtel and, specifically, to its group chief human resources officer Aileen Tan, for giving us a platform to experiment with starting a culture movement in her HR team. I learned a huge amount doing this, as documented in these pages. I am proud to see the outcomes every time I visit or, as is more often the case these days, through various social and professional media postings! My deepest gratitude goes to my wife, Luyuan. The support and love she provides, both to our two young children, Aureli and Agnes, and to me (despite my frequent absences due to work commitments), is what keeps me going.

—Andy Parker
*Singapore*

# About the Authors

Scott D. Anthony is a senior partner who has been based in Innosight's Singapore office since 2010. During that time, he led the regional expansion of Innosight's consulting business, served as Innosight's elected managing partner from 2012 to 2018, and oversaw bounded experiments in venture capital and online platforms (Innosight Ventures and Innosight X). *Eat, Sleep, Innovate* will be the eighth book he has authored or coauthored. His previous work includes *Dual Transformation* (2017), *The Little Black Book of Innovation* (2011), and *Seeing What's Next* (2004, with Harvard professor and Innosight cofounder Clayton Christensen). In 2019, he was named one of the world's ten most influential management thinkers by Thinkers50, and in 2017 he received the T50 Innovation Award. Scott received a BA in economics, summa cum laude, from Dartmouth College and an MBA with high distinction from Harvard Business School, where he was a Baker Scholar. He and his wife, Joanne, are the proud parents of four children: Charlie, Holly, Harry, and Teddy. His Twitter handle is @ScottDAnthony.

Paul Cobban has been the chief data and transformation officer at DBS Bank since 2009. Based in Singapore, Paul has led multiple bankwide transformation programs to drive a fundamental cultural change through process reengineering, human-centered design, journey thinking, innovation, data analytics, and artificial intelligence.

His leadership has been a major contributor to the transformation journey that led DBS to becoming the first bank to simultaneously hold the titles Bank of the Year (*The Banker*), Best Bank in the World (*Global Finance*), and World's Best Bank (*Euromoney*).

As part of his work at DBS, he has helped many international companies, startups, governments, and public sector departments with their own transformations.

Considered one of the world's leading cultural transformation practitioners, Paul is regularly sought after and asked to share his experiences at global speaking engagements.

Paul currently chairs the Institute of Banking and Finance (IBF) Future-Enabled Skills Work Group and is an IBF fellow. He also sits on the FinTech advisory council for the Institute of International Finance (IIF) and on the board of the European Financial Management and Marketing Association (EFMA).

Prior to DBS Paul worked for Standard Chartered, JP Morgan, and IBM. He holds a first-class honors degree from Aston University, United Kingdom.

Paul is married to Fiona and has two sons, Ross and Ewan.

Natalie Painchaud is the director of learning at Innosight. An experienced strategy and innovation consultant and coach, Natalie has extensive experience developing leaders, including more than fifteen years helping *Fortune 500* companies develop the strategies, capabilities, and early proof points required to successfully innovate. She was a faculty member of an accelerated leadership development program for one of the world's largest healthcare companies for close to ten years and collaborated on the initial design of the program.

As director of learning, Natalie leads Innosight's internal training strategy by designing and delivering development programs for the global consulting team and professional staff. In her role, she supports broader talent development initiatives, including performance management and leadership training.

Before working at Innosight, Natalie was a senior associate with an MIT-founded executive-education company. In this position, Natalie led a team that developed and presented technology-based prototypes and business cases to hundreds of global CEOs and CIOs who were invited by the sponsoring companies, HP and Oracle.

Natalie holds a BA with distinction in industrial relations from McGill University in Montreal and advanced certification in Executive Coaching from the Columbia University Coaching Program. Natalie lives in Concord, Massachusetts, with her husband, Jonathan, and dog, Leela.

Andy Parker was elected partner at Innosight in 2017. He has spent his career in management consulting, beginning with Accenture's Strategy practice, based in London. He moved to Singapore in 2011 to take up a post at Accenture's Management Consulting Innovation Center. In that role he developed a specialism for helping clients with their innovation-driven growth agendas. That led him to Innosight, where he helps clients navigate disruptive change and set growth strategies. Andy has worked with clients in diverse industries, from higher education to commodity chemicals and cement. He has worked in nearly every market across Asia-Pacific.

Andy's previous publications include the 2017 *Sloan Management Review* article "The Next Wave of Business Models in Asia." Andy served as the lead author of Innosight's 2019 research report on successful business transformation in Australia and a similar 2020 report on successful business transformation in ASEAN. Most recently Andy authored a report on the imperative for incumbent institutions in Australian higher education to respond to digital disruption.

Andy holds a bachelor of business administration from Bath University's School of Management, United Kingdom. He lives in Singapore with his wife, Luyuan, and their two young children, Aureli and Agnes.